PRENTICE HALL

Chemistry

Guided Reading and Study Workbook

Boston, Massachusetts
Upper Saddle River, New Jersey

Cover photograph: Image from Getty Images, Inc.

ISBN 0-13-190362-4

10 10 09 08 07

CONTENTS

Name ______________________ Date ______________ Class ______________

1 INTRODUCTION TO CHEMISTRY

SECTION 1.1 CHEMISTRY (pages 7–11)

This section defines chemistry and differentiates among its traditional divisions. It also distinguishes pure from applied chemistry and provides several reasons to study chemistry.

▶ What Is Chemistry? (page 7)

1. What is matter?

____

2. What is chemistry?

____

____

____

▶ Areas of Study (page 8)

3. What are the five major areas of chemistry?

a. ______________________

b. ______________________

c. ______________________

d. ______________________

e. ______________________

4. Is the following sentence true or false? The boundaries between the five areas of chemistry are not firm. ______________

5. Complete the table by filling in the appropriate subdivision of chemistry.

	Investigating ways to slow down the rusting of steel
	Developing a better insulin-delivery system for diabetics
	Determining the amount of mercury present in a soil sample
	Comparing the hardness of copper and silver
	Developing a new carbon-based fiber for clothing

CHAPTER 1, Introduction to Chemistry *(continued)*

▶ Pure and Applied Chemistry (page 9)

6. ________________ chemistry is research that is directed toward a practical goal or application; ________________ chemistry is the pursuit of chemical knowledge for its own sake.

▶ Why Study Chemistry? (pages 10–11)

7. Why is the study of chemistry important?

   a. ____

   b. ____

   c. ____

8. List three careers that require some knowledge of chemistry.

   ____

Reading Skill Practice

Outlining can help you understand and remember what you have read. Write an outline for Section 1.1, Chemistry. Begin your outline by copying the headings in the textbook. Under each heading, write the main idea. Then list the details that support the main idea. Do your work on a separate sheet of paper.

SECTION 1.2 CHEMISTRY FAR AND WIDE (pages 12–17)

This section summarizes ways in which chemistry affects many aspects of life.

▶ Materials (page 12)

1. Is the following statement true or false? Chemists design materials to fit general needs. ________________

2. In George de Mestral's hook-and-loop tapes, were the hooks macroscopic or microscopic? ______________________________

▶ Energy (page 13)

3. List two ways to meet the demand for energy.

   a. ______________________

   b. ______________________

4. How does insulation help conserve energy?

____

5. How are soybeans used as a source of energy?

____

____

6. Circle the letter of the statement that is always true about a battery.

   a. All batteries are able to be recharged.

   b. Batteries use chemicals to store energy.

   c. Batteries are devices that conserve energy.

   d. NASA developed batteries that are thrown away after use.

▶ Medicine and Biotechnology (page 14)

7. What is the role of chemistry in the development of medicines?

____

____

____

8. List three new materials chemists have developed that have medical applications.

   a. ______________________________

   b. ______________________________

   c. ______________________________

9. The field that applies science to the production of biological products is ______________________ .

Name ____________ Date ____________ Class ____________

10. Complete the concept map about genes.

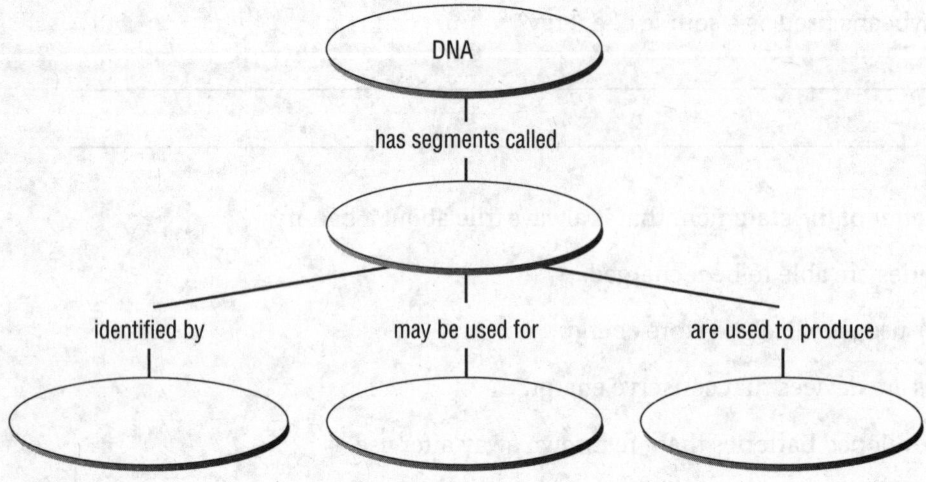

▶ Agriculture (page 15)

11. How do chemists contribute to agriculture?

____

____

____

12. How can a potato plant modified with a jellyfish gene help a farmer to conserve water?

____

____

____

13. What type of chemicals do chemists design to protect crops from pests?

____

____

____

14. In Figure 1.11, how does the plastic tube around the tomato stem protect the plant?

____

____

____

Name ______________________ Date ______________ Class ______________

▶ The Environment (page 16)

15. What are two ways that chemists work to protect the environment?

a. ____

b. ____

16. Define a pollutant.

____

____

17. How is lead harmful to humans?

____

____

18. What strategies have been used to prevent lead poisoning in children?

____

____

____

▶ The Universe (page 17)

19. Scientists can learn about the chemical composition of stars by analyzing the ______________ they transmit.

20. Why won't the method used to discover the chemical composition of stars work for the moon and planets?

____

____

21. What did chemists learn about the moon's surface by analyzing moon rocks?

____

____

____

22. Look at Figure 1.14 on page 17. What is the key difference in the methods scientists used to analyze rocks from Earth's moon and Mars?

____

____

Name ______________ Date ______________ Class ______________

SECTION 1.3 THINKING LIKE A SCIENTIST (pages 20–25)

This section describes the development of an experimental approach to chemistry and steps involved in the scientific method. It also discusses the role of collaboration and communication in science.

▶ Alchemy (page 20)

1. Practical alchemy focused on

____

____

2. Alchemists developed processes for separating ______________ and purifying ______________.

▶ An Experimental Approach to Science (page 21)

3. How did Lavoisier help to transform chemistry?

____

____

4. Circle the letter of the word that identifies what Lavoisier demonstrated was necessary for materials to burn.

a. phlogiston

b. nitrogen

c. oxygen

d. metals

▶ The Scientific Method (pages 22–23)

5. What is the scientific method?

____

____

Name ______________________ Date ________________ Class ______________

6. Complete the flowchart about the scientific method.

A scientific problem is often discovered when an ______________ is made, which leads to a question.

↓

A ______________ is formed when an explanation is proposed for an observation.

↓

Testing a proposed explanation requires designing an ______________ .

↓

For the results of the test to be accepted, the test must produce the same results ______________ .

↓

An explanation may become a ______________ if the same results are found after many tests.

7. Circle the letter of the activity that involves using the senses to gather information directly.

a. forming a hypothesis

b. making an observation

c. planning an experiment

d. analyzing data

8. What do scientists do if the results of an experiment do not support the hypothesis?

____

____

9. The variable that you change during an experiment is the ______________ .

The variable that is observed during an experiment is the ______________ .

CHAPTER 1, Introduction to Chemistry *(continued)*

10. Is the following sentence true or false? Once a theory has been proven, no experiment will ever disprove it. ______________

11. What is a scientific law?

____

____

12. Circle the letter of each statement that expresses a scientific law.

a. As the temperature of a balloon increases, the balloon expands.

b. Increasing the temperature of a balloon might cause it to burst.

c. If all other variables are kept constant, the volume of a gas increases as the temperature increases.

d. Sometimes increasing the temperature of a gas causes the gas to expand.

▶ Collaboration and Communication (pages 24–25)

13. Several scientists working together to solve a problem is ______________.

14. Is the following statement true or false? Scientists from different disciplines may need to work together on a problem because the problem is too complex for one person to solve. ______________

15. Exchanging ideas about science is called ______________.

16. How are journals helpful to scientists?

____

____

17. Is the following statement true or false? Experts in an author's field review articles after they are published in a journal. ______________.

Name ______________________ Date ________________ Class ________________

SECTION 1.4 PROBLEM SOLVING IN CHEMISTRY (pages 28–32)

This section describes effective approaches for solving numeric problems and conceptual problems.

▶ Skills Used in Solving Problems (page 28)

1. Name an everyday situation that requires problem-solving skills.

____

____

2. What is involved in effective problem solving?

____

▶ Solving Numeric Problems (pages 29–30)

3. What are the three steps for solving numeric problems?

a. ____________________

b. ____________________

c. ____________________

4. What must you determine first when solving a word problem?

____

____

5. What are two skills that you may need to use as you calculate an answer to a problem?

____

____

____

6. If your answer to a problem does not seem reasonable, list two things you can do.

____

____

____

Name ______________________ Date ______________ Class ______________

CHAPTER 1, Introduction to Chemistry *(continued)*

7. For the following word problem, fill in the table, listing the known and unknown information: A person can walk a mile in 20 minutes. The person is going for a 10-mile walk. How many hours will it take for the person to complete the walk?

Known	Unknown

▶ Solving Conceptual Problems (pages 31–32)

8. After you identify the known and unknown in a conceptual problem, what should you do next?

____

9. What are the steps for solving conceptual problems?

____

Name ____________________ Date ______________ Class ______________

2 MATTER AND CHANGE

SECTION 2.1 PROPERTIES OF MATTER (pages 39–42)

This section helps you distinguish extensive from intensive properties and identify substances by their properties. It teaches you how to differentiate the three states of matter. It also defines a physical property and lists examples of physical properties and physical changes.

▶ Describing Matter (page 39)

1. The ____________________ of an object is a measure of the amount of matter the object contains.

2. How does an extensive property differ from an intensive property?

____

____

▶ Identifying Substances (page 40)

3. Matter that has a uniform and definite composition is called a ____________________ .

4. Is the following sentence true or false? All samples of a substance have different physical properties. ____________________

5. A physical property is a quality or condition of a substance that can be ____________________ or ____________________ without changing the substance's composition.

6. Circle the letter of the term that is NOT a physical property.

a. hardness **c.** boiling point

b. color **d.** melting

7. Look at Table 2.1 on page 40. What is the melting point of bromine? ______

8. Look at Table 2.1 on page 40. Circle the letter of the substance that is a yellow solid and melts at 115°C.

a. sulfur

b. chlorine

c. gold

d. copper

Name ____________________ Date ______________ Class ______________

9. Is the following sentence true or false? Physical properties can help a chemist identify a substance. ____________

▶ States of Matter (pages 41–42)

10. Circle the letter of the term that is NOT a physical state of matter.

a. water

b. gas

c. liquid

d. solid

11. Complete the table about properties of three states of matter. Use these terms: *definite, indefinite, easily,* and *not easily.*

Properties of the States of Matter			
Property	**Solid**	**Liquid**	**Gas or Vapor**
Shape		indefinite	
Volume	definite		indefinite
Can be compressed			easily

12. Match each arrangement of the particles in matter with a physical state.

Physical State	**Arrangement**
_____ gas	**a.** packed tightly together
_____ liquid	**b.** close, but free to flow
_____ solid	**c.** spaced relatively far apart

13. Is the following sentence true or false? The words *gas* and *vapor* can be used interchangeably. ____________

14. The term gas is limited to those substances that exist in the gaseous state at ____________.

15. What does *vapor* describe?

____

____

▶ Physical Changes (page 42)

16. A physical change alters a given material without changing its chemical

______________ .

17. What are some words that describe physical changes?

____

____

18. What is true about all physical changes that involve a change of state?

____

SECTION 2.2 MIXTURES (pages 44–47)

This section explains how to classify a mixture as heterogeneous or homogeneous. It also describes ways to separate mixtures.

▶ Classifying Mixtures (pages 44–45)

1. Is the following sentence true or false? Most samples of matter are mixtures.

   ____

2. What is a mixture?

   ____

3. Is the following sentence true or false? A heterogeneous mixture is one that has a completely uniform composition. ______________

4. What is another name for a homogeneous mixture?

   ____

5. Circle the letter of the term that describes a part of a sample with uniform composition and properties.

   a. solution

   b. mixture

   c. state

   d. phase

Name ______________________ Date ______________ Class ______________

6. How many phases exist in these types of mixtures?

a. Homogeneous ________________

b. Heterogeneous ________________

▶ Separating Mixtures (pages 46–47)

7. In general, what is used to separate mixtures?

____

____

8. The process that separates a solid from a liquid in a heterogeneous mixture is called ____________________.

9. What happens during a distillation?

____

____

Match each term with its location in the diagram.

_____ **15.** condenser

_____ **16.** heat source

_____ **17.** thermometer

_____ **18.** tap water

_____ **19.** distilled water

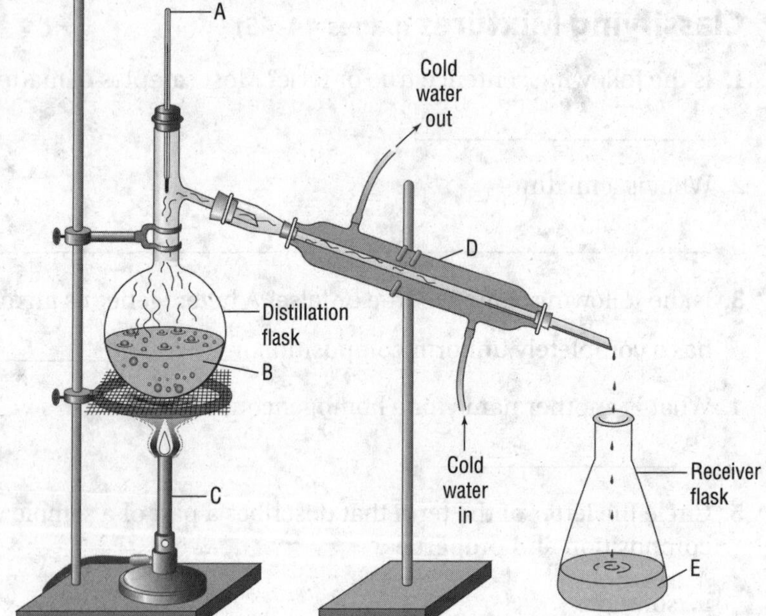

Name ______________ Date ______________ Class ______________

Reading Skill Practice

By looking carefully at photographs and drawings in textbooks, you can better understand what you have read. Look carefully at Figure 2.8 on page 47. What important idea does this drawing communicate?

SECTION 2.3 ELEMENTS AND COMPOUNDS (pages 48–52)

This section explains a key difference between an element and a compound, and describes how chemical symbols and formulas are used to represent elements and compounds. It also summarizes the process for classifying substances and mixtures.

▶ Distinguishing Elements and Compounds (pages 48–49)

1. Each ______________ has a unique set of properties.
2. What are the two groups into which substances can be classified?

____

____

3. Is the following sentence true or false? Elements can be easily separated into simpler substances. ______________
4. Compounds are substances that can be separated into simpler substances only by ______________ means.
5. Is the following sentence true or false? The properties of compounds are different from those of their component elements. ______________
6. Complete this sentence.
   Sodium chloride (table salt) is a ______________ of sodium, which is a soft ______________, and chlorine, which is a pale yellow ______________.

▶ Distinguishing Substances and Mixtures (page 50)

7. Describe one way to decide whether a sample of matter is a substance or a mixture.

____

____

____

CHAPTER 2, Matter and Change *(continued)*

8. Complete the labels in the diagram below.

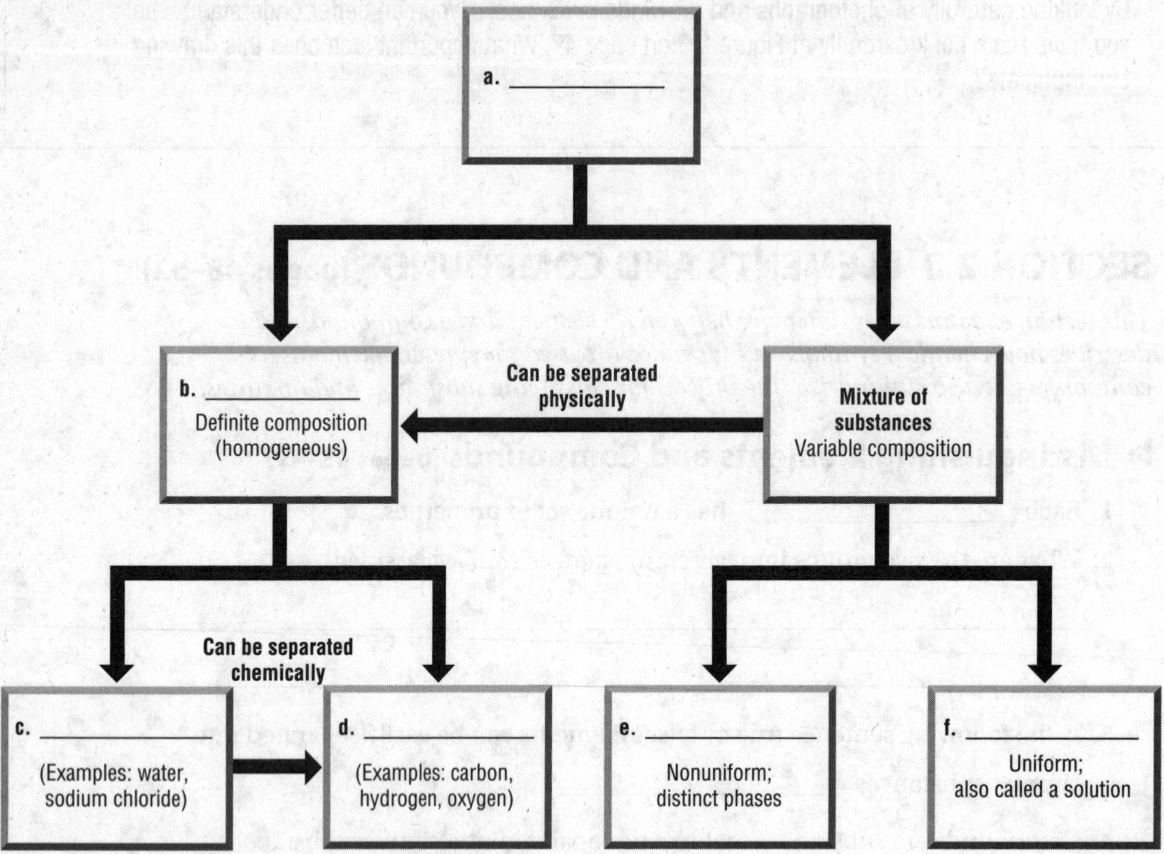

▶ Symbols and Formulas (pages 51–52)

9. What is used to represent an element?

____

____

10. What are chemical symbols used for?

____

____

11. Subscripts in chemical formulas are used to indicate the relative proportions of the elements in a ______________.

12. Is the following sentence true or false? The elements that make up a compound are always present in the same proportions. ______________

13. Use Table 2.2 on page 52 to answer the following questions.

a. Pb is the symbol for what element? ______________

b. What is the symbol for gold? ______________

c. Stibium is the Latin name for which element? ______________

SECTION 2.4 CHEMICAL REACTIONS (pages 53–55)

This section provides clues to help you recognize a chemical change. It also teaches the law of conservation of mass.

▶ Chemical Changes (page 53)

1. What is a chemical property?

____

____

____

2. Is the following sentence true or false? Chemical properties are observed only when a substance undergoes a chemical change. ______________

3. What happens during a chemical reaction?

____

4. In chemical reactions, the substances present at the start of the reaction are called ______________ and the substances produced are called ______________.

5. Circle the letter of the term that best completes the sentence. A change in the composition of matter ______ occurs during a chemical reaction.

a. sometimes

b. rarely

c. always

d. never

6. Which representation of a chemical reaction is correct?

a. products → reactants

b. reactants → products

Name ______________ Date ______________ Class ______________

▶ Recognizing Chemical Changes (page 54)

7. List four possible clues to a chemical change?

____

____

____

8. Is the following statement true or false? If you observe a clue for chemical change, you can be certain that a chemical change has taken place. ______________

9. Define a precipitate.

____

____

▶ Conservation of Mass (page 55)

10. During a chemical reaction, the mass of the products is always equal to the mass of the ______________ .

11. The law of conservation of mass states that in any physical change or chemical reaction, mass is neither ______________ nor ______________ .

12. Look at Figure 2.15 on page 55. How do you know that mass was conserved?

____

Name ______________________ Date ______________ Class ______________

3 SCIENTIFIC MEASUREMENT

SECTION 3.1 MEASUREMENTS AND THEIR UNCERTAINTY (pages 63–72)

This section describes the concepts of accuracy, precision, and error in measurements. It also explains the proper use of significant figures in measurements and calculations.

▶ Using and Expressing Measurements (page 63)

1. Why are numbers used in chemistry often expressed in scientific notation?

____

____

____

____

2. Circle the letter of each sentence that is true about numbers expressed in scientific notation.

a. A number expressed in scientific notation is written as the product of a coefficient and a power of 10.

b. The power of 10 is called the exponent.

c. The coefficient is always a number greater than or equal to one and less than ten.

d. For numbers less than one, the exponent is positive.

3. Circle the letter of the answer in which 503,000,000 is written correctly in scientific notation.

a. 5.03×10^{-7}

b. 503×10^{6}

c. 5.03×10^{8}

d. 503 million

▶ Accuracy, Precision, and Error (pages 64–65)

4. Is the following sentence true or false? To decide whether a measurement has good precision or poor precision, the measurement must be made more than once. ______________

Name ______________________ Date ______________ Class ______________

CHAPTER 3, Scientific Measurement *(continued)*

Label each of the three following sentences that describes accuracy with an *A*. Label each sentence that describes precision with a *P*.

_________ **5.** Four of five repetitions of a measurement were numerically identical, and the fifth varied from the others in value by less than 1%.

_________ **6.** Eight measurements were spread over a wide range.

_________ **7.** A single measurement is within 1% of the correct value.

8. On a dartboard, darts that are closest to the bull's-eye have been thrown with the greatest accuracy. On the second target, draw three darts to represent three tosses of lower precision, but higher accuracy than the darts on the first target.

First target

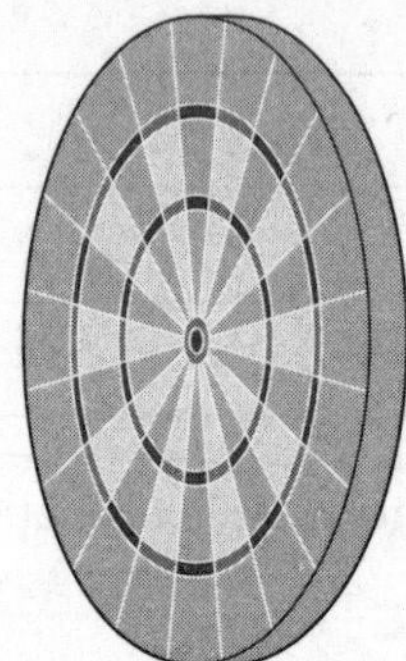

Second target

9. What is the meaning of "accepted value" with respect to an experimental measurement?

____

10. Complete the following sentence. For an experimental measurement, the experimental value minus the accepted value is called the ______________ .

11. Is the following sentence true or false? The value of an error must be positive. ______________

12. Relative error is also called ______________________ .

13. The accepted value of a length measurement is 200 cm, and the experimental value is 198 cm. Circle the letter of the value that shows the percent error of this measurement.

a. 2%

b. −2%

c. 1%

d. −1%

Name ____________ Date ____________ Class ____________

▶ Significant Figures in Measurements (pages 66–67)

14. If a thermometer is calibrated to the nearest degree, to what part of a degree can you estimate the temperature it measures? ____________

15. Circle the letter of the correct digit. In the measurement 43.52 cm, which digit is the most uncertain?

a. 4 **c.** 5

b. 3 **d.** 2

16. Circle the letter of the correct number of significant figures in the measurement 6.80 m.

a. 2 **c.** 4

b. 3 **d.** 5

17. List two situations in which measurements have an unlimited number of significant figures.

a. ____________

b. ____________

____

____

18. Circle the letter of each sentence that is true about significant figures.

a. Every nonzero digit in a reported measurement is assumed to be significant.

b. Zeros appearing between nonzero digits are never significant.

c. Leftmost zeros acting as placeholders in front of nonzero digits in numbers less than one are not significant.

d. All rightmost zeros to the right of the decimal point are always significant.

e. Zeros to the left of the decimal point that act as placeholders for the first nonzero digit to the left of the decimal point are not significant.

▶ Significant Figures in Calculations (pages 68–71)

19. Is the following sentence true or false? An answer is as precise as the most precise measurement from which it was calculated. ____________

Round the following measurements as indicated.

20. Round 65.145 meters to 4 significant figures. ____________

21. Round 100.1°C to 1 significant figure. ____________

Name ______________ Date ______________ Class ______________

22. Round 155 cm to two significant figures. ______________

23. Round 0.000 718 kilograms to two significant figures. ______________

24. Round 65.145 meters to three significant figures. ______________

SECTION 3.2 THE INTERNATIONAL SYSTEM OF UNITS (pages 73–79)

This section defines units of measurement for length, volume, mass, temperature, and energy in the International System of Units (SI).

▶ Units and Quantities (pages 74–79)

1. Complete the table showing selected SI base units of measurement.

Units of Measurement		
Quantity	SI base unit	Symbol
Length		
Mass		
Temperature		
Time		

2. All metric units of length are based on multiples of ______ .

3. The International System of Units (SI) is a revised version of the ______________ .

4. Explain what is meant by a "derived unit."

____

5. Give at least one example of a derived unit.

____

Name ______________________ Date ______________ Class ______________

6. Complete the following table showing some metric units of length. Remember that the meter is the SI base unit for length.

Metric Units of Length		
Unit	**Symbol**	**Factor Multiplying Base Unit**
Meter	m	1
Kilometer		
Centimeter		
Millimeter		
Nanometer		

Match each metric unit with the best estimate of its length or distance.

_____ 7. Height of a stove top above the floor — **a.** 1 km

_____ 8. Thickness of about 10 sheets of paper — **b.** 1 m

_____ 9. Distance along a road spanning about 10 telephone poles — **c.** 1 cm

_____ 10. Width of a key on a computer keyboard — **d.** 1 mm

11. The space occupied by any sample of matter is called its ______________.

12. Circle the letter of each sentence that is true about units of volume.

a. The SI unit for volume is derived from the meter, the SI unit for length.

b. The liter (L) is a unit of volume.

c. The liter is an SI unit.

d. There are 1000 cm^3 in 1 L, and there are also 1000 mL in 1 L, so 1 cm^3 is equal to 1 mL.

Match each of the three descriptions of a volume to the appropriate metric unit of volume.

	Example	**Unit of Volume**
_____	13. Interior of an oven	**a.** 1 L
_____	14. A box of cookies	**b.** 1 m^3
_____	15. One-quarter teaspoon	**c.** 1 mL

Name ______________________ Date ________________ Class ________________

16. A volume of 1 L is also equal to

a. 1000 mL

b. 1 dm^3

c. 1000 cm

17. The volume of any solid, liquid, or gas will change with

______________________.

18. A kilogram was originally defined as the mass of ______________________.

19. Circle the letter of the unit of mass commonly used in chemistry that equals 1/1000 kilogram.

a. gram **b.** milligram **c.** milliliter

Match each unit of mass with the object whose mass would be closest to that unit.

	Mass	Unit of Mass
_______	**20.** A few grains of sand	**a.** 1 kg
_______	**21.** A liter bottle of soda	**b.** 1 g
_______	**22.** Five aspirin tablets	**c.** 1 mg

23. Circle the letter of the instrument shown that is used to measure mass.

a. scale

b. balance beam

c. platform balance

d. analytical balance

24. Is the following sentence true or false? The mass of an object changes with location. ______________________

25. When brought to the surface of the moon, will a mass have more or less weight than it did on the surface of Earth, or will it be the same weight? Explain.

____

____

26. Draw an arrow below the diagram, showing the direction of heat transfer between two objects.

lower temperature	higher temperature

Name ______________________ Date ______________ Class ______________

27. What properties explain the behavior of liquid-filled thermometers?

____

____

____

____

28. What are the two reference temperatures on the Celsius scale?

____

____

29. What is the zero point, 0 K, on the Kelvin scale called?

____

30. A change of temperature equal to one Kelvin is equal to a change of temperature of how many degrees Celsius? ______________

31. Complete the diagram to show the reference temperatures in the Celsius and Kelvin scales.

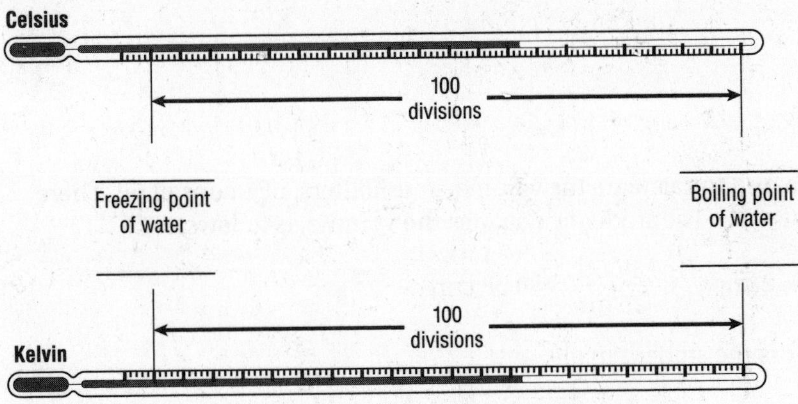

32. One calorie is the quantity of heat that raises the temperature of ______________ of pure water by ______________.

SECTION 3.3 CONVERSION PROBLEMS (pages 80–87)

This section explains how to construct conversion factors from equivalent measurements. It also describes how to apply the techniques of dimensional analysis to a variety of conversion problems.

▶ Conversion Factors (pages 80–81)

1. How are the two parts of a conversion factor related?

____

Name ______________________ Date ______________ Class ______________

CHAPTER 3, Scientific Measurement *(continued)*

2. Look at Figure 3.11. In a conversion factor, the smaller number is part of the quantity that has the ______________ unit. The larger number is part of the quantity that has the ______________ unit.

3. Is the following sentence true or false? The actual size of a measurement multiplied by a conversion factor remains the same, because the measurement being converted is multiplied by unity. ______________

4. Write two conversion factors based on the relationship between hours and minutes.

____

5. The average lead for a mechanical pencil is 6.0 cm long when it is new. Circle the letter of the conversion factor you would use to find its length in inches.

a. $\frac{2.54\ \text{cm}}{1\ \text{in.}}$

b. $\frac{1\ \text{in.}}{2.54\ \text{cm}}$

c. $\frac{1\ \text{in.}}{6.0\ \text{cm}}$

d. $\frac{6.0\ \text{cm}}{1\ \text{in.}}$

6. A student is asked to calculate the volume, in milliliters, of 2 cups of oil. There are 225 mL per cup. The student calculates the volume as follows:

$$\text{Volume} = 2\ \text{cups} \times \frac{1\ \text{cup}}{25\ \text{mL}} = 0.08\ \text{cup}$$

List three errors the student made.

____

____

____

▶ Dimensional Analysis (pages 81–83)

7. What is dimensional analysis?

____

____

____

8. Reread Sample Problem 3.5. The correct conversion factor has the ______________ unit in the denominator and the ______________ unit in the numerator.

Name ______________________ Date ________________ Class ________________

9. A container can hold 65 g of water. Circle the conversion factor needed to find the mass of water that 5 identical containers can hold.

a. $\frac{\text{5 containers}}{\text{65 g water}}$

b. $\frac{\text{1 container}}{\text{65 g water}}$

c. $\frac{\text{65 g water}}{\text{1 container}}$

d. $\frac{\text{65 g water}}{\text{5 containers}}$

▶ Converting Between Units (pages 84–85)

10. Converting between units is easily done using ______________________.

11. Circle the letter of the conversion factor that you would use to convert tablespoons to milliliters.

a. $\frac{\text{4 fluid ounces}}{\text{1 tablespoon}}$

b. $\frac{\text{1 tablespoon}}{\text{4 fluid ounces}}$

c. $\frac{\text{1 tablespoon}}{\text{15 mL}}$

d. $\frac{\text{15 mL}}{\text{1 tablespoon}}$

12. Show the calculation you would use to convert the following:

a. 0.25 m to centimeters ______________________

b. 9.8 g to kilograms ______________________

c. 35 ms to seconds ______________________

d. 4.2 dL to liters ______________________

13. Complex conversions between units may require using ______________________ conversion factor.

14. How many conversion factors would you need to use to find the number of liters in a cubic decimeter? What are they?

____

____

Name ____________________ Date ____________________ Class ____________________

15. How would you calculate the number of nanometers in 8.1 cm?

____

16. What is the equivalent of 0.35 lb in grams?

____

17. A scientist has 0.46 mL of a solution. How would she convert this volume to microliters?

____

18. Describe the steps you would use to solve this problem. In a scale drawing of a dining room floor plan, 10 mm equals 2 meters. If the homeowners wanted to purchase flooring that costs $10.89 per square yard, how much would they spend on flooring for the dining room? The dimensions of the dining room on the floor plan are 40 mm × 32 mm.

____

____

____

19. Name three common measurements that are expressed as a ratio of two units.

____

20. What technique can be used to convert complex units?

____

21. A normal concentration of glucose, or sugar, in the blood is 95 mg/dL. How many grams of sugar would be present per liter of blood? Show the conversion factors you use.

____

22. Replace each question mark in the table with the conversion factors needed to obtain the given units of density.

Mass	Volume	Density
g	$mm^3 \times$?	g/m^3
kg × ?	$cm^3 \times$?	g/m^3

23. A man can run a mile in 4 minutes. Calculate his average speed in kilometers per hour. Show your work. (1 mile = 1.61 km)

____

____

Name ______________________ Date ______________ Class ______________

24. A baseball player's batting average is .254 (254 hits per 1000 at bats). If she is at bat an average of 3 times per game, how many hits will she make in 52 games? Show your work.

____

____

SECTION 3.4 DENSITY (pages 89–93)

This section defines density. It explains that density is a characteristic property that depends on the composition of a substance, not on the size of the sample.

▶ Determining Density (page 89–90)

1. Is the mass of one pound of lead greater than, less than, or equal to the mass of one pound of feathers? ______________

2. Which material has a greater density, lead or feathers? ______________

3. How is density defined?

____

4. The mass of a sample is measured in grams, and its volume is measured in cubic centimeters. In what units would its density be reported?

____

5. Look at Table 3.6 on page 90. Circle the letter of the material that will sink in liquid water at 4°C.

   a. aluminum

   b. corn oil

   c. ice

   d. gasoline

▶ Density and Temperature (pages 91–92)

6. The density of a substance generally decreases as its temperature increases. Are there any exceptions to this statement? Explain.

____

____

____

Name ______________________ Date ______________ Class ______________

GUIDED PRACTICE PROBLEMS

GUIDED PRACTICE PROBLEM 3 (page 69)

3. Round 87.073 meters to three significant figures. Write your answer in scientific notation.

Step 1. To round to three significant figures, round to the nearest tenth. 87.073 rounds to ______

Step 2. Write the number in scientific notation. ______________ meters

GUIDED PRACTICE PROBLEM 34 (page 85)

34. The radius of a potassium atom is 0.227 nm. Express this radius in centimeters. Complete the following steps to solve the problem.

Step 1. Use the conversion factors for nanometers and centimeters. $0.227 \text{ nm} \times \frac{\square}{1 \times 10^9 \text{ nm}} \times \square$

Step 2. Simplify. $= \frac{0.227 \times 10^2}{10^9}$ $\square$

Step 3. Divide. $= \square$ cm

EXTRA PRACTICE (similar to Practice Problem 36, page 86)

36. Gold has a density of about 20 g/cm^3. Estimate this density in kg/m^3.

Name ______________________ Date ________________ Class ________________

GUIDED PRACTICE PROBLEM 46 (page 91)

46. A student finds a shiny piece of metal that she thinks is aluminum. In the lab, she determines that the metal has a volume of 245 cm^3 and a mass of 612 g. Calculate the density. Is the metal aluminum?

Analyze

Step 1. List the known values.

Volume = 245 cm^3

Mass = ______ g

Step 2. List the unknown. ________________

Calculate

Step 3. Use the following relationship to find the density. Remember to round your answer to three significant figures.

$$\text{Density} = \frac{\text{mass}}{\text{volume}}$$

$$= \frac{612\ \text{g}}{\_\_\_\_\_\ \text{cm}^3}$$

$$= \_\_\_\_\_\ \text{g/cm}^3$$

Step 4. To determine whether the piece of metal is aluminum, compare the density of the metal to the density of aluminum given in Table 3.7 on page 90. Is the metal aluminum? ________________

Evaluate

Step 5. Underline the correct word(s) that complete(s) this statement. Because the mass of the metal is about two and one-half times the volume, a density of about 2.5 g/cm^3 is reasonable. Because a density of 2.50 g/cm^3 is nearly 10% less than 2.7 g/cm^3, the density of aluminum, the metal (is, is not) aluminum.

EXTRA PRACTICE (similar to Practice Problem 48a, page 92)

48a. Use dimensional analysis to convert 4.68 g of boron to cubic centimeters of boron. The density of boron is 2.34 g/cm^3.

Name ____________________ Date ______________ Class ______________

4 ATOMIC STRUCTURE

SECTION 4.1 DEFINING THE ATOM (pages 101–103)

This section describes early atomic theories of matter and provides ways to understand the tiny size of individual atoms.

▶ Early Models of the Atom (pages 101–102)

1. Democritus, who lived in Greece during the fourth century B.C., suggested that matter is made up of tiny particles that cannot be divided. He called these particles ______________ .

2. List two reasons why the ideas of Democritus were not useful in a scientific sense. ______________________________

3. The modern process of discovery about atoms began with the theories of an English schoolteacher named ______________ .

4. Circle the letter of each sentence that is true about Dalton's atomic theory.

   a. All elements are composed of tiny, indivisible particles called atoms.

   b. An element is composed of several types of atoms.

   c. Atoms of different elements can physically mix together, or can chemically combine in simple, whole-number ratios to form compounds.

   d. Chemical reactions occur when atoms are separated, joined, or rearranged; however, atoms of one element are never changed into atoms of another element by a chemical reaction.

5. In the diagram, use the labels *mixture* and *compound* to identify the mixture of elements A and B and the compound that forms when the atoms of elements A and B combine chemically.

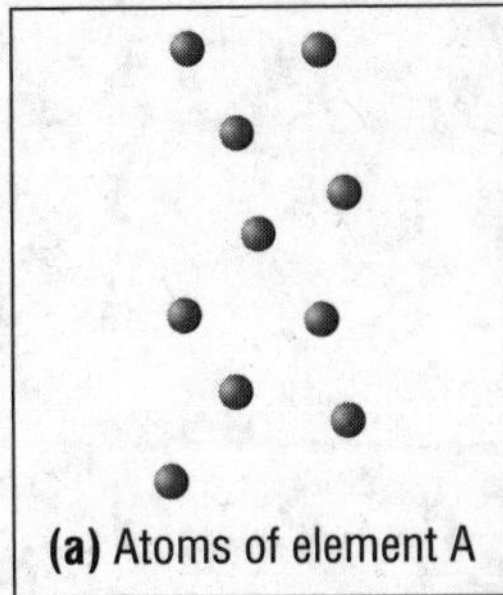
(a) Atoms of element A

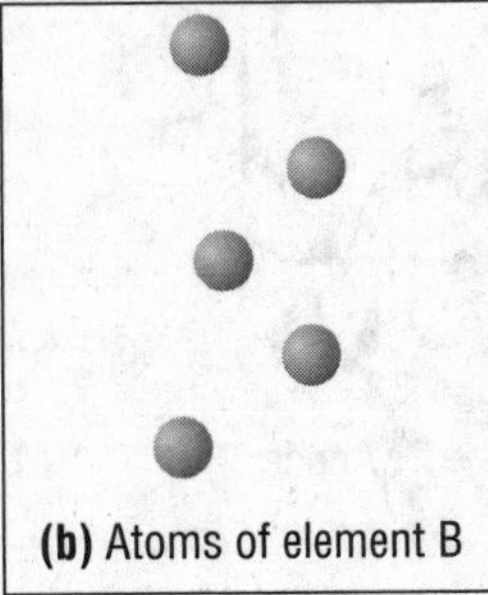
(b) Atoms of element B

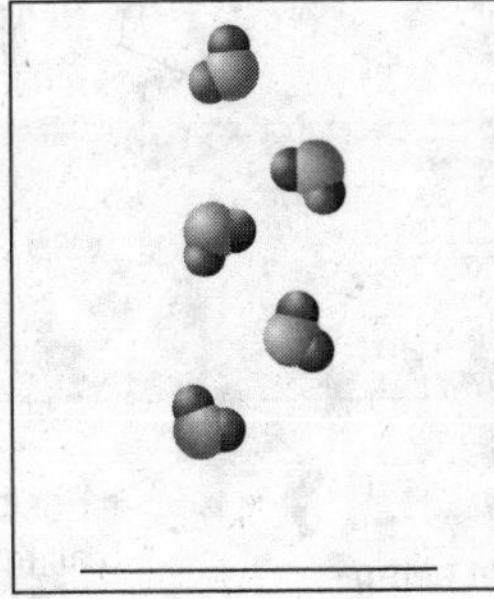
____

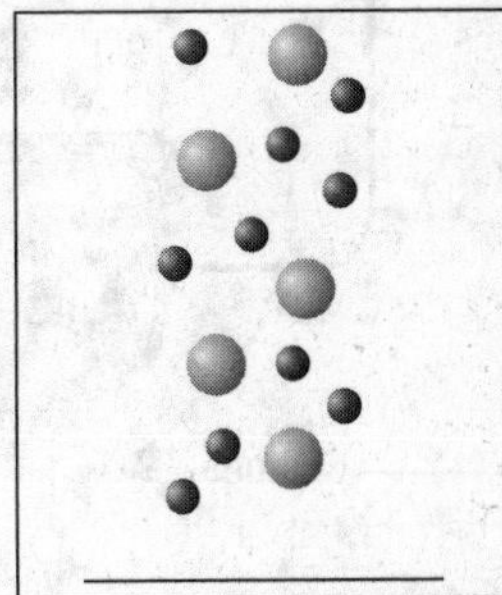
____

▶ Sizing up the Atom (page 103)

6. Suppose you could grind a sample of the element copper into smaller and smaller particles. The smallest particle that could no longer be divided, yet still has the chemical properties of copper, is ______________________.
7. About how many atoms of copper when placed side by side would form a line 1 cm long? ______________

SECTION 4.2 STRUCTURE OF THE NUCLEAR ATOM (pages 104–108)

This section describes the experiments that led to the discovery of subatomic particles and their properties.

▶ Subatomic Particles (pages 104–106)

1. How is the atomic theory that is accepted today different from Dalton's atomic theory? ____

____

2. Which subatomic particles carry a negative charge? ______________

Match each term from the experiments of J. J. Thomson with the correct description.

______	3. anode	a. an electrode with a negative charge
______	4. cathode	b. a glowing beam traveling between charged electrodes
______	5. cathode ray	c. an electrode with a positive charge
______	6. electron	d. a negatively charged particle

7. The diagram shows electrons moving from left to right in a cathode-ray tube. Draw an arrow showing how the path of the electrons will be affected by the placement of the negatively and positively charged plates.

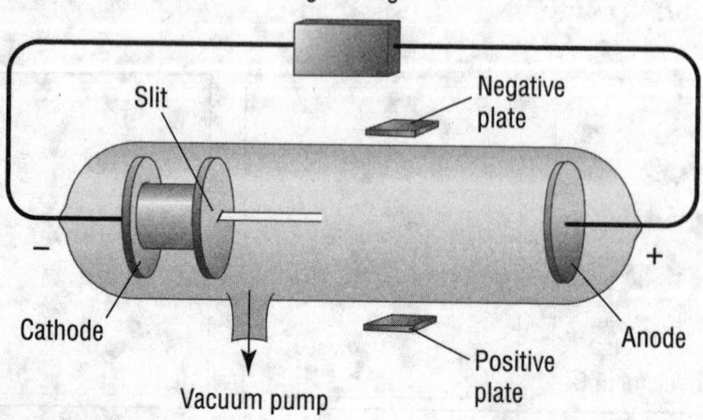

Name ______________________ Date ______________ Class ______________

8. Thomson observed that the production of cathode rays did not depend on the kind of gas in the tube or the type of metal used for the electrodes. What conclusion did he draw from these observations?

____

9. What two properties of an electron did Robert Millikan determine from his experiments?

____

10. Circle the letter of each sentence that is true about atoms, matter, and electric charge.

   a. All atoms have an electric charge.

   b. Electric charges are carried by particles of matter.

   c. Electric charges always exist in whole-number multiples of a single basic unit.

   d. When a given number of positively charged particles combines with an equal number of negatively charged particles, an electrically neutral particle is formed.

11. Circle the letter next to the number of units of positive charge that remain if a hydrogen atom loses an electron.

   a. 0 b. 1 c. 2 d. 3

12. The positively charged subatomic particle that remains when a hydrogen atom loses an electron is called ______________.

13. What charge does a neutron carry? ______________.

14. Complete the table about the properties of subatomic particles.

Properties of Subatomic Particles				
Particle	**Symbol**	**Relative Electrical Charge**	**Relative Mass (mass of proton = 1)**	**Actual Mass (g)**
Electron	e^-			9.11×10^{-28}
Proton	p^+			1.67×10^{-24}
Neutron	n^0			1.67×10^{-24}

Name ______________________ Date ______________ Class ______________

▶ The Atomic Nucleus (pages 106–108)

15. Is the following sentence true or false? An alpha particle has a double positive charge because it is a helium atom that has lost two electrons. ______________

16. Explain why in 1911 Rutherford and his coworkers were surprised when they shot a narrow beam of alpha particles through a thin sheet of gold foil.

____

____

____

____

____

17. Circle the letter of each sentence that is true about the nuclear theory of atoms suggested by Rutherford's experimental results.

a. An atom is mostly empty space.

b. All the positive charge of an atom is concentrated in a small central region called the nucleus.

c. The nucleus is composed of protons.

d. The nucleus is large compared with the atom as a whole.

e. Nearly all the mass of an atom is in its nucleus.

SECTION 4.3 DISTINGUISHING AMONG ATOMS (pages 110–119)

This section explains how atomic number identifies an element; how to use atomic number and mass number to find the number of protons, neutrons, and electrons in an atom; how isotopes differ; and how to calculate average atomic mass.

▶ Atomic Number (page 110)

1. Circle the letter of the term that correctly completes the sentence. Elements are different because their atoms contain different numbers of _______.

a. electrons

b. protons

c. neutrons

d. nuclei

Name ______________________ Date ______________ Class ______________

2. Complete the table showing the number of protons and electrons in atoms of six elements.

Atoms of Six Elements				
Name	**Symbol**	**Atomic Number**	**Number of Protons**	**Number of Electrons**
Hydrogen	H	1		
Helium	He		2	
Lithium	Li	3		
Boron	B	5		
Carbon	C	6		
Oxygen	O			8

▶ Mass Number (pages 111–112)

3. The total number of protons and neutrons in an atom is its

______________________.

4. What is the mass number of a helium atom that has two protons and two neutrons? ______________________

5. How many neutrons does a beryllium atom with four protons and a mass number of nine have? ______________________

6. Place the labels *chemical symbol, atomic number,* and *mass number* in the shorthand notation below.

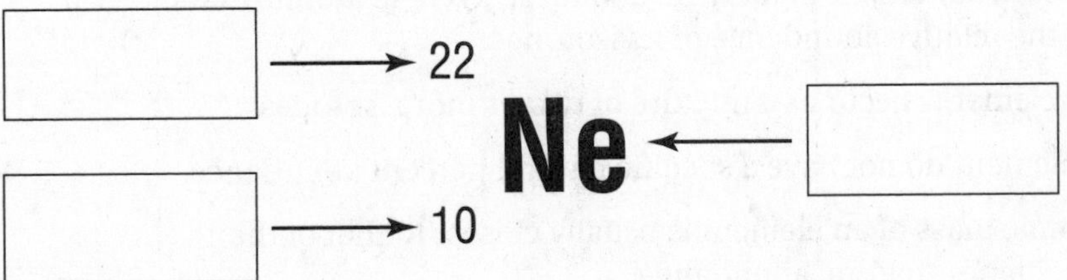

7. Designate the atom shown in Question 6 in the form "name of element"-"mass number." ______________________

8. How many protons, neutrons, and electrons are in the atom discussed in Questions 6 and 7? Protons: ☐ Neutrons: ☐ Electrons: ☐

CHAPTER 4, Atomic Structure *(continued)*

▶ Isotopes (pages 112–113)

9. How do atoms of neon-20 and neon-22 differ?

____

____

10. Neon-20 and neon-22 are called ____________________.

11. Is the following sentence true or false? Isotopes are chemically alike because they have identical numbers of protons and electrons. ____________________

Match the designation of each hydrogen isotope with its commonly used name.

______	**12.** hydrogen-1	**a.** tritium
______	**13.** hydrogen-2	**b.** hydrogen
______	**14.** hydrogen-3	**c.** deuterium

▶ Atomic Mass (pages 114–117)

15. Why is the atomic mass unit (amu), rather than the gram, usually used to express atomic mass?

____

____

16. What isotope of carbon has been chosen as the reference isotope for atomic mass units? What is the defined atomic mass in amu of this isotope?

____

17. Is the following sentence true or false? The atomic mass of an element is always a whole number of atomic mass units. ____________________

18. Circle the letter of each statement that is true about the average atomic mass of an element and the relative abundance of its isotopes.

    a. In nature, most elements occur as a mixture of two or more isotopes.

    b. Isotopes of an element do not have a specific natural percent abundance.

    c. The average atomic mass of an element is usually closest to that of the isotope with the highest natural abundance.

    d. Because hydrogen has three isotopes with atomic masses of about 1 amu, 2 amu, and 3 amu, respectively, the average atomic mass of natural hydrogen is 2 amu.

19. Circle the letter of the correct answer. When chlorine occurs in nature, there are three atoms of chlorine-35 for every one atom of chlorine-37. Which atomic mass number is closer to the average atomic mass of chlorine?

    a. 35 amu   **b.** 37 amu

Name ______________________ Date ______________ Class ______________

20. In the periodic table, the elements are organized into groups based on

____.

▶ The Periodic Table—A Preview (page 118)

21. What are the horizontal rows in the periodic table called?

____

Reading Skill Practice

Outlining can help you understand and remember what you have read. Prepare an outline of Section 4.3, *Distinguishing Among Atoms.* Begin with the headings in the textbook. Under each heading, write the main idea. Then list the details that support the main idea. Do your work on a separate sheet of paper.

Name ______________ Date ______________ Class ______________

GUIDED PRACTICE PROBLEMS

Fill in the write-on lines and boxes provided as you work through the guided practice problems.

GUIDED PRACTICE PROBLEM 18 (page 112)

18. Use Table 4.2 to express the compositions of carbon-12, fluorine-19, and beryllium-9 in shorthand notation.

Analyze

Carbon-12

Step 1. The number of protons in an atom is called its ______________ number.

The number of protons in an atom of carbon-12 is __________.

Calculate

Step 2. The number of protons plus the number of neutrons in an atom is called its ______________ number. For carbon-12, this number is __________.

Step 3. The shorthand notation for carbon-12 is:

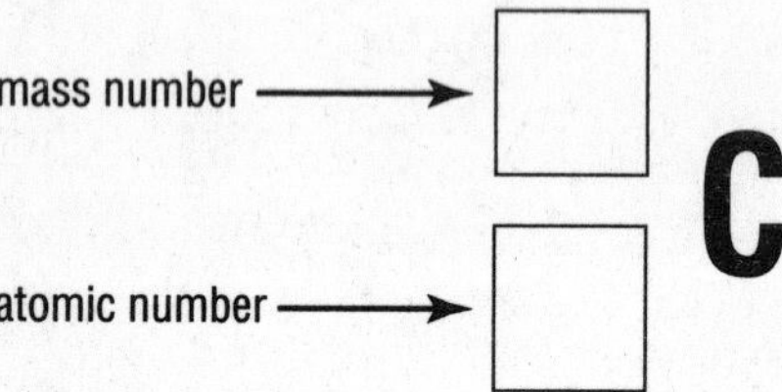

C

Evaluate

Step 4. Except for hydrogen-1, the mass number of an isotope is always greater than its atomic number. Is the mass number reasonable? __________

Fluorine-19

Step 1. The atomic number of fluorine-19 is __________.

Step 2. Its mass number is __________.

Step 3. The shorthand notation for fluorine-19 is: F

Step 4. Is your answer reasonable? Why?

____

____

Name ____________________ Date ______________ Class ______________

Beryllium-9

Step 1. The atomic number of beryllium-9 is ________.

Step 2. Its mass number is ________.

Step 3. The shorthand notation for beryllium-9 is: $^{\square}_{\square}\text{Be}$

Step 4. Is your answer reasonable? Why?

____

____

EXTRA PRACTICE (similar to Practice Problem 19, page 113)

19. Three isotopes of sulfur are sulfur-32, sulfur-33, and sulfur-34. Write the complete symbol for each isotope, including the atomic number and the mass number.

sulfur-32 $^{\square}_{\square}\text{S}$ sulfur-33 $^{\square}_{\square}\text{S}$ sulfur-34 $^{\square}_{\square}\text{S}$

GUIDED PRACTICE PROBLEM 23 (page 117)

23. The element copper has naturally occurring isotopes with mass numbers of 63 and 65. The relative abundance and atomic masses are 69.2% for mass = 62.93 amu and 30.8% for mass = 64.93 amu. Calculate the average atomic mass of copper.

Analyze

Step 1. Will the average atomic mass be closer to 63 or to 65? Explain.

____

____

Calculate

Step 2. For Cu-63: 69.2% × 62.93 amu = 0.692 × 62.93 amu = ☐

Step 3. For Cu-65: 30.8% × 64.93 amu = ☐ × ☐ = ☐

Step 4. Average mass: 43.6 amu + ☐ = ☐

Evaluate

Step 5. Explain why your answer is reasonable.

____

EXTRA PRACTICE (similar to Practice Problem 24, page 117)

24. Calculate the atomic mass of rubidium. The two isotopes of rubidium have atomic masses and relative abundancies of 84.91 amu (72.16%) and 86.91 amu (27.84%). ______________

Name ______________________ Date __________ Class ______________

5 ELECTRONS IN ATOMS

SECTION 5.1 MODELS OF THE ATOM (pages 127–132)

This section summarizes the development of atomic theory. It also explains the significance of quantized energies of electrons as they relate to the quantum mechanical model of the atom.

▶ The Development of Atomic Models (pages 127–128)

1. Complete the table about atomic models and the scientists who developed them.

Scientist	Model of Atom
Dalton	
Thomson	
Rutherford	
Bohr	

2. Is the following sentence true or false? The electrons in an atom can exist between energy levels. ______________

▶ The Bohr Model (pages 128–129)

3. What are the fixed energies of electrons called?

____

4. Circle the letter of the term that completes the sentence correctly. A quantum of energy is the amount of energy required to

a. move an electron from its present energy level to a lower one

b. maintain an electron in its present energy level

c. move an electron from its present energy level to a higher one

5. In general, the higher the electron is on the energy ladder, the ______________ it is from the nucleus.

Name ______________________ Date ______________ Class ______________

▶ The Quantum Mechanical Model (page 130)

6. What is the difference between the previous models of the atom and the modern quantum mechanical model? ______________________________________

____

____

7. Is the following sentence true or false? The quantum mechanical model of the atom estimates the probability of finding an electron in a certain position.

____

▶ Atomic Orbitals (pages 131–132)

8. A(n) ______________________ is often thought of as a region of space in which there is a high probability of finding an electron.

9. Circle the letter of the term that is used to label the energy levels of electrons?

a. atomic orbitals

b. quantum mechanical numbers

c. quantas

d. principal quantum numbers (n)

10. The letter ______________ is used to denote a spherical orbital.

11. Label each diagram below p_x, p_y, or p_z.

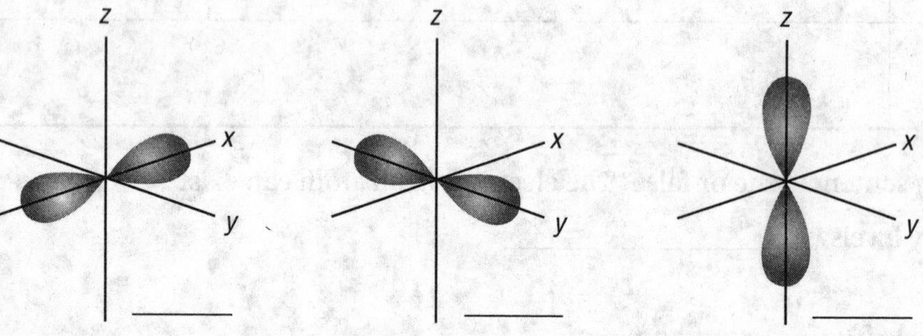

12. Use the diagram above. Describe how the p_x, p_y, and p_z orbitals are similar.

____

13. Describe how the p_x, p_y, and p_z orbitals are different. ______________________

____

14. Circle the letter of the formula for the maximum number of electrons that can occupy a principal energy level. Use n for the principal quantum number.

a. $2n^2$ **b.** n^2 **c.** $2n$ **d.** n

Name ______________________ Date ______________ Class ______________

SECTION 5.2 ELECTRON ARRANGEMENT IN ATOMS (pages 133–136)

This section shows you how to apply the aufbau principle, the Pauli exclusion principle, and Hund's rule to help you write the electron configurations of elements. It also explains why the electron configurations for some elements are exceptions to the aufbau principle.

▶ Electron Configurations (pages 133–135)

1. The ways in which electrons are arranged into orbitals around the nuclei of atoms are called ______________________.

Match the name of the rule used to find the electron configurations of atoms with the rule itself.

_____ **2.** aufbau principle

_____ **3.** Pauli exclusion principle

_____ **4.** Hund's rule

a. When electrons occupy orbitals of equal energy, one electron enters each orbital until all the orbitals contain one electron with the same spin direction.

b. Electrons occupy orbitals of lowest energy first.

c. An atomic orbital may describe at most two electrons.

5. Look at the aufbau diagram, Figure 5.7 on page 133. Which atomic orbital is of higher energy, a 4*f* or a 5*p* orbital? ______

6. Fill in the electron configurations for the elements given in the table. Use the orbital filling diagrams to complete the table.

Electron Configurations for Some Selected Elements

Element	Orbital filling 1s	2s	$2p_x$	$2p_y$	$2p_z$	3s	Electron configuration
☐	↑	☐	☐	☐	☐	☐	$1s^1$
He	↑↓	☐	☐	☐	☐	☐	☐
☐	↑↓	↑	☐	☐	☐	☐	$1s^22s^1$
C	↑↓	↑↓	↑	↑	☐	☐	☐
☐	↑↓	↑↓	↑	↑	↑	☐	$1s^22s^22p^3$
O	↑↓	↑↓	↑↓	↑	↑	☐	☐
☐	↑↓	↑↓	↑↓	↑↓	↑	☐	$1s^22s^22p^5$
Ne	↑↓	↑↓	↑↓	↑↓	↑↓	☐	☐
☐	↑↓	↑↓	↑↓	↑↓	↑↓	↑	$1s^22s^22p^63s^1$

7. In an electron configuration, what does a superscript stand for?

____

8. In an electron configuration, what does the sum of the superscripts equal?

____

▶ Exceptional Electron Configurations (page 136)

9. Is the following sentence true or false?
Every element in the periodic table follows the aufbau principle.

____

10. Filled energy sublevels are more _______________ than partially filled sublevels.

11. Half-filled levels are not as stable as _______________ levels, but are more stable than other configurations.

Reading Skill Practice

Outlining can help you understand and remember what you have read. Prepare an outline of Section 5.2, *Electron Arrangement in Atoms.* Begin your outline by copying the headings from the textbook. Under each heading, write the main idea. Then list the details that support, or back up, the main idea. Do your work on a separate sheet of paper.

SECTION 5.3 PHYSICS AND THE QUANTUM MECHANICAL MODEL (pages 138–146)

This section describes the variables used to describe light. It also explains how atomic emission spectra are produced, and compares the dual wave-particle nature of light and electrons.

▶ Light (pages 138–140)

1. Match each term describing waves to its definition.

______	amplitude	**a.** the distance between two crests
______	wavelength	**b.** the wave's height from zero to the crest
______	frequency	**c.** the number of wave cycles to pass a given point per unit of time

2. The units of frequency are usually cycles per second. The SI unit of cycles per second is called a(n) ______________.

3. Label the parts of a wave in this drawing. Label the wavelength, the amplitude, the crest, and the origin.

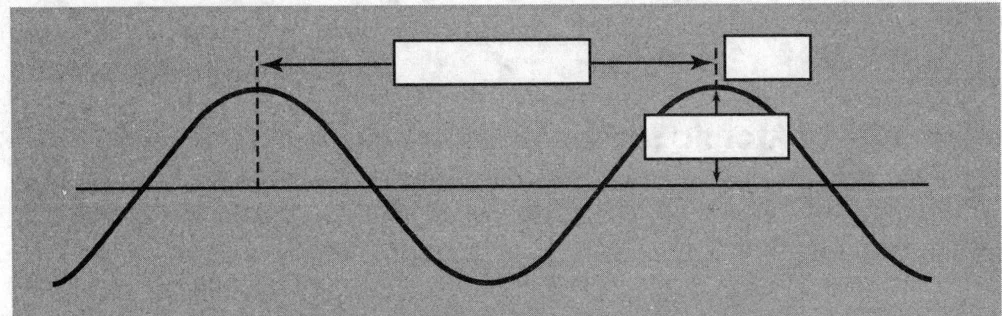

4. The product of wavelength and frequency always equals a(n) ______________, the speed of light.

5. Is the following sentence true or false? The wavelength and frequency of light are inversely proportional to each other. ______________

6. Light consists of electromagnetic waves. What kinds of visible and invisible radiation are included in the electromagnetic spectrum?

____

____

____

7. When sunlight passes through a prism, the different wavelengths separate into a(n) ______________ of colors.

8. Put the visible colors in order of increasing frequency.

______ orange	______ violet
______ green	______ yellow
______ blue	______ red

9. Look at Figure 5.10 on page 139. The electromagnetic spectrum consists of radiation over a broad band of wavelengths. What type of radiation has the lowest frequency? The highest frequency?

____

▶ Atomic Spectra (page 141)

10. What happens when an electric current is passed through the gas or vapor of an element?

____

CHAPTER 5, Electrons in Atoms *(continued)*

11. Passing the light emitted by an element through a prism gives the

    ________________________________ of the element.

12. Is the following sentence true or false? The emission spectrum of an element can be the same as the emission spectrum of another element.

    ____

▶ An Explanation of Atomic Spectra (pages 142–143)

13. What is the lowest possible energy of an electron called? ____________________

14. Only electrons moving from ______________ to ______________ energy levels lose energy and emit light.

▶ Quantum Mechanics (pages 381–382)

15. What did Albert Einstein call the quanta of light energy?

    ____

16. What does de Broglie's equation predict about the behavior of particles?

    ____

17. Is the following sentence true or false? Quantum mechanics describes the motions of subatomic particles and atoms as waves.

    ____

18. According to the Heisenberg uncertainty principle, it is impossible to know exactly both the ____________ and the ____________ of a particle at the same time.

19. Does the Heisenberg uncertainty principle apply to cars and airplanes?

    ____

Name ______________________ Date ________________ Class ________________

GUIDED PRACTICE PROBLEM

GUIDED PRACTICE PROBLEM 14 (page 140)

14. What is the wavelength of radiation with a frequency of 1.50×10^{13} Hz? Does this radiation have a longer or shorter wavelength than red light?

Analyze

Step 1. What is the equation for the relationship between frequency and wavelength? ________________

Step 2. What does *c* represent and what is its value?

____

Step 3. What is the wavelength of red light in cm?

____

____

Calculate

Step 4. Solve the equation for the unknown. $\lambda =$ __________

Step 5. Substitute the known quantities into the equation and solve.

$$\frac{2.998 \times 10^{8}\ \text{m/s}}{\boxed{}} = \boxed{}$$

Step 6. Compare the answer with the wavelength of red light. Does the given radiation have a wavelength longer or shorter than that of red light?

____

____

Evaluate

Step 7. Explain why you think your result makes sense?

____

____

____

Step 8. Are the units in your answer correct? How do you know?

____

Name ______________________ Date ______________ Class ______________

6 THE PERIODIC TABLE

SECTION 6.1 ORGANIZING THE ELEMENTS (pages 155–160)

This section describes the development of the periodic table and explains the periodic law. It also describes the classification of elements into metals, nonmetals, and metalloids.

▶ Searching For An Organizing Principle (page 155)

1. How many elements had been identified by the year 1700? ______________

2. What caused the rate of discovery to increase after 1700?

____

____

3. What did chemists use to sort elements into groups?

____

____

▶ Mendeleev's Periodic Table (page 156)

4. Who was Dmitri Mendeleev? ____

____

5. What property did Mendeleev use to organize the elements into a periodic table?

____

6. Is the following sentence true or false? Mendeleev used his periodic table to predict the properties of undiscovered elements. ______________

▶ The Periodic Law (page 157)

7. How are the elements arranged in the modern periodic table?

____

8. Is the following statement true or false? The periodic law states that when elements are arranged in order of increasing atomic number, there is a periodic repetition of physical and chemical properties. ______________

▶ Metals, Nonmetals, and Metalloids (pages 158–160)

9. Explain the color coding of the squares in the periodic table in Figure 6.5.

____

____

Name ______________________ Date ________________ Class ________________

10. Which property below is not a general property of metals.

a. ductile

b. poor conductor of heat

c. malleable

d. high luster

11. Is the following statement true or false? The variation in properties among metals is greater than the variation in properties among nonmetals. ________________

12. Under some conditions, a metalloid may behave like a ________________. Under other conditions, a metalloid may behave like a ________________.

SECTION 6.2 CLASSIFYING THE ELEMENTS (pages 161–167)

This section explains why you can infer the properties of an element based on the properties of other elements in the periodic table. It also describes the use of electron configurations to classify elements.

▶ Squares In The Periodic Table (pages 161–163)

1. Label the sample square from the periodic table below. Use the labels *element name, element symbol, atomic number,* and *average atomic mass.*

2. List three things, other than the name, symbol, atomic number, and average atomic mass, you can discover about an element using the periodic table in Figure 6.9.

a. ____

b. ____

c. ____

▶ Electron Configurations In Groups (pages 164–165)

3. Is the following sentence true or false? The subatomic particles that play the key role in determining the properties of an element are electrons. ________________

4. Why are Group A elements called representative elements?

____

____

Name ______________________ Date ______________ Class ______________

5. Classify each of the following elements as a (an) *alkali metal, alkaline earth metal, halogen,* or *noble gas.*

a. sodium ______________________ **e.** xenon ______________________

b. chlorine ______________________ **f.** potassium ______________________

c. calcium ______________________ **g.** magnesium ______________________

d. fluorine ______________________

6. For elements in each of the following groups, how many electrons are in the highest occupied energy level?

a. Group 3A ______________________

b. Group 1A ______________________

c. Group 8A ______________________

▶ Transition Elements (page 166)

7. Complete the table about classifying elements according to the electron configuration of their highest occupied energy level.

Category	Description of Electron Configuration
Noble gases	
Representative elements	
	s sublevel and nearby *d* sublevel contain electrons
	s sublevel and nearby *f* sublevel contain electrons

8. Circle the letter of the elements found in the *p* block.

a. Groups 1A and 2A and helium

b. Groups 3A, 4A, 5A, 6A, 7A, and 8A except for helium

c. transition metals

d. inner transition metals

Match the category of elements with an element from that category.

______ **9.** Noble gases **a.** gallium

______ **10.** Representative elements **b.** nobelium

______ **11.** Transition metals **c.** argon

______ **12.** Inner transition metals **d.** vanadium

Name ______________ Date ______________ Class ______________

13. Use Figure 6.12 on page 166. Write the electron configurations for the following elements.

a. magnesium ______________

b. cobalt ______________

c. sulfur ______________

SECTION 6.3 PERIODIC TRENDS (pages 170–178)

This section explains how to interpret group trends and periodic trends in atomic size, ionization energy, ionic size, and electronegativity.

▶ Trends in Atomic Size (pages 170–171)

1. Is the following sentence true or false? The radius of an atom can be measured directly. ______________

2. What are the atomic radii for the following molecules?

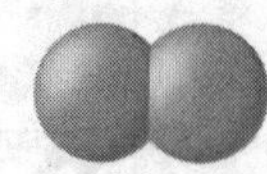

Hydrogen	**Oxygen**	**Nitrogen**	**Chlorine**
atomic radius =	atomic radius =	atomic radius =	atomic radius =
______	______	______	______

3. What is the general trend in atomic size within a group? Within a period?

____

____

4. What are the two variables that affect atomic size within a group?

a. ____

b. ____

5. For each pair of elements, pick the element with the largest atom.

a. Helium and argon ______________

b. Potassium and argon ______________

▶ Ions (page 172)

6. What is an ion?

____

Name ______________________ Date ______________ Class ______________

7. How are ions formed?

____

8. An ion with a positive charge is called a(n) ________________ ; an ion with a negative charge is called a(n) ________________ .

9. Complete the table about anions and cations.

	Anions	Cations
Charge		
Metal/Nonmetal		
Minus sign/Plus sign		

▶ Trends in Ionization Energy (pages 173–175)

10. ________________ is the energy required to overcome the attraction of protons in the nucleus and remove an electron from a gaseous atom.

11. Why does ionization energy tend to decrease from top to bottom within a group?

____

____

____

12. Why does ionization energy tend to increase as you move across a period?

____

____

____

____

13. There is a large increase in ionization energy between the second and the third ionization energies of a metal. What kind of ion is the metal likely to form? Include the charge in your answer.

____

▶ Trends in Ionic Size (page 176)

14. Metallic elements tend to ________________ electrons and form ________________ ions.

Nonmetallic elements tend to ________________ electrons and form ________________ ions.

15. Circle the letter of the statement that is true about ion size.

a. Cations are always smaller than the neutral atoms from which they form.

b. Anions are always smaller than the neutral atoms from which they form.

c. Within a period, a cation with a greater charge has a larger ionic radius.

d. Within a group, a cation with a higher atomic number has a smaller ionic radius.

16. Which ion has the larger ionic radius: Ca^{2+} or Cl^-? ________

▶ Trends in Electronegativity (page 177)

17. What property of an element represents its tendency to attract electrons when it chemically combines with another element? ______________________

18. Use Table 6.2 on page 177. What trend do you see in the relative electronegativity values of elements within a group? Within a period?

____

____

19. Circle the letter of each statement that is true about electronegativity values.

a. The electronegativity values of the transition elements are all zero.

b. The element with the highest electronegativity value is sodium.

c. Nonmetals have higher electronegativity values than metals.

d. Electronegativity values can help predict the types of bonds atoms form.

▶ Summary of Trends (page 178)

20. Use Figure 6.22 on page 178. Circle the letter of each property for which aluminum has a higher value than silicon.

a. first ionization energy

b. atomic radius

c. electronegativity

d. ionic radius

Reading Skill Practice

A graph can help you understand comparisons of data at a glance. Use graph paper to make a graph of the data in Table 6.2 on page 177. Plot electronegativity values on the vertical axis. Use a range from 0 to 4. Plot atomic number on the horizontal axis. Label each period and the first element in each period.

Name ______________________ Date ______________ Class ______________

GUIDED PRACTICE PROBLEM

GUIDED PRACTICE PROBLEM 8 (page 167)

8. Use Figure 6.9 and Figure 6.12 to write the electron configurations of these elements.

a. carbon **b.** strontium **c.** vanadium

Analyze

a. What is the number of electrons for each element?

C ______ Sr ______ V ______

b. What is the highest occupied energy sublevel for each element, according to its position on the periodic table? Remember that the energy level for the *d* block is always one less than the period.

C ______ Sr ______ V ______

c. According to its position on the periodic table, how many electrons does each element have in the sublevel listed above?

C ______ Sr ______ V ______

Solve

d. Begin filling in electron sublevels. Start from the top left and move right across each period in Figure 6.12 until you reach the highest occupied sublevel for each element. Make sure the *d*-block is in the correct energy level.

C ______________ Sr ______________________

V ______________________

e. How can you check whether your answers are correct?

____

____

f. Check your answers as outlined above.

C ____

Sr ____

V ____

Name ______________ Date ______________ Class ______________

IONIC AND METALLIC BONDING

SECTION 7.1 IONS (pages 187–193)

This section explains how to use the periodic table to infer the number of valence electrons in an atom and draw its electron dot structure. It also describes the formation of cations from metals and anions from nonmetals.

▶ Valence Electrons (pages 187–188)

1. What are valence electrons? ______________________________

____

2. The valence electrons largely determine the ______________ of an element and are usually the only electrons used in ______________.

3. Is the following sentence true or false? The group number of an element in the periodic table is related to the number of valence electrons it has. ______________

4. What is an electron dot structure? ______________________________

____

5. Draw the electron dot structure of each of the following atoms.

   a. argon ______________

   b. calcium ______________

   c. iodine ______________

▶ The Octet Rule (page 188)

6. What is the octet rule? ______________________________

____

____

7. Metallic atoms tend to lose valence electrons to produce a(n) ______________, or a positively charged ion. Most nonmetallic atoms achieve a complete octet by gaining or ______________ electrons.

Name ________________ Date ________________ Class ________________

▶ Formation of Cations (pages 188–190)

8. Write the electron configurations for these metals and circle the electrons lost when each metal forms a cation.

a. Mg ________________________________

b. Al ________________________________

c. K ________________________________

Match the noble gas with its electron configuration.

______	**9.** argon	**a.** $1s^2$
______	**10.** helium	**b.** $1s^22s^22p^6$
______	**11.** neon	**c.** $1s^22s^22p^63s^23p^6$
______	**12.** krypton	**d.** $1s^22s^22p^63s^23p^63d^{10}4s^24p^6$

13. What is the electron configuration called that has 18 electrons in the outer energy level and all of the orbitals filled?

____

14. Write the electron configuration for zinc.

____

15. Fill in the electron configuration diagram for the copper(I) ion.

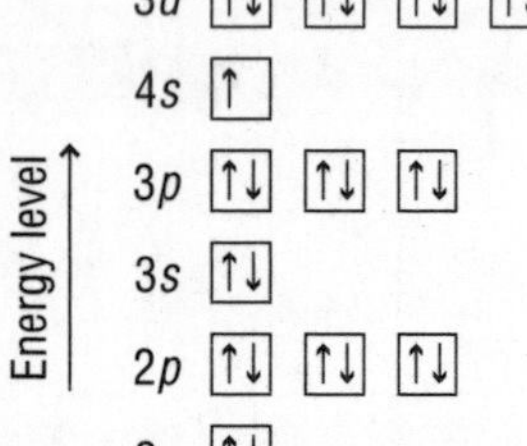

Copper atom
Cu

Copper(I) ion
Cu+

▶ Formation of Anions (pages 191–192)

16. Atoms of most nonmetallic elements achieve noble-gas electron configurations by gaining electrons to become ________________, or negatively charged ions.

17. What property of nonmetallic elements makes them more likely to gain electrons than lose electrons?

____

Name ____________ Date ____________ Class ____________

18. Is the following sentence true or false? Elements of the halogen family lose one electron to become halide ions. ____________

19. How many electrons will each element gain in forming an ion?

a. nitrogen ____________

b. oxygen ____________

c. sulfur ____________

d. bromine ____________

20. Write the symbol and electron configuration for each ion from Question 19, and name the noble gas with the same configuration.

a. nitride ____________

b. oxide ____________

c. sulfide ____________

d. bromide ____________

SECTION 7.2 IONIC BONDS AND IONIC COMPOUNDS (pages 194–199)

This section lists the characteristics of an ionic bond. It also describes the use of these characteristics to explain the electrical conductivity of ionic compounds when melted and when in aqueous solutions.

▶ Formation of Ionic Compounds (pages 194–195)

1. What is an ionic bond? ____________

____

2. In an ionic compound, the charges of the ____________ and ____________ must balance to produce an electrically ____________ substance.

3. Complete the electron dot structures below to show how beryllium fluoride (BeF_2) is formed. Use the diagram on page 194 as a model.

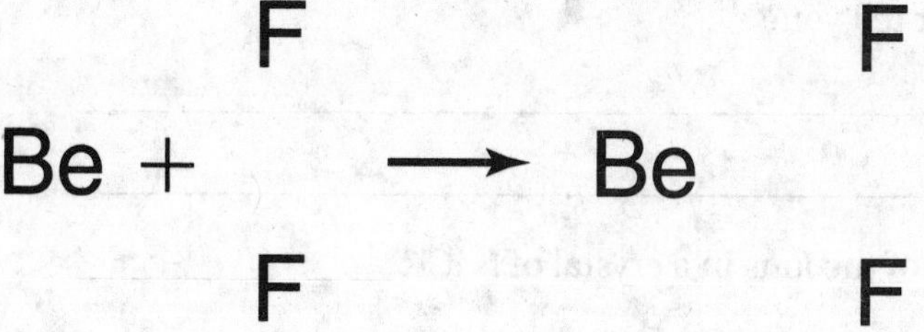

Name ______________ Date ______________ Class ______________

4. Why do beryllium and fluorine combine in a 1 : 2 ratio?

____

____

____

5. A chemical formula shows the types and _______________ of atoms in the smallest representative unit of a substance.

6. List the numbers and types of atoms represented by these chemical formulas.

a. Fe_2O_3 _______________

b. $KMnO_4$ _______________

c. CH_3 _______________

d. NH_4NO_3 _______________

7. What is a formula unit?

____

8. Explain why the ratio of magnesium ions to chloride ions in $MgCl_2$ is 1 : 2.

____

____

9. Describe the structure of ionic compounds.

____

____

▶ Properties of Ionic Compounds (pages 196–198)

10. Most ionic compounds are _______________ at room temperature.

11. Is the following sentence true or false? Ionic compounds generally have low melting points. _______________

12. What does a coordination number tell you?

____

____

13. What is the coordination number of the ions in a crystal of NaCl? _______________

Name ______________ Date ______________ Class ______________

14. Circle the letter of each statement that is true about ionic compounds.

a. When dissolved in water, ionic compounds can conduct electricity.

b. When melted, ionic compounds do not conduct electricity.

c. Ionic compounds have very unstable structures.

d. Ionic compounds are electrically neutral.

Reading Skill Practice

By looking carefully at photographs and drawings in textbooks, you can better understand what you have read. Look carefully at Figure 7.10 on page 198. What important idea does this drawing communicate? Do your work on a separate sheet of paper.

SECTION 7.3 BONDING IN METALS (pages 201–203)

This section uses the theory of metallic bonds to explain the physical properties of metals. It also describes the arrangements of atoms in some common metallic crystal structures.

▶ Metallic Bonds and Metallic Properties (pages 201–202)

1. Is the following sentence true or false? Metals are made up of cations, not neutral atoms. ______________

2. What are metallic bonds? ______________

____

____

3. Name three properties of metals that can be explained by metallic bonding.

a. ______________

b. ______________

c. ______________

4. What happens to an ionic crystal when a force is applied to it?

____

____

▶ Crystalline Structure of Metals (page 202)

5. Metal atoms in crystals are arranged into very ______________ and orderly patterns.

Name ______________________ Date ______________ Class ______________

6. Label each of the following arrangements of atoms with the correct name.

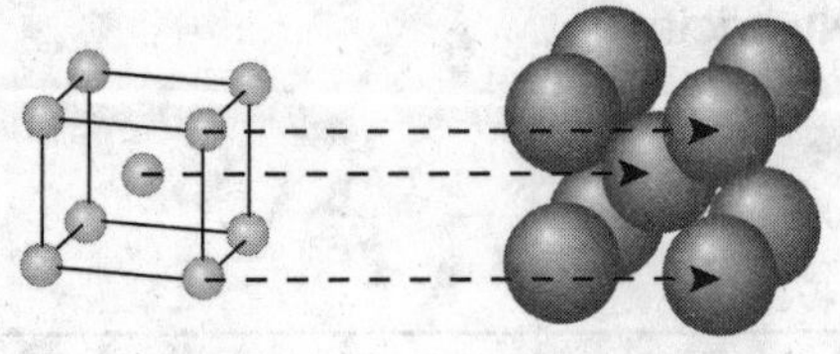

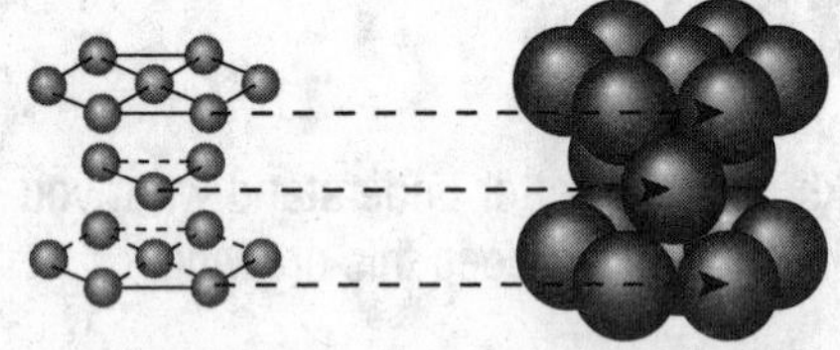

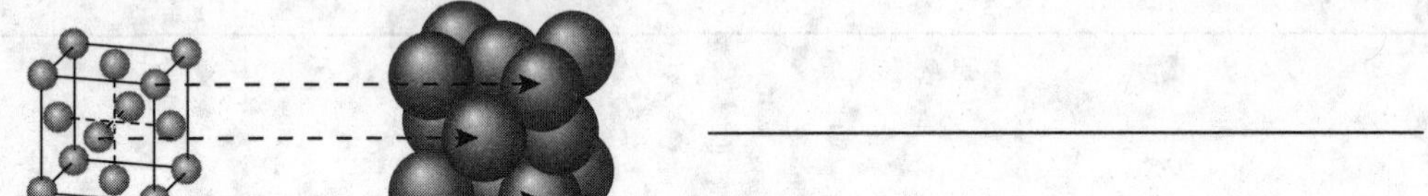

7. Circle the letter of each metal whose atoms form a face-centered cubic pattern.

a. magnesium **c.** sodium

b. copper **d.** aluminum

Match the arrangement with the number of neighbors each atom in the arrangement has.

_____ **8.** body-centered cubic **a.** 12

_____ **9.** face-centered cubic **b.** 8

_____ **10.** hexagonal close-packed

▶ Alloys (page 203)

11. A mixture of two or more elements, at least one of which is a metal, is called a(n) ______________ .

12. Is the following sentence true or false? Pure metals are usually harder and more durable than alloys. ______________

13. The most common use of nonferrous alloys is in ______________ .

14. **What four properties make steel an important alloy?**

a. ______________________

b. ______________________

c. ______________________

d. ______________________

15. **What are the component elements for the following alloys?**

a. sterling silver ______________________

b. brass ______________________

c. surgical steel ______________________

d. cast iron ______________________

16. ______________ alloys have smaller atoms that fit into the spaces between larger atoms. ______________ alloys have component atoms that are roughly equal in size.

GUIDED PRACTICE PROBLEM

GUIDED PRACTICE PROBLEM 12 (page 196)

12. Use electron dot structures to determine formulas of the ionic compounds formed when
a. potassium reacts with iodine.
b. aluminum reacts with oxygen.

a. Potassium reacts with iodine.

Analyze

Step 1. Is one of the elements a metal? If so, which one? ______________

Step 2. Metal atoms ________ their valence electrons when forming ionic compounds.

Nonmetal atoms ________ electrons when forming ionic compounds.

Solve

Step 3. Draw the electron dot structures for potassium and iodine.

potassium ______________ iodine ______________

Step 4. The metal atom, ____________, must lose _____ electron(s) in order to achieve an octet in the next-lowest energy level. The nonmetal atom, ________, must gain _____ electron(s) in order to achieve a complete octet.

Step 5. Using electron dot structures, write an equation that shows the formation of the ionic compound from the two elements. Make sure that the electrons lost equals the electrons gained.

Step 6. The chemical formula for the ionic compound formed is ____________.

Name ____________________ Date ______________ Class ______________

b. Aluminum reacts with oxygen.

Analyze

Step 1. Is one of the elements a metal? If so, which one? ______________

Step 2. Metal atoms ________ valence electrons when forming ionic compounds.

Nonmetal atoms ________ electrons when forming ionic compounds.

Solve

Step 3. Draw the electron dot structures for aluminum and oxygen.

aluminum ______________ oxygen ______________

Step 4. The metal atom, ____________, must lose _____ electron(s) in order to achieve an octet in the next-lowest energy level. The nonmetal atom, ________, must gain _____ electron(s) in order to achieve a complete octet.

Step 5. Using electron dot structures, write an equation that shows the formation of the ionic compound from the two elements. Make sure that the electrons lost equals the electrons gained.

Step 6. The chemical formula for the ionic compound formed is ___________.

Name ______________________ Date ______________ Class ______________

8 COVALENT BONDING

SECTION 8.1 MOLECULAR COMPOUNDS (pages 213–216)

This section explains how to distinguish between ionic and molecular compounds.

▶ Molecules and Molecular Compounds (pages 213–214)

1. What is a covalent bond?

____

2. Many elements found in nature exist as ______________ .

3. What is a molecule?

____

____

4. Compounds that are formed when two or more atoms combine to form molecules are called ______________ .

5. Circle the letter of the substances that do NOT exist as molecules in nature.

a. oxygen

b. water

c. neon

d. ozone

e. helium

6. List two general properties of molecular compounds.

a. ____

b. ____

Name ______________________ Date ______________ Class ______________

CHAPTER 8, Covalent Bonding *(continued)*

▶ Molecular Formulas (pages 215–216)

7. What is a molecular formula?

____

____

Match each compound with its molecular formula.

______ **8.** carbon dioxide **a.** C_2H_6

______ **9.** ethane **b.** CO_2

______ **10.** ammonia **c.** NH_3

11. Is the following sentence true or false? A molecular formula shows the arrangement of the atoms in a molecule. ______________

In the diagram, match the type of model or formula with its representation.

a. ball-and-stick model
b. molecular formula
c. perspective drawing
d. space-filling molecular model
e. structural formula

$NH_3(g)$

12. ____________

13. ____________

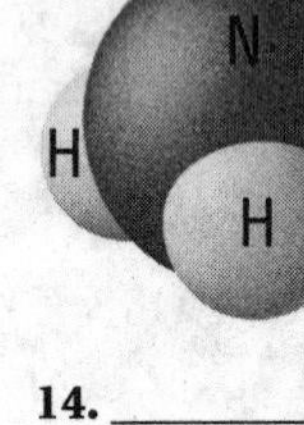

14. ____________

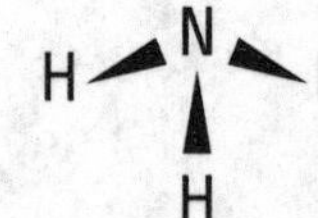

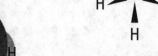

15. ____________

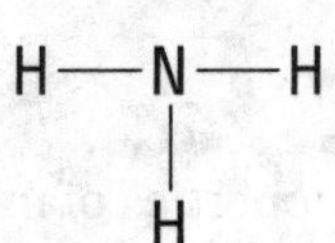

16. ____________

17. What is the arrangement of atoms within a molecule called?

____

Name ______________________ Date ______________ Class ______________

SECTION 8.2 THE NATURE OF COVALENT BONDING (pages 217–220)

This section uses electron dot structures to show the formation of single, double, and triple covalent bonds. It also describes and gives examples of coordinate covalent bonding, resonance structures, and exceptions to the octet rule.

▶ The Octet Rule in Covalent Bonding (page 217)

1. What usually happens to the electron configuration of an atom when it forms a covalent bond?

____

____

▶ Single Covalent Bonds (pages 217–220)

2. Is the following sentence true or false? In a structural formula a shared pair of electrons is represented by a two dashes. ______________

3. Structural formulas show the arrangement of ______________ in molecules.

4. Use the electron dot structure below. Circle each unshared pair of electrons in a water molecule.

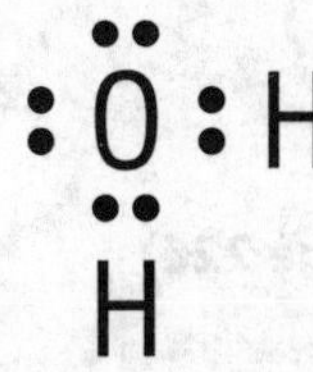

5. Complete the electron dot structure for each molecule. Each molecule contains only single covalent bonds.

a. NH_3	b. H_2O_2	c. CH_4
H N H H	H O O H	H H C H H

▶ Double and Triple Covalent Bonds (pages 221–222)

6. A chemical bond formed when atoms share two pairs of electrons is called a(n) ____.

7. How many covalent bonds are in a nitrogen molecule?

____

CHAPTER 8, Covalent Bonding *(continued)*

8. Is the following sentence true or false? All diatomic molecules contain double bonds. ______________

▶ Coordinate Covalent Bonds (pages 223–225)

9. What is a coordinate covalent bond?

____

____

10. Look at Table 8.2 on page 224. Which two nitrogen compounds contain coordinate covalent bonds?

____

11. Complete the electron dot structure for the chlorate ion (ClO_3^-) by filling in the bonds and unpaired electrons.

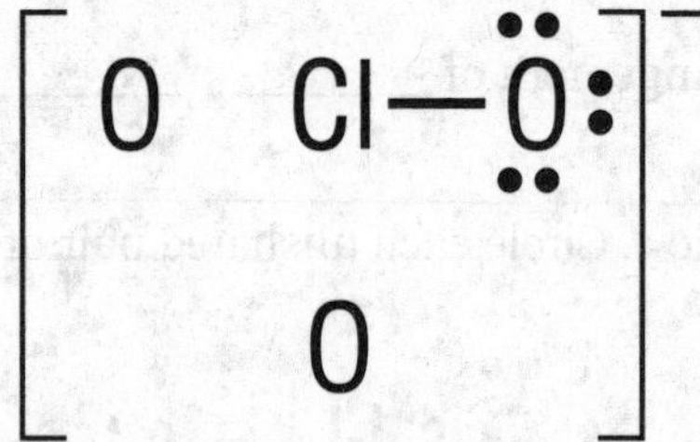

▶ Bond Dissociation Energies (page 226)

12. What is bond dissociation energy?

____

____

13. Is the following sentence true or false? Molecules with high bond dissociation energies are relatively unreactive. ______________

14. What is the bond dissociation energy for a typical C — C covalent bond?

____

Name ______________ Date ______________ Class ______________

▶ Resonance (pages 227–228)

15. The actual bonding in ozone is a ______________ of the extremes represented by its ______________.

16. When can resonance structures be written for a molecule?

____

____

▶ Exceptions to the Octet Rule (pages 228–229)

17. Why does the NO_2 molecule not follow the octet rule?

____

SECTION 8.3 BONDING THEORIES (pages 230–236)

This section describes the molecular orbital model of covalent bonding, including orbital hybridization. It also explains the use of VSEPR theory to predict the shapes of some molecules.

▶ Molecular Orbitals (pages 230–231)

1. What is a molecular orbital?

____

____

2. Is the following sentence true or false? Electrons fill the antibonding molecular orbital first to produce a stable covalent bond. ______________

3. When two *s* atomic orbitals combine and form a molecular orbital, the bond that forms is called a(n) ______________ bond.

4. Circle the letter of each type of covalent bond that can be formed when *p* atomic orbitals overlap.

a. pi **b.** beta **c.** sigma **d.** alpha

▶ VSEPR Theory (pages 232–233)

5. What is VSEPR theory?

____

____

6. When the central atom of a molecule has unshared electrons, the bond angles will be ______________ than when all the central atom's electrons are shared.

CHAPTER 8, Covalent Bonding *(continued)*

7. What is the bond angle in carbon dioxide? Why?

____

8. What are the names of these common molecular shapes?

____

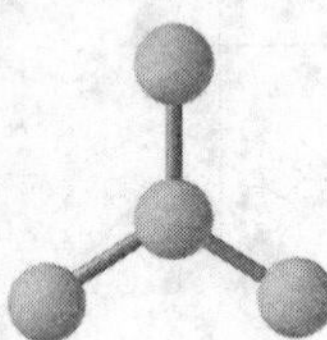

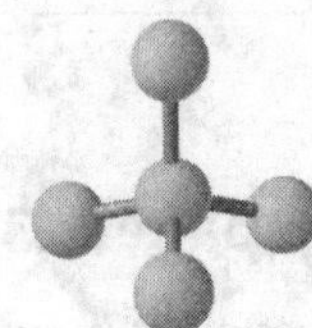

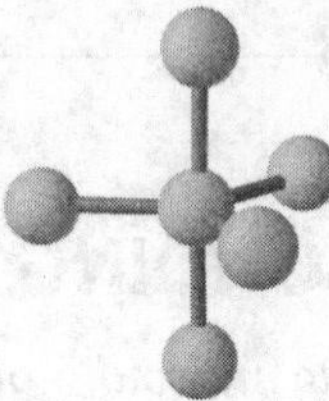

____

▶ Hybrid Orbitals (pages 234–236)

9. Is the following sentence true or false? Orbital hybridization theory can describe both the shape and bonding of molecules. ______________

10. What is orbital hybridization?

____

____

Match the hybrid orbitals formed by carbon with the carbon compound in which they are found.

_____ **11.** sp^3	**a.** ethyne
_____ **12.** sp^2	**b.** ethene
_____ **13.** sp	**c.** methane

Name ______________ Date ______________ Class ______________

Reading Skill Practice

You can increase your understanding of what you have read by making comparisons. A compare/contrast table can help you do this. On a separate sheet of paper, draw a table to compare the three types of hybrid orbitals as explained on pages 234–236. The three heads for the rows should be *sp*, sp^2, and sp^3. Then list the characteristics that will form the basis of your comparison above each column. The column heads should be *Number of Hybrid Orbitals, Component Orbitals, Number of Bonds,* and *Bond Angle.*

SECTION 8.4 POLAR BONDS AND MOLECULES (pages 237–244)

This section explains the use of electronegativity values to classify a bond as nonpolar covalent, polar covalent, or ionic. It also names and describes the weak attractive forces that hold groups of molecules together.

▶ Bond Polarity (pages 237–238)

1. Is the following statement true or false? Covalent bonds differ in the way electrons are shared by the bonded atoms, depending on the kind and number of atoms joined together. ______________

2. Describe how electrons are shared in each type of bond. Write *equally* or *unequally*.

a. Nonpolar bond ______________ **b.** Polar bond ______________

3. Why does the chlorine atom in hydrogen chloride acquire a slightly negative charge? ______________

____

4. What symbols are used to represent the charges on atoms in a polar covalent bond? The polarity of the bond? ______________

Match the electronegativity difference range with the most probable type of bond that will form.

______ **5.** 0.0–0.4	**a.** ionic
______ **6.** 0.4–1.0	**b.** nonpolar covalent
______ **7.** 1.0–2.0	**c.** very polar covalent
______ **8.** > 2.0	**d.** moderately polar covalent

▶ Polar Molecules (pages 239–240)

9. Circle the letter of each sentence that is true about polar molecules.

a. Some regions of a polar molecule are slightly negative and some are slightly positive.

b. A molecule containing a polar bond is always polar.

c. A molecule that has two poles is called a dipolar molecule.

d. When polar molecules are placed in an electric field, they all line up with the same orientation in relation to the charged plates.

10. Are the following molecules polar or nonpolar?

a. H_2O ______________ **c.** NH_3 ______________

b. CO_2 ______________ **d.** HCl ______________

▶ Attractions Between Molecules (pages 240–241)

11. What causes dispersion forces?

____

____

12. Is the following sentence true or false? Dispersion forces generally increase in strength as the number of electrons in a molecule increases. ______________

13. The strongest of the intermolecular forces are ______________ .

▶ Intermolecular Attractions and Molecular Properties (pages 243–244)

14. What determines the physical properties of a compound?

____

____

15. Use Table 8.4 on page 244. Complete the following table comparing ionic and covalent compounds.

Characteristic	Ionic Compound	Covalent Compound
Representative unit		
Physical state		
Melting point		
Solubility in water		

Name ________________ Date ________________ Class ________________

GUIDED PRACTICE PROBLEM

GUIDED PRACTICE PROBLEM 19 (page 239)

19. Identify the bonds between atoms of each pair of elements as nonpolar covalent, moderately polar covalent, very polar covalent, or ionic.

a. H and Br **b.** K and Cl **c.** C and O **d.** Br and Br

Analyze

Step 1. What is the most probable type of bond for each electronegativity difference range?

Electronegativity Difference Range	Most Probable Type of Bond
0.0–0.4	________________
0.4–1.0	________________
1.0–2.0	________________
$\geq$ 2.0	________________

Solve

Step 2. From Table 6.2 on page 177, determine the electronegativity values and differences for each pair of elements.

a. H = 2.1, Br = [ ]; difference = [ ]

b. K = [ ], Cl = 3.0; difference = [ ]

c. C = [ ], O = 3.5; difference = [ ]

d. Br = 2.8, Br = [ ]; difference = [ ]

Step 3. Refer to Table 8.3 on page 238 to determine the most probable type of bond for each compound.

a. ________________

b. ________________

c. ________________

d. ________________

Name ____________________ Date ____________________ Class ____________________

CHEMICAL NAMES AND FORMULAS

SECTION 9.1 NAMING IONS (pages 253–258)

This section explains the use of the periodic table to determine the charge of an ion. It also defines polyatomic ion *and gives the names and formulas for the most common polyatomic ions.*

▶ Monatomic Ions (pages 253–256)

1. What are monatomic ions?

____

2. How is the ionic charge of a Group 1A, 2A, or 3A ion determined?

____

3. How is the ionic charge of a Group 5A, 6A, or 7A ion determined?

____

____

4. Circle the letter of the type of element that often has more than one common ionic charge.

   a. alkali metal

   b. alkaline earth metal

   c. transition metal

   d. nonmetal

5. The ____________________ of naming transition metal cations uses a Roman numeral in parentheses to indicate the numeric value of the ionic charge.

6. An older naming system uses the suffix *-ous* to name the cation with the ____________________ charge, and the suffix *-ic* to name the cation with the ____________________ charge.

7. What is a major advantage of the Stock system over the old naming system?

____

Name ______________________ Date ______________ Class ______________

CHAPTER 9, Chemical Names and Formulas *(continued)*

8. Use the periodic table to write the name and formula (including charge) for each ion in the table below.

Element	Name	Formula
Fluorine		
Calcium		
Oxygen		

▶ Polyatomic Ions (pages 257–258)

9. What is a polyatomic ion?

____

____

10. Is the following sentence true or false? The names of polyatomic anions always end in *-ide.* ____________________

11. What is the difference between the sulfite and sulfate anions?

____

12. Look at Table 9.3 on page 257. Circle the letter of a polyatomic ion that is a cation.

a. ammonium

b. acetate

c. oxalate

d. phosphate

13. How many atoms make up the oxalate ion and what is its charge?

____

____

14. What three hydrogen-containing polyatomic anions are essential components of living systems?

a. ____

b. ____

c. ____

Name ______________________ Date ______________ Class ______________

15. Look at Figure 9.5 on page 257. Identify each of the ions shown below.

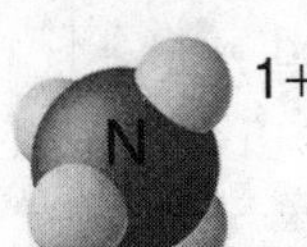

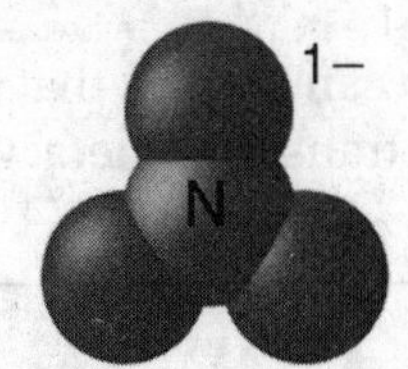

a. ______________ b. ______________ c. ______________

SECTION 9.2 NAMING AND WRITING FORMULAS FOR IONIC COMPOUNDS (pages 260–266)

This section explains the rules for naming and writing formulas for binary ionic compounds and compounds containing a polyatomic ion.

▶ Binary Ionic Compounds (pages 260–263)

1. Traditionally, common names were based on some ______________ of a compound or its ______________.

2. What is the general name for compounds composed of two elements?

   ____

3. When writing the formula for any ionic compound, the charges of the ions must ______________.

4. What are two methods for writing a balanced formula?

   a. ______________________________

   b. ______________________________

5. What are the formulas for the compounds formed by the following pairs of ions?

   a. Fe^{2+}, Cl^{-} ______________

   b. Cr^{3+}, O^{2-} ______________

   c. Na^{+}, S^{2-} ______________

6. What are the formulas for these compounds?

   a. lithium bromide ______________

   b. cupric nitride ______________

   c. magnesium chloride ______________

7. The name of a binary ionic compound is written with the name of the ______________ first followed by the name of the ______________.

Name ______________________ Date ______________ Class ______________

8. How can you tell that cobalt(II) iodide is a binary ionic compound formed by a transition metal with more than one ionic charge?

____

____

9. Write the names for these binary ionic compounds.

a. PbS ______________________

b. $MgCl_2$ ______________________

c. Al_2Se_3 ______________________

▶ Compounds with Polyatomic Ions (pages 264–266)

10. What is a polyatomic ion?

____

11. How do you write the formula for a compound containing a polyatomic ion?

____

____

____

12. Why are parentheses used to write the formula $Al(OH)_3$?

____

13. Complete the table for these ionic compounds containing polyatomic ions.

Cation	Anion	Name	Formula
NH_4^+	S^{2-}		
Fe^{3+}		iron(III) carbonate	
	NO_3^-		$AgNO_3$
		potassium cyanide	KCN

Name ______________ Date ______________ Class ______________

SECTION 9.3 NAMING AND WRITING FORMULAS FOR MOLECULAR COMPOUNDS (pages 268–270)

This section explains the rules for naming and writing formulas for binary molecular compounds.

▶ Naming Binary Molecular Compounds (pages 268–269)

1. Circle the letter of the type(s) of elements that form binary molecular compounds.

   a. two nonmetallic elements

   b. a metal and a nonmetal

   c. two metals

2. Is the following sentence true or false? Two nonmetallic elements can combine in only one way. ______________

3. What method is used to distinguish between different molecular compounds that contain the same elements? ______________

Match the prefix with the number it indicates.

______	**4.** *octa-*	**a.** 4
______	**5.** *tetra-*	**b.** 7
______	**6.** *hepta-*	**c.** 8
______	**7.** *nona-*	**d.** 9

8. What are the names of the following compounds?

   a. BF_3 ______________

   b. N_2O_4 ______________

   c. P_4S_7 ______________

▶ Writing Formulas for Binary Molecular Compounds (page 270)

9. What are the formulas for the following compounds?

   a. carbon tetrabromide ______________

   b. nitrogen triiodide ______________

   c. iodine monochloride ______________

   d. tetraiodine nonaoxide ______________

Name ______________________ Date ________________ Class ______________

Reading Skill Practice

Writing a summary can help you remember the information you have read. When you write a summary, include only the most important points. Write a summary of the information in Section 9.3 on pages 268–269. Your summary should be shorter than the text on which it is based. Do your work on a separate sheet of paper.

SECTION 9.4 NAMING AND WRITING FORMULAS FOR ACIDS AND BASES (pages 271–273)

This section explains the three rules for naming acids and shows how these rules can also be used to write the formulas for acids. Names and formulas for bases are also explained.

▶ Naming Common Acids (pages 271–272)

1. Acids produce ____________________ ions when dissolved in water.

2. When naming acids, you can consider them to be combinations of ____________________ connected to as many ____________________ ions as are necessary to create an electrically neutral compound.

3. What is the formula for hydrobromic acid? ________________

4. What are the components of phosphorous acid? What is its formula?

   ____

▶ Writing Formulas for Acids (page 272)

5. Use Table 9.5 on page 272 to help you complete the table about acids.

Acid Name	Formula	Anion Name
acetic acid		
carbonic acid		
hydrochloric acid		
nitric acid		
phosphoric acid		
sulfuric acid		

Name ______________________ Date ______________ Class ______________

▶ Names and Formulas for Bases (page 273)

6. A base is a compound that produces ______________ when dissolved in water.

7. How are bases named?

____

SECTION 9.5 THE LAWS GOVERNING FORMULAS AND NAMES (pages 274–279)

This section uses data to demonstrate that a compound obeys the law of definite proportions. It also explains how to use flow charts to write the name and formula of a compound.

▶ The Laws of Definite and Multiple Proportions (pages 274–275)

1. What is the law of definite proportions?

____

____

____

2. Circle the whole-number mass ratio of Li to Cl in LiCl. The atomic mass of Li is 6.9; the atomic mass of Cl is 35.5.

   a. 42 : 1

   b. 5 : 1

   c. 1 : 5

3. Circle the whole-number mass ratio of carbon to hydrogen in C_2H_4. The atomic mass of C is 12.0; the atomic mass of H is 1.0.

   a. 1 : 6 **c.** 1 : 12

   b. 6 : 1 **d.** 12 : 1

4. In the compound sulfur dioxide, a food preservative, the mass ratio of sulfur to oxygen is 1 : 1. An 80-g sample of a compound composed of sulfur and oxygen contains 48 g of oxygen. Is the sample sulfur dioxide? Explain.

____

____

5. What is the law of multiple proportions?

____

____

____

Name ______________________ Date ______________ Class ______________

6. Complete the table using the law of multiple proportions.

	Mass of Cu	Mass of Cl	Mass Ratio Cl : Cu	Whole-number Ratio of Cl
Compound A	8.3 g	4.6 g		
Compound B	3.3 g	3.6 g		

▶ Practicing Skills: Naming Chemical Compounds (pages 276–277)

7. How can a flowchart help you to name chemical compounds?

____

8. Use the flowchart in Figure 9.20 on page 277 to write the names of the following compounds:

a. CsCl ______________________

b. $SnSe_2$ ______________________

c. NH_4OH ______________________

d. HF ______________________

e. Si_3N_4 ______________________

9. Complete the following five rules for writing a chemical formula from a chemical name.

a. In an ionic compound, the net ionic charge is ______________.

b. An *-ide* ending generally indicates a ______________ compound.

c. An *-ite* or *-ate* ending means there is a ______________ ion that includes oxygen in the formula.

d. ______________ in a name generally indicate that the compound is molecular and show the number of each kind of atom in the molecule.

e. A ______________ after the name of a cation shows the ionic charge of the cation.

Name ______________________ Date ______________________ Class ______________________

▶ Practicing Skills: Writing Chemical Formulas (page 278)

10. Fill in the missing labels from Figure 9.22 on page 278.

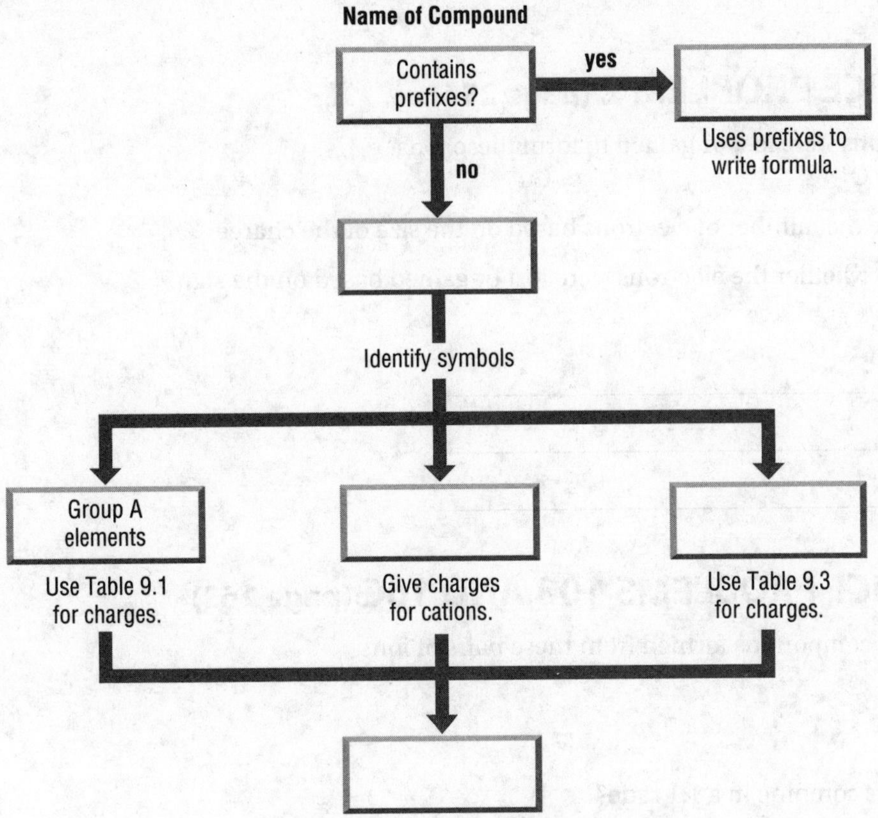

Name of Compound
Contains prefixes?
yes
Uses prefixes to write formula.
no
Identify symbols
Group A elements
Use Table 9.1 for charges.
Give charges for cations.
Use Table 9.3 for charges.
Use crisscross method. Add parentheses for any multiple polyatomic ions.

11. Use the flowchart in Figure 9.22 to write the formulas of the following compounds:

a. potassium silicate ______________________

b. phosphorus pentachloride ______________________

c. manganese(II) chromate ______________________

d. lithium hydride ______________________

e. diiodine pentoxide ______________________

GUIDED PRACTICE PROBLEMS

GUIDED PRACTICE PROBLEM 2 (page 256)

2. How many electrons were lost or gained to form these ions?
a. Fe^{3+} **b.** O^{2-} **c.** Cu^{+}

Step 1. Determine the number of electrons based on the size of the charge.

Step 2. Determine whether the electrons were lost or gained based on the sign of the charge.

a. ______________________________

b. ______________________________

c. ______________________________

GUIDED PRACTICE PROBLEMS 10B AND 10C (page 263)

10. Write formulas for compounds formed from these pairs of ions.

b. Li^{+}, O^{2-}

Analyze

Step 1. Do the ions combine in a 1:1 ratio?

____

Solve

Step 2. Use the crisscross method to balance the formula.

Write the formula. __________

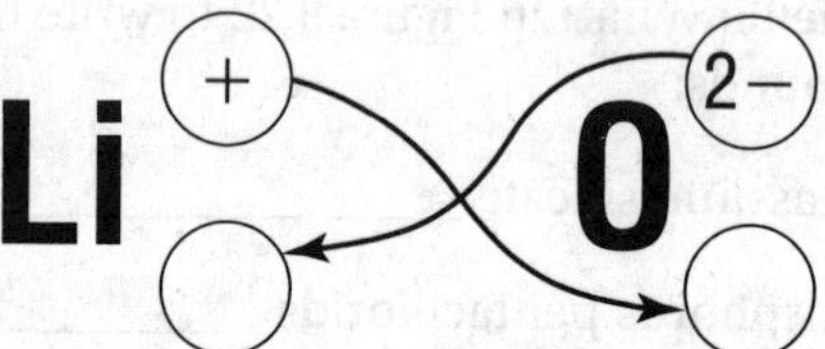

Name ______________________ Date ________________ Class ______________

c. Ca^{2+}, N^{3-}

Analyze

Step 1. Will the calcium (Ca^{2+}) and nitride (N^{3-}) ions combine in a 1 : 1 ratio? How do you know?

____

____

Solve

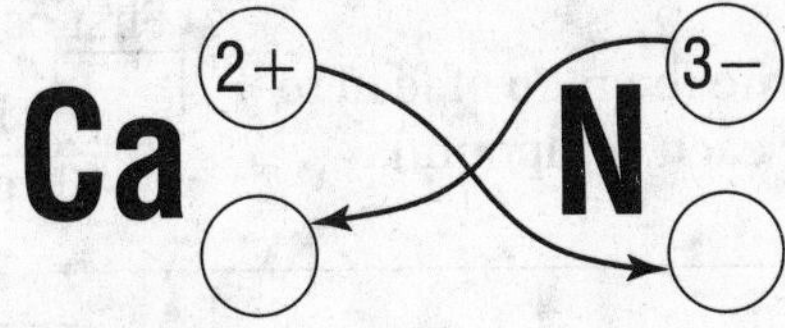

Step 2. Use the crisscross method to balance the formula.

Write the formula. ________

GUIDED PRACTICE PROBLEM 13B (page 265)

13b. Write the formula for chromium(III) nitrate.

- Is the compound ionic or molecular? Explain.

____

- Use Table 9.3 on page 257 to write the formula for the nitrate ion. ________
- Use the crisscross method to balance the formula.
- Write the formula. ________________

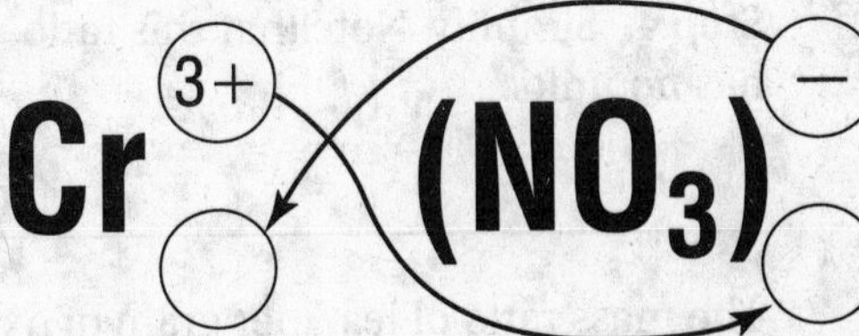

GUIDED PRACTICE PROBLEM 34 (page 275)

34. Lead forms two compounds with oxygen. One compound contains 2.98 g of lead and 0.461 g of oxygen. The other contains 9.89 g of lead and 0.763 g of oxygen. For a given mass of oxygen, what is the lowest whole-number mass ratio of lead in the two compounds?

Complete the following steps to solve the problem.

	First compound	Second compound
Step 1. Write the ratio of lead to oxygen for each compound.	$\frac{\boxed{}\text{ g lead}}{0.461\text{ g oxygen}}$	$\frac{9.89\text{ g lead}}{\boxed{}\text{ g oxygen}}$
Step 2. Divide the numerator by the denominator in each ratio.	$\frac{6.46\ \boxed{}}{\boxed{}}$	$\frac{\boxed{}\text{ g lead}}{\text{g oxygen}}$
Step 3. Write a ratio comparing the first compound to the second.	$\frac{\boxed{}\ \cancel{\text{g lead/g oxygen}}}{13.0\ \cancel{\text{g lead/g oxygen}}}$	
Step 4. Simplify. Note that this ratio has no units.	$\frac{0.497}{1} = \text{roughly } \frac{1}{\boxed{}}$	

The mass ratio of lead per gram of oxygen in the two compounds is ____________.

Name ______________________ Date ______________ Class ______________

10 CHEMICAL QUANTITIES

SECTION 10.1 THE MOLE: A MEASUREMENT OF MATTER (pages 287–296)

This section defines the mole and explains how the mole is used to measure matter. It also teaches you how to calculate the mass of a mole of any substance.

▶ Measuring Matter (pages 287–289)

1. What do the questions "how much?" and "how many?" have in common?

____

____

2. List two or three ways to measure matter.

____

▶ What Is a Mole? (pages 290–293)

3. Circle the letter of the term that is an SI unit for measuring the amount of a substance.

   a. dozen b. ounce c. pair d. mole

4. What is Avogadro's number?

____

5. Circle the letter of the term that is NOT a representative particle of a substance.

   a. molecule b. atom c. grain d. formula unit

6. List the representative particle for each of the following types of substances.

   a. molecular compounds ______________

   b. ionic compounds ______________

   c. elements ______________

7. Is the following sentence true or false? To determine the number of representative particles in a compound, you count the molecules by viewing them under a microscope. ______________

8. How can you determine the number of atoms in a mole of a molecular compound?

____

____

Name ______________________ Date ______________ Class ______________

CHAPTER 10, Chemical Quantities *(continued)*

9. Complete the table about representative particles and moles.

Representative Particles and Moles			
	Representative Particle	Chemical Formula	Representative Particles in 1.00 mol
Atomic oxygen		O	
Oxygen gas	Molecule		
Sodium ion			
Sodium chloride			

▶ The Mass of a Mole of an Element (pages 293–294)

10. What is the atomic mass of an element?

____

11. Circle the letter of the phrase that completes this sentence correctly. The atomic masses of all elements

a. are the same.

b. are based on the mass of the carbon isotope C-12.

c. are based on the mass of a hydrogen atom.

▶ The Mass of a Mole of a Compound (pages 295–296)

12. How do you determine the mass of a mole of a compound?

____

____

____

13. Complete the labels on the diagram below.

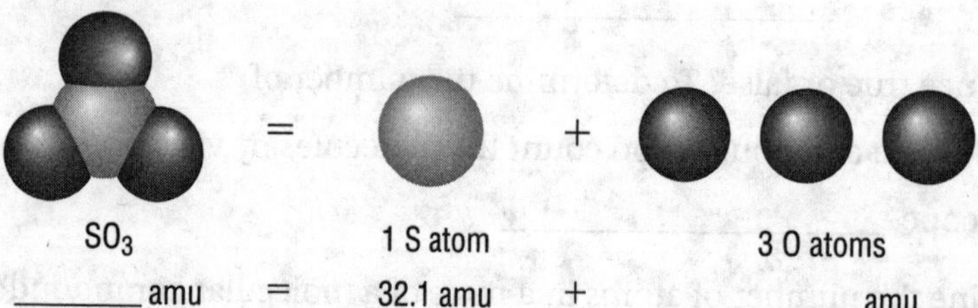

SO_3 = 1 S atom + 3 O atoms

________ amu = 32.1 amu + ________ amu

Name ______________________ Date ______________ Class ______________

14. What is the molar mass of a compound?

____

15. Is the following sentence true or false? Molar masses can be calculated directly from atomic masses expressed in grams. ______________

SECTION 10.2 MOLE–MASS AND MOLE–VOLUME RELATIONSHIPS (pages 297–303)

This section explains how to use molar mass and molar volume to convert among measurements of mass, volume, and number of particles.

▶ The Mole–Mass Relationship (pages 297–299)

1. What is the molar mass of a substance?

____

2. What is the molar mass of KI (potassium iodide)?

____

▶ The Mole–Volume Relationship (pages 300–302)

3. Is the following sentence true or false? The volumes of one mole of different solid and liquid substances are the same. ______________

4. Circle the letter of each term that can complete this sentence correctly. The volume of a gas varies with a change in

   a. temperature.
   b. the size of the container.
   c. pressure.
   d. the amount of light in the container.

5. Circle the letter of the temperature that is defined as standard temperature.

   a. 0 K
   b. 100 K
   c. 0°C
   d. 100°C

6. Is the following sentence true or false? Standard pressure is 101.3 kPa or 1 atmosphere (atm). ______________

7. What is the molar volume of a gas at standard temperature and pressure (STP)? ______________

8. What units do you normally use to describe the density of a gas?

____

Name ______________________ Date ______________ Class ______________

9. What is Avogadro's hypothesis?

____

____

10. Look at Figure 10.9 on page 300 to help you answer this question. Why is Avogadro's hypothesis reasonable?

____

____

____

11. How many gas particles occupy a volume of 22.4 L at standard temperature and pressure? ______________

▶ The Mole Road Map (page 303)

12. The figure below shows how to convert from one unit to another unit. Write the missing conversion factors below.

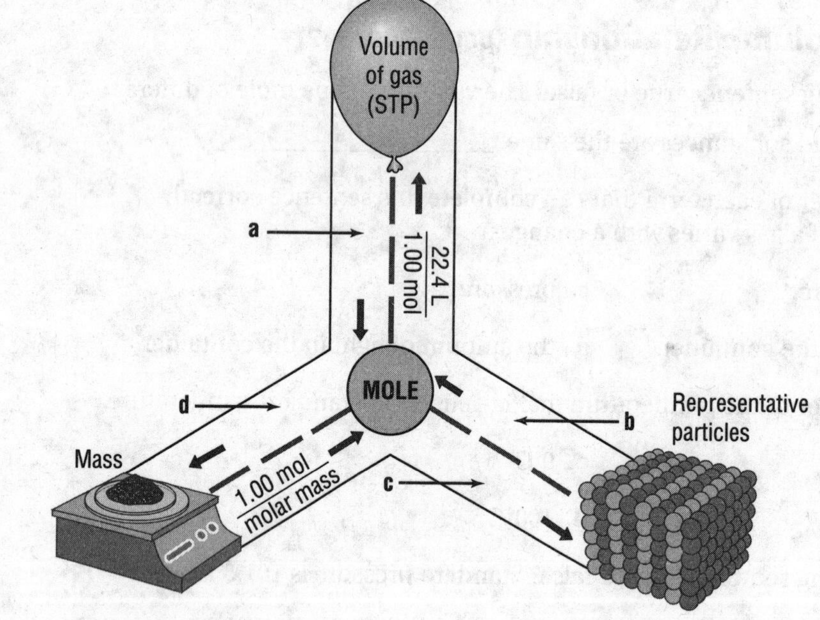

a. ______________________ **c.** ______________________

b. ______________________ **d.** ______________________

Name ______________________ Date ______________ Class ______________

SECTION 10.3 PERCENT COMPOSITION AND CHEMICAL FORMULAS (pages 305–312)

This section explains how to calculate percent composition from chemical formulas or experimental data, and how to derive empirical and molecular formulas.

▶ Percent Composition of a Compound (pages 305–308)

1. How do you express relative amounts of each element in a compound?

____

2. Circle the letter of the phrase that completes this sentence correctly. The number of percent values in the percent composition of a compound is

a. half as many as there are different elements in the compound.

b. as many as there are different elements in the compound.

c. twice as many as there are different elements in the compound.

3. What is the formula for the percent by mass of an element in a compound?

____

4. In the diagram below, which compound has a greater percent composition of chromium? ______________________

How much greater is this percent? __________

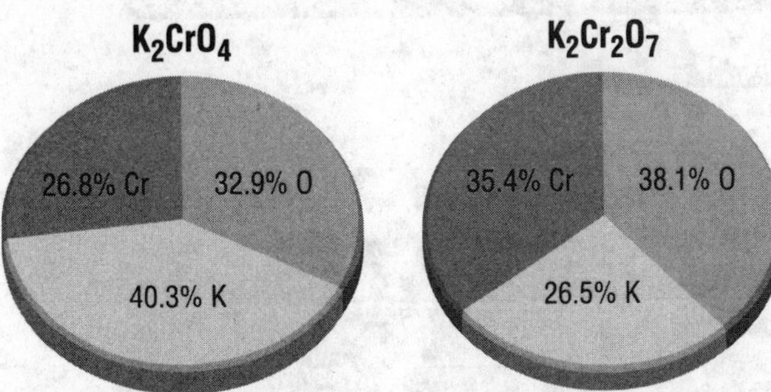

Potassium chromate, K_2CrO_4 Potassium dichromate, $K_2Cr_2O_7$

5. To calculate the percent composition of a known compound, start with the chemical formula of the compound and calculate the ________________, which gives the mass of one mole of the compound.

6. Is the following sentence true or false? You can use percent composition to calculate the number of grams of an element in a given amount of a compound. ________________

7. How do you calculate the grams of an element in a specific amount of a compound?

____

____

▶ Empirical Formulas (pages 309–310)

8. An empirical formula of a compound gives the ______________ whole-number ratio of the atoms of the elements in a compound.

9. Is the following sentence true or false? The empirical formula of a compound is always the same as the molecular formula. ______________

10. Look at Figure 10.16 and Table 10.3. Name three compounds that have an empirical formula of CH.

____

11. Fill in the labels on the diagram below.

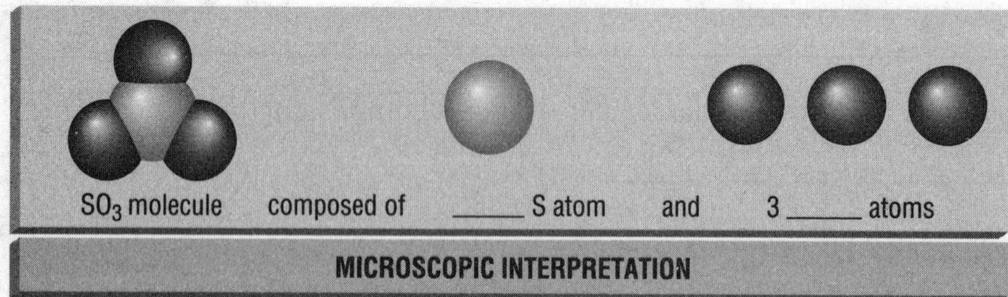

Name ______________________ Date ______________ Class ______________

▶ Molecular Formulas (pages 311–312)

12. The molecular formula of a compound is either the same as its empirical formula or a ______________________________ of it.

13. What do you need to know to calculate the molecular formula of a compound?

____

14. If you divide the molar mass of a compound by the empirical formula mass, what is the result?

____

15. What factor would you use to convert the empirical formula of a compound to a molecular formula?

____

Reading Skill Practice

By looking carefully at photographs and illustrations in textbooks, you can better understand what you have read. Look carefully at Figure 10.15 on page 309. What important idea does this illustration communicate?

GUIDED PRACTICE PROBLEMS

GUIDED PRACTICE PROBLEM 1 (page 289)

1. If 0.20 bushels is 1 dozen apples and a dozen apples has a mass of 2.0 kg, what is the mass of 0.50 bushel of apples?

Analyze

Step 1. List the knowns and the unknown.
Knowns

____

____

____

Unknown

____

Use dimensional analysis to convert the number of bushels to the mass of apples, by following this sequence of conversions:

Number of bushels → dozens of apples → mass of apples

Calculate

Step 2. Solve for the unknown.
The first conversion factor is:

The second conversion factor is:

Multiplying the number of bushels by these two conversion factors gives the answer in kilograms.

The mass of 0.50 bushel of apples is __________.

Evaluate

Step 3. Does the result make sense?

____

____

____

Name ______________________ Date ______________ Class ______________

GUIDED PRACTICE PROBLEM 3 (page 291)

3. How many moles is 2.80×10^{24} atoms of silicon?

Step 1. List what you know.

2.80×10^{24} atoms of Si

[ ] atoms in one mole

Step 2. Multiply the atoms of silicon by a mol/atoms conversion factor.

2.80×10^{24} atoms Si $\times \dfrac{1 \text{ mol}}{\square \text{ atoms Si}}$

Step 3. Divide.

[ ] mol

GUIDED PRACTICE PROBLEM 5 (page 292)

5. How many atoms are in 1.14 mol SO_3?

Analyze

Step 1. List the knowns and the unknown.

Knowns

____

____

____

Unknown

____

Calculate

Step 2. Solve for the unknown.

The first conversion factor is $\dfrac{6.02 \times 10^{23} \text{ molecules of water}}{1 \text{ mol water}}$

The second conversion factor is $\dfrac{4 \text{ atoms}}{1 \text{ molecule } SO_3}$.

Multiply moles of SO_3 by these conversion factors:

number of atoms $= 1.14 \cancel{\text{mol } SO_3} \times \dfrac{6.02 \times 10^{23} \cancel{\text{molecules of } SO_3}}{\cancel{1 \text{ mol } SO_3}} \times \dfrac{4 \text{ atoms}}{\cancel{1 \text{ molecule } SO_3}}$.

= ______________________

Evaluate

Step 3. Does the result make sense?

____

____

Name ______________________ Date ________________ Class ________________

EXTRA PRACTICE (similar to Practice Problem 5, page 292)

4. How many molecules is 0.360 mol of water?

Analyze

Step 1. List the knowns and the unknown.
Knowns

____

____

Unknown

____

Calculate

Step 2. Solve for the unknown.
The conversion factor is $\frac{6.02 \times 10^{23} \text{ molecules of water}}{1 \text{ mol water}}$

Multiplying mols of water by this conversion factor will give the answer

$$\text{molecules of water} = 0.360 \cancel{\text{mol water}} \times \frac{6.02 \times 10^{23} \text{ molecules of water}}{1 \cancel{\text{mol water}}}$$

= ______________________

Evaluate

Step 3. Does the result make sense?

____

____

GUIDED PRACTICE PROBLEM 7 (page 296)

7. Find the molar mass of PCl_3.

Analyze

Step 1. List the knowns and the unknown.
Knowns

____

____

____

Name ____________________ Date ______________ Class ______________

Unknown

____

Calculate

Step 2. Solve for the unknown.
Convert moles of phosphorus and chlorine to grams of phosphorus and chlorine. Then add to get the results.

$$1 \cancel{\text{mol P}} \times \frac{31.0 \text{ g P}}{1 \cancel{\text{mol P}}} = 31.0 \text{ g P}$$

$$3 \cancel{\text{mol Cl}} \times \frac{35.5 \text{ g Cl}}{1 \cancel{\text{mol Cl}}} = 106.5 \text{ g Cl}$$

molar mass of PCl_3 = ______________

Evaluate

Step 3. Does the result make sense?

____

____

EXTRA PRACTICE (similar to Practice Problem 5, page 292)

5. How many atoms are there in 2.00 moles of SO_3?

EXTRA PRACTICE (similar to Practice Problem 7, page 296)

7. Find the molar mass of table salt (sodium chloride).

EXTRA PRACTICE (similar to Practice Problem 8, page 296)

8. What is the mass of 1 mole of ozone (O_3)?

GUIDED PRACTICE PROBLEM 16 (page 298)

16. Find the mass, in grams, of 4.52×10^{-3} mol $C_{20}H_{42}$.

Analyze

Step 1. List the known and the unknown.
Known

____

Unknown

____

Calculate

Step 2. Solve for the unknown.
Determine the molar mass of $C_{20}H_{42}$:

1 mol $C_{20}H_{42}$ = 20 × 12.0 g + 42 × 1.0 g = 282 g

Multiply the given number of moles by the conversion factor:

$$\text{mass} = 4.52 \times 10^{-3}\ \cancel{\text{mol } C_{20}H_{42}} \times \frac{282\ \text{g } C_{20}H_{42}}{\cancel{1\ \text{mol } C_{20}H_{42}}} = \underline{\hspace{4cm}}$$

Evaluate

Step 3. Does the result make sense?

____

____

EXTRA PRACTICE (similar to Practice Problem 17, page 298)

17. Calculate the mass, in grams, of 10 mol of sodium sulfate (Na_2SO_4).

Calculate the mass, in grams, of 10 mol of iron(II) hydroxide ($Fe(OH)_2$).

Name ______________________ Date ______________ Class ______________

GUIDED PRACTICE PROBLEM 18 (page 299)

18. Find the number of moles in 3.70×10^{-1} g of boron.

Analyze

Step 1. List the known and the unknown.
Known

____

Unknown

____

The unknown number of moles is calculated by converting the known mass to the number of moles using a conversion factor of mass → moles.

Calculate

Step 2. Solve for the unknown.
Determine the molar mass of boron: 1 mol B = 10.8 g B

Multiply the given mass by the conversion factor relating mass of boron to moles of boron:

$$\text{mass} = 3.70 \times 10^{-1}\ \cancel{\text{g B}} \times \frac{1\ \text{mol B}}{10.8\ \cancel{\text{g B}}}$$

= ______________________

Evaluate

Step 3. Does the result make sense?

____

____

GUIDED PRACTICE PROBLEM 20 (page 301)

20. What is the volume of these gases at STP?
a. 3.20×10^{-3} mol CO_2
b. 3.70 mol N_2

a. 3.20×10^{-3} mol CO_2

Analyze

Step 1. List the knowns and the unknown.
Knowns

____

____

Unknown

____

To convert moles to liters, use the relationship 1 mol CO_2 = 22.4 L CO_2 (at STP).

Calculate

Step 2. Solve for the unknown.
Multiply the given number of moles of CO_2 by the conversion factor to give the result.

$$\text{volume} = 3.20 \times 10^{-3}\ \cancel{\text{mol } CO_2} \times \frac{22.4 \text{ L } CO_2}{1\ \cancel{\text{mol } CO_2}}$$

= ______________

Evaluate

Step 3. Does the result make sense?

____

____

b. 3.70 mol N_2

Analyze

Step 1. List the knowns and the unknown.
Knowns

____

____

Unknown

____

Use the relationship 1 mol N_2 = 22.4 L N_2 (at STP) to convert moles to liters.

Calculate

Step 2. Solve for the unknown.
Multiply the given number of moles of N_2 by the conversion factor to give the result.

$$\text{volume} = 3.70\ \cancel{\text{mol } N_2} \times \frac{22.4 \text{ L } N_2}{1\ \cancel{\text{mol } N_2}}$$

= ______________

Name ______________________ Date ______________ Class ______________

Evaluate

Step 3. Does the result make sense?

____

____

GUIDED PRACTICE PROBLEM 22 (page 302)

22. A gaseous compound composed of sulfur and oxygen, which is linked to the formation of acid rain, has a density of 3.58 g/L at STP. What is the molar mass of this gas?

Analyze

Step 1. List the knowns and the unknown.
Knowns

____

____

Unknown

____

To convert density (g/L) to molar mass (g/mol), a conversion factor of L/mol is needed.

Calculate

Step 2. Solve for the unknown.
Multiply the density by the conversion factor relating liters and moles.

$$\text{molar mass} = \frac{3.58\ \text{g}}{1\ \text{L}} \times \frac{22.4\ \text{L}}{1\ \text{mol}}$$

$= \_\_\_\_\_\_\_\_\_\_\_\_\_\_$

Evaluate

Step 3. Does the result make sense?

____

____

GUIDED PRACTICE PROBLEM 32 (page 306)

32. A compound is formed when 9.03 g Mg combines with 3.48 g N. What is the percent composition of this compound?

Analyze

Step 1. List the known and the unknowns.
Knowns

____

____

____

Unknowns

____

____

The percent of an element in a compound is the mass of the element in the compound divided by the mass of the compound. To be expressed as a percentage, the ratio must be multiplied by 100%.

Calculate

Step 2. Solve for the unknown.

$$\text{percent Mg} = \frac{9.03 \text{ g Mg}}{12.51 \text{ g compound}} \times 100\% = \_\_\_\_\_\_\_\_$$

$$\text{percent N} = \frac{3.48 \text{ g N}}{12.51 \text{ g compound}} \times 100\% = \_\_\_\_\_\_\_\_$$

Evaluate

Step 3. Does the result make sense?

____

____

Name ______________________ Date ______________ Class ______________

GUIDED PRACTICE PROBLEM 34 (page 307)

34. Calculate the percent composition of these compounds.
a. ethane (C_2H_6)
b. sodium hydrogen sulfate ($NaHSO_4$)

a. ethane (C_2H_6)

Analyze

Step 1. List the knowns and the unknowns.

Knowns

____

____

____

Unknowns

____

____

Because no masses are given, the percent composition can be determined based on the molar mass of the substance. The percent of an element in a compound is the mass of the element in the compound divided by the mass of the compound. To express the ratio as a percent, the ratio is multiplied by 100%.

Calculate

Step 2. Solve for the unknown.

$$\text{percent C} = \frac{24.0\ \text{g C}}{30.0\ \text{g compound}} \times 100\% = \_\_\_\_\_\_\_\_\_\_$$

$$\text{percent H} = \frac{6.0\ \text{g H}}{30.0\ \text{g compound}} \times 100\% = \_\_\_\_\_\_\_\_\_\_$$

Evaluate

Step 3. Does the result make sense?

____

____

Name ______________ Date ______________ Class ______________

b. sodium hydrogen sulfate ($NaHSO_4$)

Analyze

Step 1. List the knowns and the unknowns.

Knowns

____

____

____

____

____

Unknowns

____

____

____

____

Because no masses are given, the percent composition can be determined based on the molar mass of the substance. The percent of an element in a compound is the mass of the element in the compound divided by the mass of the compound. To express the ratio as a percent, the ratio is multiplied by 100%.

Calculate

Step 2. Solve for the unknown.

$$\text{percent Na} = \frac{23.0\ \text{g Na}}{120.1\ \text{g compound}} \times 100\% = \underline{\qquad\qquad}$$

$$\text{percent H} = \frac{1.0\ \text{g H}}{120.1\ \text{g compound}} \times 100\% = \underline{\qquad\qquad}$$

$$\text{percent S} = \frac{32.1\ \text{g S}}{120.1\ \text{g compound}} \times 100\% = \underline{\qquad\qquad}$$

$$\text{percent O} = \frac{64.0\ \text{g O}}{120.1\ \text{g compound}} \times 100\% = \underline{\qquad\qquad}$$

Evaluate

Step 3. Does the result make sense?

____

____

GUIDED PRACTICE PROBLEM 36 (page 310)

36. Calculate the empirical formula of each compound.
a. 94.1% O, 5.9% H
b. 67.6% Hg, 10.8% S, 21.6% O

a. 94.1% O, 5.9% H

Analyze

Step 1. List the knowns and the unknown.

Knowns

____

____

____

Unknown

____

Use the percent composition to convert to mass, recalling that percent means parts per hundred. Then use the molar mass to convert to number of moles. Finally, determine whole number ratios based on the number of moles of each element per 100 grams of compound.

Calculate

Step 2. Solve for the unknown.
One hundred grams of compound has 5.9 g H and 94.1 g O.
Multiply by conversion factors relating moles of the elements to grams.

$$5.9\ \cancel{\text{g H}} \times \frac{1\ \text{mol H}}{1.0\ \cancel{\text{g H}}} = 5.9\ \text{mol H}$$

$$94.1\ \cancel{\text{g O}} \times \frac{1\ \text{mol O}}{16.0\ \cancel{\text{g O}}} = 5.88\ \text{mol O}$$

So the mole ratio for 100 g of the compound is $H_{5.9}O_{5.9}$. But formulas must have whole number subscripts. Divide each molar quantity by the smaller number of moles. This will give 1 mol for the element with the smaller number of moles. In this case, the ratio is one-to-one and so the empirical formula is simply H_1O_1. However, a subscript of one is never written, so the answer is ______.

Evaluate

Step 3. Does the result make sense?

____

____

b. 67.6% Hg, 10.8% S, 21.6% O

Analyze

Step 1. List the knowns and the unknown.

Knowns

____

____

____

____

Unknown

____

Use the percent composition to convert to mass. Then use molar mass to convert to number of moles. Finally, determine whole number ratios based on the number of moles of each element per 100 grams of compound.

Calculate

Step 2. Solve for the unknown.

One hundred grams of compound has 67.6 g Hg, 10.8 g S, and 21.6 g O. Multiply by a conversion factor relating moles to grams.

$$67.6\ \cancel{g\ Hg} \times \frac{1\ mol\ Hg}{200.6\ \cancel{g\ Hg}} = 0.337\ mol\ Hg$$

$$10.8\ \cancel{g\ S} \times \frac{1\ mol\ S}{32.1\ \cancel{g\ S}} = 0.336\ mol\ S$$

$$21.6\ \cancel{g\ O} \times \frac{1\ mol\ O}{16.0\ \cancel{g\ O}} = 1.35\ mol\ O$$

So the mole ratio for 100 g of the compound is $Hg_{0.34}S_{0.34}O_{1.35}$.

Divide each molar quantity by the smaller number of moles.

$$\frac{0.34\ mol\ Hg}{0.34} = 1\ mol\ Hg$$

$$\frac{0.34\ mol\ S}{0.34} = 1\ mol\ S$$

$$\frac{1.35\ mol\ O}{1.35} = 4\ mol\ O$$

The empirical formula is ______________.

Evaluate

Step 3. Does the result make sense?

____

____

Name ______________________ Date ________________ Class ________________

GUIDED PRACTICE PROBLEM 38 (page 312)

38. Find the molecular formula of ethylene glycol, which is used as antifreeze. The molar mass is 62 g/mol and the empirical formula is CH_3O.

Analyze

Step 1. List the knowns and the unknown.
Knowns

____

____

Unknown

____

Calculate

Step 2. Solve for the unknown.
First, calculate the empirical formula mass (efm):

$$1\ \cancel{\text{mol C}} \times \frac{12\ \text{g C}}{1\ \cancel{\text{mol C}}} = 12\ \text{g C}$$

$$3\ \cancel{\text{mol H}} \times \frac{1.0\ \text{g H}}{1\ \cancel{\text{mol H}}} = 3\ \text{g H}$$

$$1\ \cancel{\text{mol O}} \times \frac{16\ \text{g O}}{1\ \cancel{\text{mol O}}} = 16\ \text{g O}$$

So efm = 12g + 3 g + 16 g = 31 g.

Divide the molar mass by the empirical formula mass:
Molar mass/efm = 62 g/31 g = 2

Multiply subscripts in the empirical formula by this value.

The molecular formula is ____________________.

Evaluate

Step 3. Does the result make sense?

____

____

Name ______________________ Date ______________ Class ______________

11 CHEMICAL REACTIONS

SECTION 11.1 DESCRIBING CHEMICAL REACTIONS (pages 321–329)

This section explains how to write equations describing chemical reactions using appropriate symbols. It also describes how to write balanced chemical equations when given the names or formulas of the reactants and products in a chemical reaction.

▶ Writing Chemical Equations (pages 321–323)

1. A chemical reaction occurs when one or more ______________ change into one or more new substances called ______________.

2. The arrow in a reaction means ____

____.

3. Is the following sentence true or false? When there are two or more reactants or products, they are separated by an arrow. ______________

4. Write a word equation that describes the following reactions.

   a. Acetylene reacts with oxygen to produce carbon dioxide and water.

   ____

   b. When heated, mercury(II) oxide reacts to form mercury and oxygen.

   ____

5. What is a chemical equation?

____

____

6. A chemical reaction that shows only the formulas, but not the relative amounts of the reactants and products is a(n) ______________.

7. Identify the reactant(s) and product(s) in the chemical equation $Li + Br_2 \longrightarrow LiBr$.

   a. reactant(s) ______________

   b. product(s) ______________

8. Circle the letter of each statement that is true about a catalyst.

   a. A catalyst is the new material produced as a result of a chemical reaction.

   b. A catalyst is not used up in a chemical reaction.

   c. A catalyst adds heat to a chemical reaction.

   d. A catalyst speeds up a chemical reaction.

Name ______________________ Date ______________ Class ______________

9. Use the symbols in Table 11.1 on page 323 to write a skeleton equation for the following chemical reaction. Hydrochloric acid reacts with zinc to produce aqueous zinc(II) chloride and hydrogen gas.

____

▶ Balancing Chemical Equations (pages 324–328)

10. What is the law of conservation of mass?

____

11. Complete the flowchart for balancing equations.

Determine the correct formulas and physical states for the ______________ and ______________.

↓

Write a ______________ with the formulas for the reactants on the left and the formulas for the products on the right of a yields sign (⟶).

↓

Count the number of ______________ of each element in the reactants and in the products.

↓

Balance the number of atoms of the elements on the two sides of the equation by placing ______________ in front of formulas. Never try to balance an equation by changing the ______________ in formulas.

↓

Check each atom or polyatomic ion to be sure the equation is ______________, and make sure that all coefficients are in the ______________ possible ratio.

Name ______________________ Date ______________ Class ______________

12. Balance the following chemical equations.

a. _______ $Na(s)$ + _______ $H_2O(l) \longrightarrow$ _______ $NaOH(aq) + H_2(g)$

b. _______ $AgNO_3(aq) + Zn(s) \longrightarrow Zn(NO_3)_2(aq)$ + _______ $Ag(s)$

SECTION 11.2 TYPES OF CHEMICAL REACTIONS (pages 330–339)

This section explains how to identify a reaction as a combination, decomposition, single-replacement, double-replacement, or combustion reaction. It also describes how to predict the products of each type of reaction.

▶ Classifying Reactions (page 330)

1. There are _______________ general types of chemical reactions.

2. Complete the diagram of a combination reaction. Which characteristic of this type of reaction is shown in the diagram?

____

____

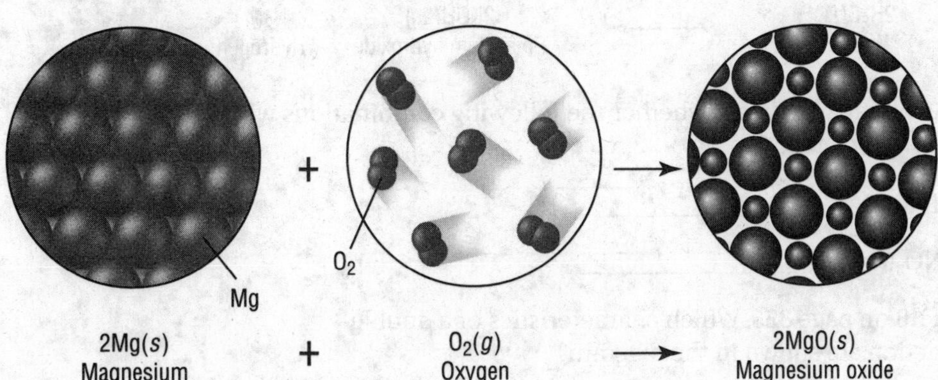

3. Is the following sentence true or false? The product of a combination reaction is always a molecular compound. _______________

4. Circle the letter of each set of reactants that can produce more than one product.

a. two nonmetals

b. a Group A metal and a nonmetal

c. a transition metal and a nonmetal

d. two metals

5. Look at Figure 11.6 on page 332. Which characteristics of a decomposition reaction are shown in the diagram?

____

____

6. Rapid decomposition reactions can cause ________________ as a result of the formation of gaseous products and heat.

7. Most decomposition reactions require the addition of ________________ in the form of heat, light, or electricity.

8. Complete the diagram of a single replacement reaction. Which characteristics of this type of reaction are shown in the diagram?

____

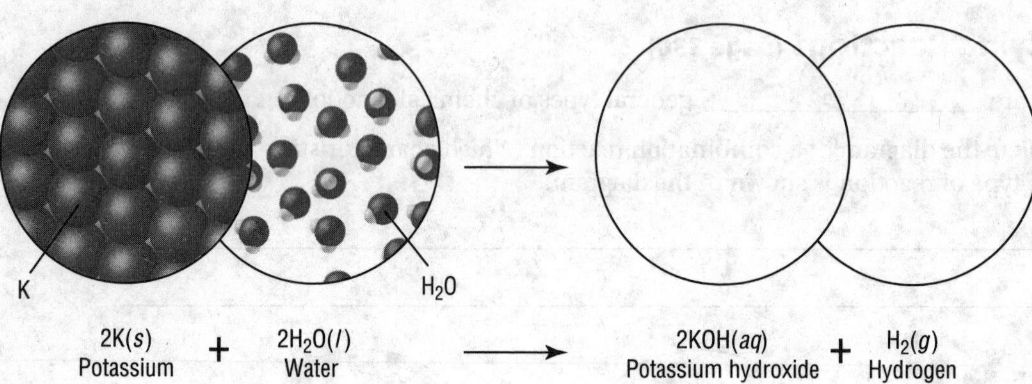

9. Using Table 11.2 on page 333, state whether the following combinations will produce a reaction or no reaction.

a. $Ag(s) + HCl(aq)$ ________________

b. $Cu(s) + AgNO_3(aq)$ ________________

10. Look at Figure 11.8 on page 335. Which characteristics of a double-replacement reaction are shown in the diagram?

____

____

____

11. When solutions of ionic compounds are mixed, what three circumstances may indicate that a double-replacement reaction has occurred?

a. ____

b. ____

c. ____

12. Look at the diagram of a combustion reaction in Figure 11.9 on page 336. Which characteristics of this type of reaction are shown in the diagram?

____

Name ______________________ Date ______________ Class ______________

13. Is the following sentence true or false? Hydrocarbons, compounds of hydrogen and carbon, are often the reactants in combustion reactions. ______________

14. Circle the letter of each compound that can be produced by combustion reactions.

a. oxygen

b. carbon dioxide

c. water

d. glucose

▶ Predicting the Products of a Chemical Reaction (pages 337–339)

15. Classify the reaction in each of the following equations.

a. $BaCl_2(aq) + K_2CrO_4(aq) \longrightarrow BaCrO_4(s) + 2KCl\ (aq)$ ______________

b. $Si(s) + 2Cl_2(g) \longrightarrow SiCl_4(l)$ ______________

c. $2C_6H_6(l) + 15O_2(g) \longrightarrow 6H_2O(l) + 12CO_2(g)$ ______________

16. Use Figure 11.10 on page 339. The equation for the combustion of pentane is $C_5H_{12} + 8O_2 \longrightarrow 5CO_2 + 6H_2O$. What numbers in this equation are represented by x and y in the general equation? ______________

SECTION 11.3 REACTIONS IN AQUEOUS SOLUTION (pages 342–344)

This section explains how to write and balance net ionic equations. It also describes the use of solubility rules to predict the formation of precipitates in double-replacement reactions.

▶ Net Ionic Equations (pages 342–343)

1. Many important chemical reactions take place in ______________.

2. An equation that shows dissolved ionic compounds as their free ions is called a(n) ______________.

3. Is the following sentence true or false? A spectator ion is not directly involved in a reaction. ______________

4. What is a net ionic equation? ______________

____

____

Name ______________________ Date ______________ Class ______________

5. Circle the letter of each sentence that is true about ionic equations.

a. A complete ionic equation shows only the ions involved in the reaction.

b. Spectator ions are left out of a net ionic equation.

c. Atoms do not need to be balanced in an ionic equation.

d. Ionic charges must be balanced in a net ionic equation.

6. Write the balanced net ionic equation for this reaction:
$Pb(NO_3)_2(aq) + KI(aq) \longrightarrow PbI_2(s) + KNO_3(aq)$. Show your work.

____

____

____

____

▶ Predicting the Formation of a Precipitate (page 344)

7. What determines whether a precipitate forms when two solutions of ionic compounds are mixed?

____

8. Use Table 11.3 on page 344 to predict whether the following compounds are soluble or insoluble.

a. $Fe(OH)_3$ ______________________

b. NaOH ______________________

c. $Ca(ClO_3)_2$ ______________________

d. $HgSO_4$ ______________________

Reading Skill Practice

A flowchart can help you to remember the order in which events occur. On a separate sheet of paper, create a flowchart that describes the steps for writing a balanced net ionic equation. This process is explained on pages 342–343 of your textbook.

Name ______________________ Date ______________ Class ______________

GUIDED PRACTICE PROBLEMS

GUIDED PRACTICE PROBLEM 2 (page 324)

2. Sulfur burns in oxygen to form sulfur dioxide. Write a skeleton equation for this chemical reaction. Include appropriate symbols from Table 11.1.

Analyze

Step 1. Write the formula for each reactant and each product. Include the common STP state of each substance.

Reactants

____

____

Products

____

Solve

Step 2. Write the skeleton equation using + between reactants on the left side and → to separate the reactants from the product:

____

GUIDED PRACTICE PROBLEM 3 (page 327)

3. Balance each equation.

a. $AgNO_3 + H_2S \rightarrow Ag_2S + HNO_3$

b. $Zn(OH)_2 + H_3PO_4 \rightarrow Zn_3(PO_4)_2 + H_2O$

a. $AgNO_3 + H_2S \rightarrow Ag_2S + HNO_3$

Analyze

Step 1. Count the number of atoms of each element on both sides of the skeleton equation.

Left side: Right side:

______________________ ______________________

______________________ ______________________

______________________ ______________________

______________________ ______________________

______________________ ______________________

Solve

Step 2. Identify any necessary coefficient.
The reactant containing Ag needs a coefficient of 2, and the product containing H needs a coefficient of 2. Rewrite the equation with these coefficients and count again.

____

Left side:	Right side:
______________	______________
______________	______________
______________	______________
______________	______________
______________	______________

Because the number of atoms of each element is the same on both sides, the equation is balanced.

b. $Zn(OH)_2 + H_3PO_4 \rightarrow Zn_3(PO_4)_2 + H_2O$

Analyze

Step 1. Look at the zinc ions on both sides of the equation. Make the number of zinc ions in zinc hydroxide match the number in zinc phosphate.

_____ $Zn(OH)_2 + H_3PO_4 \longrightarrow Zn_3(PO_4)_2 + H_2O$

____

Step 2. Look at the phosphate ions on both sides of the equation. Make the number of phosphate ions in phosphoric acid match the number of phosphate ions in zinc phosphate.

$3Zn(OH)_2$ + _____ $H_3PO_4 \longrightarrow Zn_3(PO_4)_2 + H_2O$

____

Step 3. Look at the remaining ions in the reactants (OH^- and H^+).

3 × _____ ions of OH^-
2 × _____ ions of H^+
⟶ will form _____ molecules of H_2O

____

Step 4. Complete the balanced equation.

_____ $Zn(OH)_2$ + _____ $H_3PO_4 \longrightarrow Zn_3(PO_4)_2$ + _____ H_2O

____

Name ______________________ Date ______________ Class ______________

GUIDED PRACTICE PROBLEM 5 (page 328)

5. Balance each equation.

a. $FeCl_3 + NaOH \rightarrow Fe(OH)_3 + NaCl$

b. $CS_2 + Cl_2 \rightarrow CCl_4 + S_2Cl_2$

a. $FeCl_3 + NaOH \rightarrow Fe(OH)_3 + NaCl$

Analyze

Step 1. Count the number of atoms of each element on both sides of the skeleton equation.

Solve

Step 2. Identify any necessary coefficient.
The product containing Cl needs a coefficient of 3. Then the reactant containing Na needs a coefficient of 3. Rewrite the equation with these coefficients and count again.

____

b. $CS_2 + Cl_2 \rightarrow CCl_4 + S_2Cl_2$

Analyze

Step 1. Count the number of atoms of each element on both sides of the skeleton equation.

Solve

Step 2. Identify any necessary coefficient.
Two products contain a total of six Cl atoms. To match this total on the left side, Cl_2 needs a coefficient of 3. Rewrite the equation with this coefficient and count again.

____

GUIDED PRACTICE PROBLEM 13 (page 331)

13. Complete and balance the equation for a combination reaction.
$Be + O_2 \rightarrow$

Analyze

Step 1. Identify the relevant concepts.
Beryllium is a Group 2A metal, which means it will combine with oxygen, a gas in Group 6A, in a 1:1 ratio. Oxygen exists as diatomic molecules.

Name ______________________ Date ______________ Class ______________

Solve

Step 2. Write the skeleton equation.

____

Step 3. Balance the equation.
A coefficient of 2 is needed before the product to balance the number of oxygen atoms. Then a coefficient of 2 is needed before the reactant Be.

____

GUIDED PRACTICE PROBLEM 15 (page 332)

15. Complete and balance the equation for a decomposition reaction.
$HI \rightarrow$

Analyze

Step 1. Identify the relevant concepts.
Remember that both hydrogen and iodine exist as diatomic molecules.

Solve

Step 2. Write the skeleton equation.

____

Step 3. Balance the equation.

____

GUIDED PRACTICE PROBLEM 17 (page 334)

17. Complete the equations for these single-replacement reactions in aqueous solution. Balance each equation. Write "no reaction" if a reaction does not occur. Use the activity series in Table 11.2.

a. $Fe(s) + Pb(NO_3)_2(aq) \rightarrow$

b. $Cl_2(aq) + NaI(aq) \rightarrow$

c. $Ca(s) + H_2O(l) \rightarrow$

a. $Fe(s) + Pb(NO_3)_2(aq) \rightarrow$

Analyze

Step 1. Identify the more active metal.
Table 11.2 shows that iron is more reactive than lead.

Name ______________________ Date ________________ Class ________________

Solve

Step 2. Write a skeleton equation.
Fe replaces Pb.

____

Step 3. Count to see if the equation is balanced.

b. $Cl_2(aq) + NaI(aq) \rightarrow$

Analyze

Step 1. Identify relevant concepts.
Cl and I are Group 7A halogens and Cl is more reactive than I. Recall that chlorine and iodine exist as a diatomic molecules.

Solve

Step 2. Write a skeleton equation.
Cl replaces I.
$Cl_2(aq) + NaI(aq) \rightarrow I_2(aq) + NaCl(aq)$

Balance the equation.

____

c. $Ca(s) + H_2O(l) \rightarrow$

Analyze

Step 1. Identify relevant concepts.
According to Table 11.2, Ca is more reactive than H and can replace H in water. Ca has a 2+ charge and OH has a 1− charge. Also, hydrogen gas exists as a diatomic molecule.

Solve

Step 2. Write a skeleton equation.
One Ca replaces one H.
$Ca(s) + H_2O(l) \rightarrow H_2(g) + Ca(OH)_2(aq)$

Step 3. Balance the equation.

____

GUIDED PRACTICE PROBLEM 18 (page 335)

18. Write the products of these double-replacement reactions. Balance each equation.

a. $NaOH(aq) + Fe(NO_3)_3(aq) \rightarrow$ (Iron(III) hydroxide is a precipitate.)

b. $Ba(NO_3)_2(aq) + H_3PO_4(aq) \rightarrow$ (Barium phosphate is a precipitate.)

a. $NaOH + Fe(NO_3)_3 \rightarrow$

Analyze

Step 1. Write the formula for iron(III) hydroxide.

____

Solve

Step 2. Write the skeleton equation.

$NaOH(aq) + Fe(NO_3)_3(aq) \rightarrow Fe(OH)_3(s) + NaNO_3(aq)$

Step 3. Balance the equation.

____

b. $Ba(NO_3)_2 + H_3PO_4 \rightarrow$

Analyze

Step 1. Write the formula for barium phosphate.

____

Solve

Step 2. Write the skeleton equation.

$Ba(NO_3)_2(aq) + H_3PO_4(aq) \rightarrow Ba_3(PO_4)_2(s) + HNO_3(aq)$

Step 3. Balance the equation.

____

Name ______________________ Date ______________ Class ______________

GUIDED PRACTICE PROBLEM 21 (page 337)

21. Write a balanced equation for the complete combustion of glucose ($C_6H_{12}O_6$).

Analyze

Step 1. Identify the second reactant and the products.
Oxygen gas is the other reactant in a combustion reaction. The products are CO_2 and H_2O. Write a skeleton equation for this reaction.

____

Solve

Step 2. Balance the equation.

____

Name ______________________ Date ______________ Class ______________

12 STOICHIOMETRY

SECTION 12.1 THE ARITHMETIC OF EQUATIONS (pages 353–358)

This section explains how to calculate the amount of reactants required or product formed in a nonchemical process. It teaches you how to interpret chemical equations in terms of interacting moles, representative particles, masses, and gas volume at STP.

▶ Using Everyday Equations (pages 353–355)

1. How can you determine the quantities of reactants and products in a chemical reaction?

____

____

2. Quantity usually means the ______________ of a substance expressed in grams or moles.

3. A bookcase is to be built from 3 shelves (Sh), 2 side boards (Sb), 1 top (T), 1 base (B), and 4 legs (L). Write a "balanced equation" for the construction of this bookcase.

____

▶ Using Balanced Chemical Equations (page 354)

4. Is the following sentence true or false? Stoichiometry is the calculation of quantities in chemical reactions. ______________

5. Calculations using balanced equations are called ______________.

▶ Interpreting Chemical Equations (pages 356–357)

6. From what elements is ammonia produced? How is it used?

____

____

7. Circle the letter of the term that tells what kind of information you CANNOT get from a chemical equation.

a. moles

b. mass

c. size of particles

d. volume

e. number of particles

8. The coefficients of a balanced chemical equation tell you the relative number of moles of ______________ and ______________ in a chemical reaction.

9. Why is the relative number of moles of reactants and products the most important information that a balanced chemical equation provides?

____

____

▶ Mass Conservation in Chemical Reactions (pages 357–358)

10. Is the following sentence true or false? A balanced chemical equation must obey the law of conservation of mass. ______________

11. Use Figure 12.3 on page 357. Complete the table about the reaction of nitrogen and hydrogen.

$N_2(g)$	+ $3H_2(g)$	→	$2NH_3(g)$
☐ atoms N	+ 6 atoms H	→	☐ atoms N and ☐ atoms H
1 molecule N_2	+ ☐ molecules H_2	→	☐ molecules NH_3
☐ × (6.02×10^{23} molecules N_2)	+ 3 × (6.02×10^{23} molecules H_2)	→	☐ × (6.02×10^{23} molecules NH_3)
1 mol N_2	+ ☐ mol H_2	→	2 mol NH_3
28 g N_2	+ 3 × ☐ g H_2	→	2 × ☐ g NH_3
	☐ g reactants	→	34 g products
Assume STP 22.4 L N_2	+ 67.2 L H_2	→	☐ L NH_3

12. Circle the letter(s) of the items that are ALWAYS conserved in every chemical reaction.

a. volume of gases

b. mass

c. formula units

d. moles

e. molecules

f. atoms

13. What reactant combines with oxygen to form sulfur dioxide? Where can this reactant be found in nature?

____

____

Name ______________________ Date ______________ Class ______________

SECTION 12.2 CHEMICAL CALCULATIONS (pages 359–366)

This section shows you how to construct mole ratios from balanced chemical equations. It then teaches you how to calculate stoichiometric quantities from balanced chemical equations using units of moles, mass, representative particles, and volumes of gases at STP.

▶ Writing and Using Mole Ratios (pages 359–362)

1. What is essential for all calculations involving amounts of reactants and products? ______________________

2. Is the following sentence true or false? If you know the number of moles of one substance in a reaction, you need more information than the balanced chemical equation to determine the number of moles of all the other substances in the reaction.

____

3. The coefficients from a balanced chemical equation are used to write conversion factors called ______________.

4. What are mole ratios used for?

____

____

____

____

5. The equation for the formation of potassium chloride is given by the equation

$2K(s) + Cl_2(g) \longrightarrow 2KCl(s)$

Write the six possible mole ratios for this equation.

______________ ______________

______________ ______________

______________ ______________

6. Is the following sentence true or false? Laboratory balances are used to measure moles of substances directly. ______________

7. The amount of a substance is *usually* determined by measuring its mass in ______________________.

Name ______________ Date ______________ Class ______________

8. Is the following sentence true or false? If a sample is measured in grams, molar mass can be used to convert the mass to moles. ______________

9. Complete the flow chart to show the steps for the mass–mass conversion of any given mass of *G* to any wanted mass of *W*. In the chemical equation, *a* moles of *G* react with *b* moles of *W*.

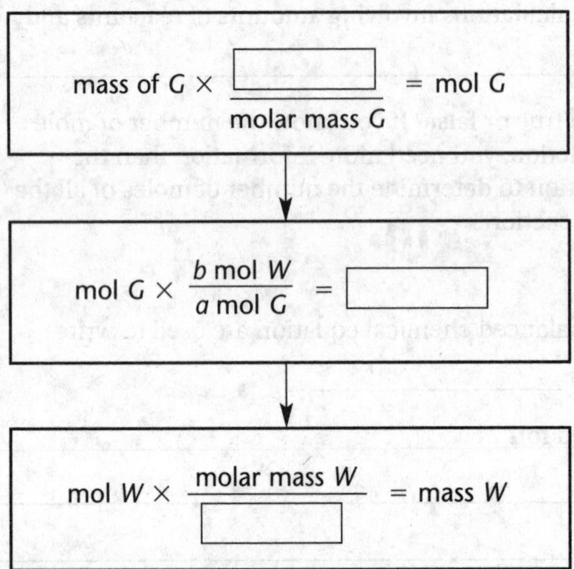

10. Use the diagram below. Describe the steps needed to solve a mass–mass stoichiometry problem.

____

____

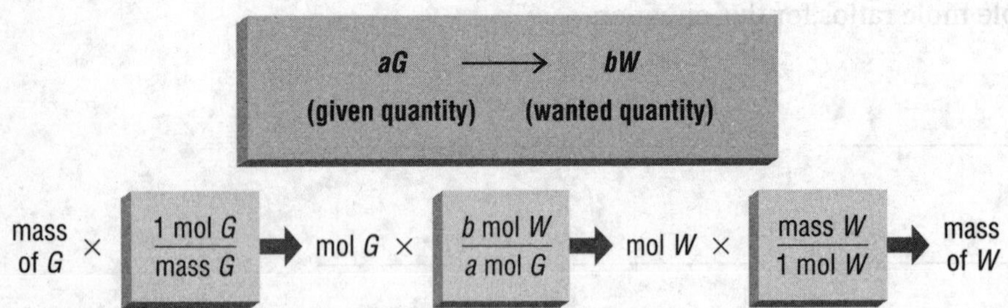

▶ Other Stoichiometric Calculations (pages 363–366)

11. Is the following sentence true or false? Stoichiometric calculations can be expanded to include any unit of measurement that is related to the mole.

____

12. List two or three types of problems that can be solved with stoichiometric calculations.

____

____

13. In any problem relating to stoichiometric calculations, the given quantity is first converted to ______________ .

14. The combustion of methane produces carbon dioxide and water. The chemical equation for this reaction is

$CH_4(g) + 2O_2(g) \longrightarrow CO_2(g) + 2H_2O(g)$

Write the three conversion factors you would use to find the volume of carbon dioxide obtained from 1.5 L of oxygen.

______________ ______________ ______________

Reading Skill Practice

Sometimes information you read is easier to remember if you write it in a different format. For example, the paragraph on page 363 and Figure 12.8 both explain how to solve stoichiometric problems. Use these explanations to make a diagram or flow chart for solving a particle–mass stoichiometry problem. Do your work on a separate sheet of paper.

SECTION 12.3 LIMITING REAGENT AND PERCENT YIELD (pages 368–375)

This section helps you identify and use the limiting reagent in a reaction to calculate the maximum amount of product(s) produced and the amount of excess reagent. It also explains how to calculate theoretical yield, actual yield, or percent yield, given appropriate information.

▶ Limiting and Excess Reagents (pages 368–371)

1. What is a limiting reagent? ______________________________

____

2. Is the following sentence true or false? A chemical reaction stops before the limiting reagent is used up. ______________

3. Circle the letter of the term that correctly completes the sentence. The reactant that is not completely used up in a chemical reaction is called the ______ .

a. spectator reagent **c.** excess reagent

b. limiting reagent **d.** catalyst

Name ____________ Date ____________ Class ____________

4. If the quantities of reactants are given in units other than moles, what is the first step for determining the amount of product?

a. Determine the amount of product from the given amount of limiting reagent.

b. Convert each given quantity of reactant to moles.

c. Identify the limiting reagent.

5. In the diagram below, which reactant is the limiting reagent and why? The chemical equation for the formation of water is $2H_2 + O_2 \longrightarrow 2H_2O$.

____

____

Experimental Conditions		
	Reactants	Products
Before reaction	2 molecules O_2 3 molecules H_2	0 molecules H_2O

▶ Percent Yield (pages 372–375)

6. What is the theoretical yield?

____

____

7. The amount of product that actually forms when a chemical reaction is carried out in a laboratory is called the ____________ yield.

8. Is the following sentence true or false? The actual yield is usually greater than the theoretical yield. ____________

9. Complete the equation for the percent yield of a chemical reaction.

$$\text{Percent yield} = \frac{\boxed{}\ \text{yield}}{\boxed{}\ \text{yield}} \times 100\%$$

10. Describe four factors that may cause percent yields to be less than 100%.

____

____

Name ______________ Date ______________ Class ______________

GUIDED PRACTICE PROBLEMS

GUIDED PRACTICE PROBLEM 11 (page 360)

11. This equation shows the formation of aluminum oxide.

$4Al(s) + 3O_2(g) \longrightarrow 2Al_2O_3(s)$

a. How many moles of oxygen are required to react completely with 14.8 moles of aluminum?

Analyze

1. What is the given information? ______________

2. What is the unknown? ______________

3. What conversion factor will you need to use? ______________

Calculate

4. Complete the solution. 14.8 ________ $\times \frac{3 \text{ mol } O_2}{\boxed{}}$ = ________ mol O_2

Evaluate

5. Why does the answer have three significant figures?

____

____

____

b. How many moles of aluminum oxide are formed when 0.78 moles of oxygen react with an excess of aluminum?

Analyze

6. What information is given? ______________

7. What information is unknown? ______________

Calculate

8. Complete the solution. ________ mol O_2 $\times \frac{\boxed{} \text{ mol } Al_2O_3}{\boxed{}}$

= ________ mol Al_2O_3

Evaluate

9. Why does the answer have two significant figures?

____

____

Name ______________ Date ______________ Class ______________

EXTRA PRACTICE (similar to Practice Problem 15, page 364)

15. How many molecules of oxygen are produced by the decomposition of 1225 grams of potassium chlorate ($KClO_3$)?

$2KClO_3(s) \longrightarrow 2KCl(s) + 3O_2(g)$

EXTRA PRACTICE (similar to Practice Problem 17, page 365)

17. The equation for the combustion of carbon monoxide is

$2CO(g) + O_2(g) \longrightarrow 2CO_2(g)$

How many liters of oxygen are needed to burn 10 liters of carbon monoxide?

GUIDED PRACTICE PROBLEM 25 (page 370)

25. The equation for the complete combustion of ethene (C_2H_4) is

$C_2H_4(g) + 3O_2(g) \longrightarrow 2CO_2(g) + 2H_2O(g)$

a. If 2.70 moles of ethene reacted with 6.30 moles of oxygen, identify the limiting reagent.

Step 1. Calculate the number of moles of oxygen needed to react with 2.70 moles of ethane. Multiply by the mole ratio.

2.70 ______ $\times \dfrac{\square \text{ mol } O_2}{1 \text{ mol } C_2H_4}$

= ______ mol O_2

Step 2. Compare the number of moles of oxygen needed to the number given.

______ O_2 given is less than ______ mol O_2 needed

Step 3. Identify the limiting reagent.

Because ______ mol O_2 are needed to react with the 2.70 mol C_2H_4 and only ______ mol O_2 are available, ______ is the limiting reagent.

Name ______________________ Date ______________ Class ______________

b. Calculate the number of moles of water produced.

Step 1. Identify the mole ratio needed.

$$\frac{\square \text{ mol } H_2O}{3 \text{ mol } O_2}$$

Step 2. Calculate the given number of moles of oxygen.

$$6.30 \underline{\hspace{2cm}} \times \frac{\square \text{ mol } H_2O}{3 \text{ mol } O_2}$$

$$= \underline{\hspace{1.5cm}} \text{ mol } H_2O$$

GUIDED PRACTICE PROBLEM 29 (page 374)

29. When 84.8 grams of iron(III) oxide reacts with an excess of carbon monoxide, 54.3 grams of iron are produced.

$Fe_2O_3(s) + 3CO(g) \longrightarrow 2Fe(s) + 3CO_2(g)$

What is the percent yield of this reaction?

Step 1. First calculate the theoretical yield. Begin by finding the molar mass of Fe_2O_3.

$2 \text{ mol Fe} \times (\underline{\hspace{1.5cm}} \text{ g Fe/mol Fe}) +$

$3 \text{ mol } O_3 \times (\underline{\hspace{1.5cm}} \text{ g } O_3/\text{mol } O_3)$

$= \underline{\hspace{1.5cm}} \text{ g} + 48.0 \text{ g}$

$= \underline{\hspace{1.5cm}} \text{ g}$

Step 2. Calculate the number of moles of iron(III) oxide. Multiply by the mole/mass conversion factor.

$$\underline{\hspace{1.5cm}} \text{ g } Fe_2O_3 \times \frac{1 \text{ mol } Fe_2O_3}{159.6 \text{ g } Fe_2O_3}$$

$$= \underline{\hspace{1.5cm}} \text{ mol}$$

Step 3. Find the number of moles of Fe expected. Multiply by the mole ratio.

$$0.531 \underline{\hspace{2cm}} \times \frac{\square \text{ mol Fe}}{1 \text{ mol } Fe_2O_3}$$

$$= \underline{\hspace{1.5cm}} \text{ mol Fe}$$

Step 4. Find the mass of iron that should be produced. Multiply by the mole/mass conversion factor.

$$1.062 \underline{\hspace{2cm}} \times \frac{\square \text{ g Fe}}{1 \text{ mol Fe}} = 59.3 \text{ g Fe}$$

Step 5. Compare the actual yield to the theoretical yield by dividing.

$$\frac{\text{actual yield}}{\text{theoretical yield}} = \frac{\square \text{ g Fe}}{\square \text{ g Fe}} = 0.916$$

Step 6. Write the answer as a percent, with the correct number of significant figures.

$0.916 = \underline{\hspace{2cm}}$

Name ______________________ Date ________________ Class ________________

13 STATES OF MATTER

SECTION 13.1 THE NATURE OF GASES (pages 385–389)

This section introduces the kinetic theory and describes how it applies to gases. It defines gas pressure and explains how temperature is related to the kinetic energy of the particles of a substance.

▶ Kinetic Theory and a Model for Gases (pages 385–386)

1. The energy an object has because of its motion is called ______________________ .

2. Circle the letter of each sentence that is true about the assumptions of the kinetic theory concerning gases.

a. A gas is composed of particles with insignificant volume that are relatively far apart from each other.

b. Strong attractive forces exist between particles of a gas.

c. Gases tend to collect near the bottom of a container.

d. The paths of uninterrupted travel of particles in a gas are relatively short because the particles are constantly colliding with each other or with other objects.

3. Is the following statement true or false? According to the kinetic theory, collisions between particles in a gas are perfectly elastic because kinetic energy is transferred without loss from one particle to another, and the total kinetic energy remains constant. ______________

▶ Gas Pressure (pages 386–387)

4. Gas pressure results from the force exerted by a gas per ______________________ ____ .

5. Simultaneous collisions of billions of particles in a gas with an object result in ______________ .

6. What force holds the particles of air in Earth's atmosphere? ______________

7. What kind of pressure is measured with a barometer?

____

Name ______________________ Date ______________ Class ______________

CHAPTER 13, States of Matter *(continued)*

8. Look at Figure 13.2 on page 386. What accounts for the difference in height of the two mercury columns shown in the figure?

____

____

____

____

9. Circle the letter next to every name of a unit of pressure.

a. mm Hg

b. standard

c. pascal

d. kPa

e. atm

f. degree

10. Standard temperature and pressure (STP) are defined as ______________________

____

▶ Kinetic Energy and Temperature (pages 388–389)

11. What happens to the temperature of a substance when the average kinetic energy of its particles increases?

____

12. Is the following statement true or false. All the particles in a substance at a given temperature have the same kinetic energy. ______________

13. The temperature 0 K, or −273.15°C, is called ______________ zero. Theoretically, particles of matter at this temperature would have no ______________.

14. On the graph below, write the labels *lower temperature* and *higher temperature* to identify the curve that depicts the kinetic energy distribution of particles in a liquid at a lower temperature and at a higher temperature.

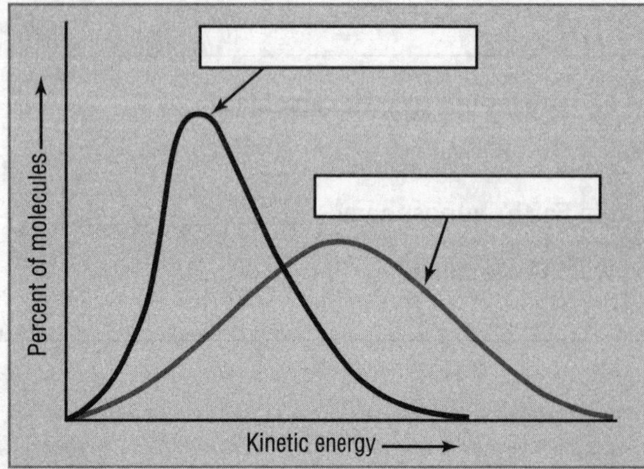

Name ______________________ Date ______________ Class ______________

15. Circle the letter of the temperature scale that correctly completes this sentence. Temperature on the ______ scale is directly proportional to the average kinetic energy of the particles of a substance.

a. Celsius

b. Kelvin

c. Fahrenheit

d. Centigrade

SECTION 13.2 THE NATURE OF LIQUIDS (pages 390–395)

This section describes a model for liquids in terms of kinetic energy and the attractive forces between the particles in a liquid. It also uses kinetic theory to distinguish evaporation from boiling.

▶ A Model for Liquids (page 390)

1. Is the following sentence true or false? The kinetic theory states that there are no attractions between the particles of a liquid.

____

2. Circle the letter next to each sentence that is true about the particles of a liquid.

a. Most of the particles in a liquid have enough kinetic energy to escape into a gaseous state.

b. Liquids are much denser than gases because intermolecular forces reduce the amount of space between the particles in a liquid.

c. Increasing pressure on a liquid has hardly any effect on its volume.

d. Liquid particles are free to slide past one another.

▶ Evaporation (page 391)

3. The conversion of a liquid to a gas or vapor is called ______________________.

4. When vaporization occurs at the surface of a liquid that is not boiling, the process is called ______________________.

5. As a liquid evaporates, why do only some of the particles break away from the surface of the liquid? Why does the liquid evaporate faster if the temperature is increased?

____

____

____

____

____

Name ______________________ Date ________________ Class ______________

6. Is the following sentence true or false? Evaporation is a cooling process because the particles in a liquid with the highest kinetic energy tend to escape first, leaving the remaining particles with a lower average kinetic energy and, thus, a lower temperature. ______________

Questions 7, 8, 9, and 10 refer to either container A or container B below. Think of each container as a system involving both liquid water and water vapor.

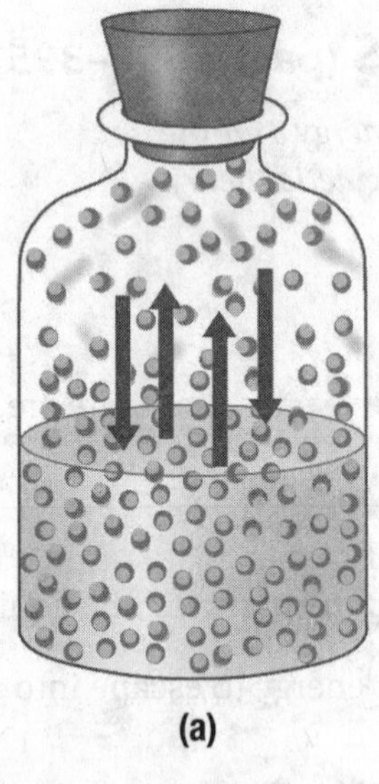

(a)

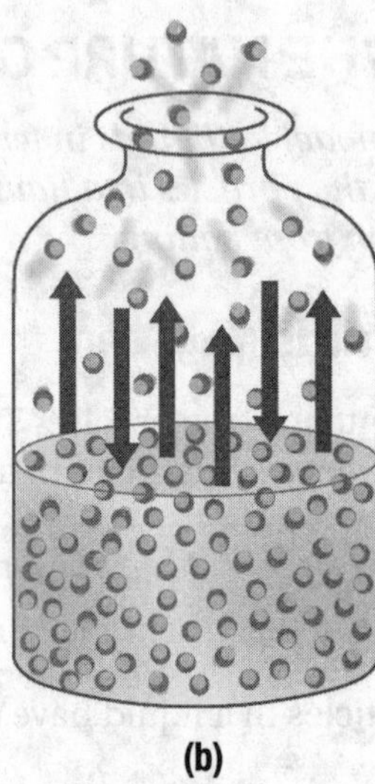

(b)

7. From which of the containers are water molecules able to escape? ____

8. In which container can a dynamic equilibrium between water molecules in the liquid state and water molecules in the vapor state be established? ____

9. In which container will the water level remain constant? ____

10. From which container is it possible for all of the liquid water to disappear through evaporation? ____

11. What causes the chill you may feel after stepping out of a swimming pool on a warm, windy day?

____

____

Name ______________________ Date ______________ Class ______________

▶ Vapor Pressure (pages 392–393)

12. Circle the letter next to each sentence that is true about vapor pressure.

a. Vapor pressure arises when particles of a liquid in a closed, partly filled container vaporize and collide with the walls of the container.

b. After a time in a closed, partly filled container, a liquid will evaporate and its vapor will condense at equal rates.

c. Look at Figure 13.6b on page 391. Condensation on the inside of the terrarium indicates that there is not a liquid-vapor equilibrium in the sealed terrarium.

d. When the temperature of a contained liquid increases, its vapor pressure increases.

13. Look at Figure 13.7 on page 393. How does the vapor pressure of the ethanol in the manometer change when the temperature is increased from 0°C to 20°C? Circle the letter of the correct answer.

a. The vapor pressure decreases by more than 4 kPa.

b. The vapor pressure remains constant.

c. The vapor pressure increases by more than 4 kPa.

d. There is no way to detect a change in vapor pressure with a manometer.

▶ Boiling Point (pages 393–395)

14. The boiling point of a liquid is the temperature at which the vapor pressure of the liquid is just equal to the ______________________.

15. Look at Figure 13.8 on page 394. Why does the boiling point decrease as altitude increases?

____

____

____

16. Use Figure 13.9 on page 394. At approximately what temperature would ethanol boil atop Mount Everest, where the atmospheric pressure is 34 kPa? Circle the letter next to the best estimate.

a. 50°C **b.** 100°C **c.** 0°C **d.** 85°C

17. Is the following sentence true or false? After a liquid reaches its boiling point, its temperature continues to rise until all the liquid vaporizes. ______________

Reading Skill Practice

Writing a summary can help you remember what you have read. When you write a summary, include only the most important points. Write a summary of the discussion of boiling point on pages 393–395. Do your work on a separate sheet of paper.

SECTION 13.3 THE NATURE OF SOLIDS (pages 396–399)

This section describes the highly organized structures of solids, distinguishes between a crystal lattice and a unit cell, and explains how allotropes of an element differ.

▶ A Model for Solids (page 396)

1. Is the following sentence true or false? Although particles in solids have kinetic energy, the motion of particles in solids is restricted to vibrations about fixed points. ______________
2. A solid melts when ______________.
3. Is the following sentence true or false? The temperature at which the liquid and solid states of a substance are in equilibrium is the same as the melting point *and* the freezing point of the substance. ______________

▶ Crystal Structure and Unit Cells (pages 396–399)

4. How are particles arranged in a crystal?

____

5. What type of solid has a relatively low melting point?

____

6. Do all solids melt when heated? Explain.

____

7. Circle the letter next to each sentence that is true about solids.
   - **a.** Most solid substances are not crystalline.
   - **b.** All crystals have sides, or faces, that intersect at angles that are characteristic for a given substance.
   - **c.** There are seven groups, or crystal systems, into which all crystals may be classified.
   - **d.** The orderly array of sodium ions and chloride ions gives crystals of table salt their regular shape.

Name ______________________ Date ______________ Class ______________

Identify the unit cell in each figure below as simple cubic, body-centered cubic, or face-centered cubic.

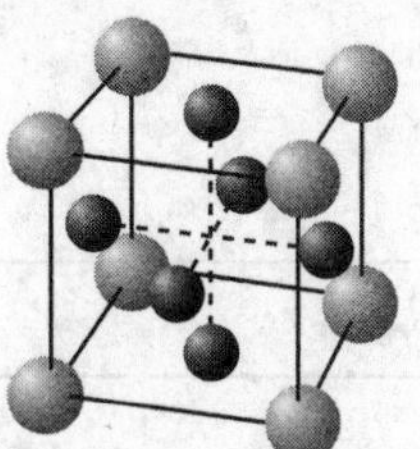
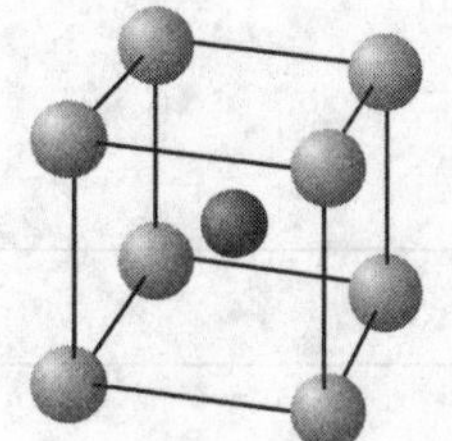
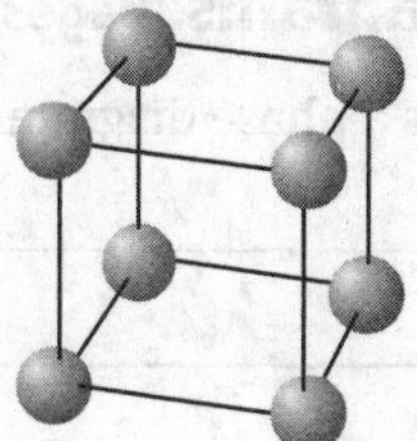

8. ______________ 9. ______________ 10. ______________

11. Is the following sentence true or false? Some solid substances can exist in more than one form. Give an example to support your answer.

____

____

12. Two or more different molecular forms of the same element in the same physical state are called ______________.

13. What is an amorphous solid?

____

14. Circle the letter next to each solid that is an amorphous solid.

a. table salt
c. plastic
b. rubber
d. glass

15. How are glasses different from crystalline solids?

____

____

____

SECTION 13.4 CHANGES OF STATE (pages 401–404)

This section describes the process of sublimation. It also explains phase changes between solid, liquid, and vapor states and how to interpret a phase diagram.

▶ Sublimation (page 401)

1. The process by which wet laundry dries on an outdoor clothesline in winter is called ______________.

2. Is the following sentence true or false? Solids have vapor pressure because some particles near the surface of a solid substance have enough kinetic energy to escape directly into the vapor phase. ______________

Name ______________ Date ______________ Class ______________

▶ Phase Diagrams (pages 402–403)

3. What does a phase diagram show?

____

____

4. What is the triple point of a substance?

____

____

5. In the phase diagram for water shown below, label the melting point and boiling point at normal atmospheric pressure, and the triple point.

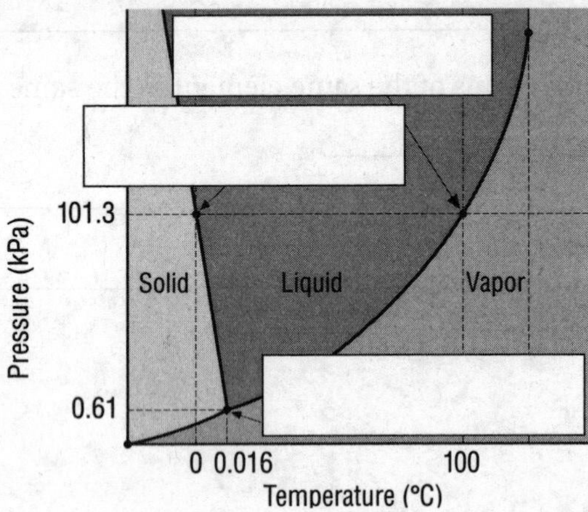

6. Use the phase diagram above to answer the following question. Why is a laboratory required to produce the conditions necessary for observing water at the triple point?

____

____

Name ______________________ Date ______________ Class ______________

GUIDED PRACTICE PROBLEM

GUIDED PRACTICE PROBLEM 2 (page 387)

2. The pressure at the top of Mount Everest is 33.7 kPa. Is that pressure greater than or less than 0.25 atm?

Analyze

Step 1. To convert kPa to atm, what conversion factor do you need to use?

____

Step 2. Why can you use an estimate to solve this problem?

____

____

Calculate

Step 3. Write the expression needed to find the answer.

____

Step 4. Which common fraction is this number close to?

____

Step 5. What is this fraction written as a decimal? Is this number greater than or less than 0.25?

____

Evaluate

Step 6. Are you confident your estimate gave a correct answer to this problem?

____

____

EXTRA PRACTICE (similar to Practice Problem 1, page 387)

1. What pressure, in atmospheres, does a gas exert at 152 mm Hg?

What is this pressure in kilopascals?

Name ______________________ Date ______________ Class ______________

14 THE BEHAVIOR OF GASES

SECTION 14.1 PROPERTIES OF GASES (pages 413–417)

This section uses kinetic theory to explain the properties of gases. This section also explains how gas pressure is affected by the amount of gas, its volume, and its temperature.

▶ Compressibility (pages 413–414)

1. Look at Figure 14.1 on page 413. How does an automobile air bag protect the crash dummy from being broken as a result of impact?

____

____

____

2. What theory explains the behavior of gases? ______________

3. Circle the letter next to each sentence that is true concerning the compressibility of gases.

   a. The large relative distances between particles in a gas means that there is considerable empty space between the particles.

   b. The assumption that particles in a gas are relatively far apart explains gas compressibility.

   c. Compressibility is a measure of how much the volume of matter decreases under pressure.

   d. Energy is released by a gas when it is compressed.

▶ Factors Affecting Gas Pressure (pages 414–417)

4. List the name, the symbol, and a common unit for the four variables that are generally used to describe the characteristics of a gas.

   a. ____

   b. ____

   c. ____

   d. ____

5. What keeps the raft in Figure 14.3 inflated?

____

____

____

Name ______________ Date ______________ Class ______________

6. How do conditions change inside a rigid container when you use a pump to add gas to the container?

____

____

7. The diagrams below show a sealed container at three pressures. Complete the labels showing the gas pressure in each container.

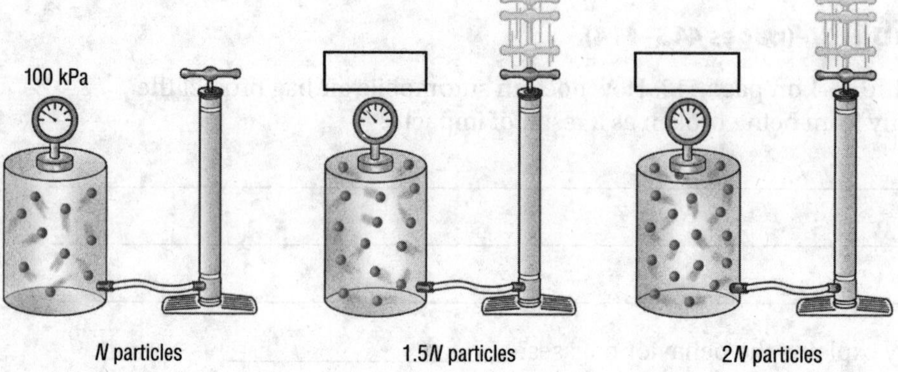

8. What can happen if too much gas is pumped into a sealed, rigid container?

____

____

9. Is the following sentence true or false? When a sealed container of gas is opened, gas will flow from the region of lower pressure to the region of higher pressure. ______________

10. Look at Figure 14.5 on page 416. What happens when the push button on an aerosol spray can is pressed?

____

____

____

11. In the diagram, complete the labels showing the pressure on the piston and the gas pressure inside the container.

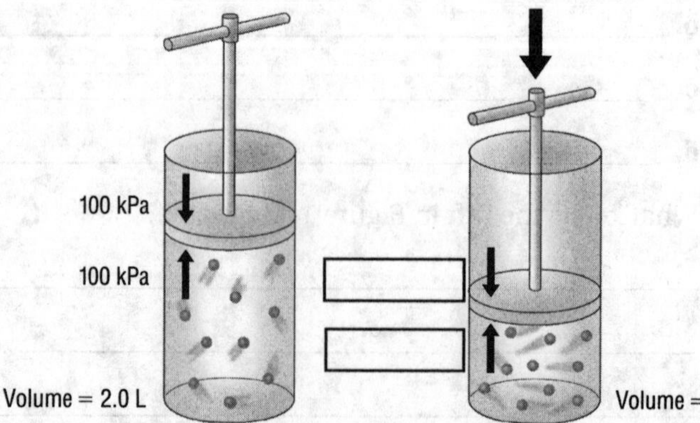

Name ______________________ Date ______________ Class ______________

12. When the volume of a gas is reduced by one half, what happens to its pressure?

____

13. Is the following sentence true or false? Raising the temperature of a contained gas causes its pressure to decrease. ______________

14. Circle the letter next to each sentence that correctly describes how gases behave when the temperature increases.

   a. The average kinetic energy of the particles in the gas increases as the particles absorb energy.

   b. Faster-moving particles impact the walls of their container with more force, exerting greater pressure.

   c. When the average kinetic energy of the enclosed particles doubles, temperature doubles and the pressure is cut in half.

15. Explain why it is dangerous to throw aerosol cans into a fire.

____

____

16. Decide whether the following sentence is true or false, and explain your reasoning. When the temperature of a sample of steam increases from 100°C to 200°C, the average kinetic energy of its particles doubles.

____

____

SECTION 14.2 THE GAS LAWS (pages 418–425)

This section explains the relationships among the volume, pressure, and temperature of gases as described by Boyle's law, Charles's law, Gay-Lussac's law, and the combined gas law.

▶ Boyle's Law: Pressure and Volume (pages 418–419)

1. Circle the letter of each sentence that is true about the relationship between the volume and the pressure of a contained gas at constant temperature.

   a. When the pressure increases, the volume decreases.

   b. When the pressure decreases, the volume increases.

   c. When the pressure increases, the volume increases.

   d. When the pressure decreases, the volume decreases.

2. ______________ law states that for a given mass of gas at constant temperature, the volume of the gas varies inversely with pressure.

Name ______________ Date ______________ Class ______________

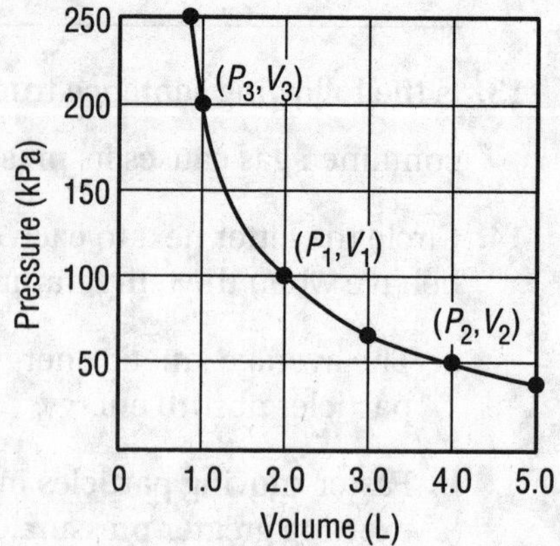

Questions 3, 4, 5, and 6 refer to the graph. This graph represents the relationship between pressure and volume for a sample of gas in a container at a constant temperature.

3. $P_1 \times V_1 =$ ______________

4. $P_2 \times V_2 =$ ______________

5. $P_3 \times V_3 =$ ______________

6. What do you notice about the product of pressure times volume at constant temperature?

____

▶ Charles's Law: Temperature and Volume (pages 420–421)

7. Look at the graph in Figure 14.10 on page 420. What two observations did Jacques Charles make about the behavior of gases from similar data?

____

____

8. What does it mean to say that two variables are directly proportional?

____

____

9. Is the following sentence true or false? Charles's law states that when the pressure of a fixed mass of gas is held constant, the volume of the gas is directly proportional to its Kelvin temperature. ______________

10. Charles's law may be written $\frac{V_1}{T_1} = \frac{V_2}{T_2}$ at constant pressure if the temperatures are measured on what scale? ______________

▶ Gay-Lussac's Law: Pressure and Temperature (pages 422–423)

11. Complete the following sentence. Gay-Lussac's law states that the pressure of a gas is ____.

12. Gay-Lussac's law may be written $\frac{P_1}{T_1} = \frac{P_2}{T_2}$ if the volume is constant and if the temperatures are measured on what scale? ______________

Name ______________________ Date ______________ Class ______________

13. Complete the missing label in the diagram below showing the pressure change when a gas is heated at constant volume.

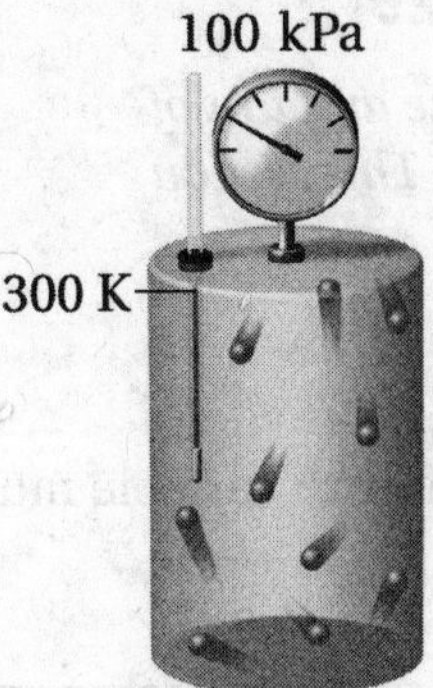

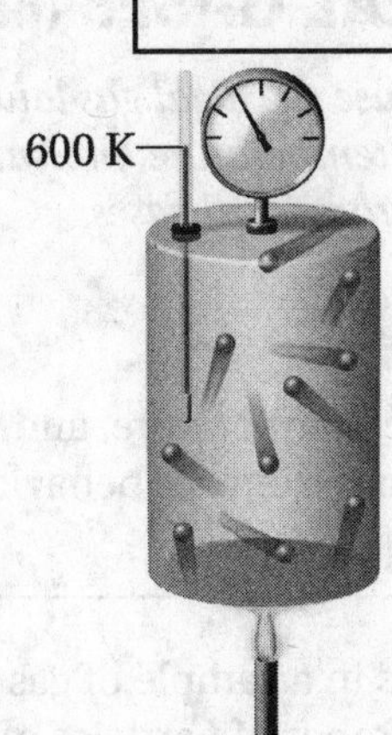

▶ The Combined Gas Law (pages 424–425)

14. Is the following sentence true or false? The gas laws of Boyle, Charles, and Gay-Lussac can be combined into a single mathematical expression.

____

Questions 15, 16, 17, and 18 refer to the following equation

$$\frac{P_1 \times V_1}{T_1} = \frac{P_2 \times V_2}{T_2}$$

15. What law does this mathematical equation represent?

____

16. Which gas law does this equation represent if temperature is held constant so that $T_1 = T_2$? ______________________

17. Which gas law does this equation represent if pressure is held constant so that $P_1 = P_2$? ______________________

18. Which gas law does this equation represent if volume is held constant so that $V_1 = V_2$? ______________________

19. In which situations does the combined gas law enable you to do calculations when the other gas laws do not apply?

____

____

Name ______________________ Date ______________ Class ______________

SECTION 14.3 IDEAL GASES (pages 426–429)

This section explains how to use the ideal gas law to calculate the amount of gas at specified conditions of temperature, pressure and volume. This section also distinguishes real gases from ideal gases.

▶ Ideal Gas Law (pages 426–427)

1. In addition to pressure, temperature, and volume, what fourth variable must be considered when analyzing the behavior of a gas?

____

2. Is the number of moles in a sample of gas directly proportional or inversely proportional to the number of particles of gas in the sample?

____

3. At a specified temperature and pressure, is the number of moles of gas in a sample directly proportional or inversely proportional to the volume of the sample? ______________________

4. Circle the letter next to the correct description of how the combined gas law must be modified to introduce the number of moles.

a. Multiply each side of the equation by the number of moles.

b. Add the number of moles to each side of the equation.

c. Divide each side of the equation by the number of moles.

5. For what kind of gas is $(P \times V) / (T \times n)$ a constant for all values of pressure, temperature, and volume under which the gas can exist? ______________

6. What constant can you calculate when you know the volume occupied by one mole of gas at standard temperature and pressure?

____

Name ____________________ Date ______________ Class ______________

7. Complete the table about the ideal gas law. Write what each symbol in the ideal gas law represents, the unit in which it is measured, and the abbreviation of the unit.

Symbol	Quantity	Unit	Abbreviation for Unit
P			
V			
n			
R			
T			

8. When would you use the ideal gas law instead of the combined gas law?

____

____

▶ Ideal Gases and Real Gases (pages 428–429)

9. Circle the letter of each sentence that is true about ideal gases and real gases.

a. An ideal gas does not follow the gas laws at all temperatures and pressures.

b. An ideal gas does not conform to the assumptions of the kinetic theory.

c. There is no real gas that conforms to the kinetic theory under all conditions of temperature and pressure.

d. At many conditions of temperature and pressure, real gases behave very much like ideal gases.

10. Is the following sentence true or false? If a gas were truly an ideal gas, it would be impossible to liquefy or solidify it by cooling or by applying pressure.

____

11. Red gases differ most from an ideal gas at ____________ temperatures and ____________ pressures.

12. Look at Figure 14.14 on page 428. What substance is shown? What change of state is occurring? How do you know this substance is not an ideal gas?

____

____

SECTION 14.4 GASES: MIXTURES AND MOVEMENTS (pages 432–436)

This section explains Dalton's law of partial pressures, and Graham's law of effusion.

▶ Dalton's Law (pages 432–434)

1. Is the following statement true or false? Gas pressure depends only on the number of particles in a given volume and on their average kinetic energy. The type of particle does not matter. ________________

2. The contribution of the pressure of each gas in a mixture to the total pressure is called the ______________________ exerted by that gas.

3. What is Dalton's law of partial pressures?

____

____

4. Container (T) in the figure below contains a mixture of the three different gases in (a), (b), and (c) at the pressures shown. Write in the pressure in container (T).

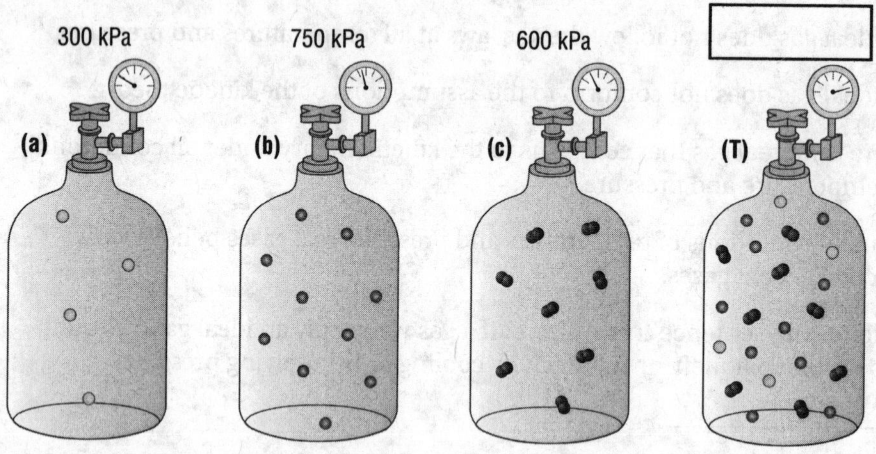

Name ______________________ Date ______________ Class ______________

▶ Graham's Law (pages 435–436)

5. The tendency of molecules in a gas to move from areas of higher concentration to areas of lower concentration is called ______________ .

6. What is Graham's law of effusion?

____

____

7. Is the following sentence true or false? If two objects with different masses have the same kinetic energy, the one with the greater mass must move faster.

____

Reading Skill Practice

You may sometimes forget the meaning of a vocabulary term that was introduced earlier in the textbook. When this happens, you can check its meaning in the Glossary on pages R107–R117. The Glossary lists all vocabulary terms in the textbook and their meanings. You'll find the terms listed in alphabetical order. Use the Glossary to review the meanings of all vocabulary terms introduced in Section 14.4. Write each term and its definition on a separate sheet of paper.

Name ______________________ Date ______________ Class ______________

GUIDED PRACTICE PROBLEMS

GUIDED PRACTICE PROBLEM 13 (page 424)

13. A gas at 155 kPa and 25°C has an initial volume of 1.00 L. The pressure of the gas increases to 605 kPa as the temperature is raised to 125°C. What is the new volume?

Analyze

a. Temperature can be converted from Celsius to Kelvin by adding ________.

b. What is the expression for the combined gas law?

____

c. What is the unknown in this problem? ________

Calculate

d. Convert degrees Celsius to kelvins.

T_1 = 25°C + [ ] = [ ] K

T_2 = 125°C + [ ] = [ ] K

e. Rearrange the combined gas law to isolate V_2.

V_2 =

f. Substitute the known quantities into the equation and solve.

$$V_2 = \frac{1.00\ \text{L} \times \boxed{}\ \cancel{\text{kPa}} \times 398\ \cancel{\text{K}}}{605\ \cancel{\text{kPa}} \times \boxed{}\ \cancel{\text{K}}} = \boxed{}$$

Evaluate

g. Explain why you think your answer is reasonable.

____

____

____

____

h. Are the units in your answer correct? How do you know?

____

Name ______________________ Date ______________ Class ______________

EXTRA PRACTICE (similar to Practice Problem 11, page 423)

11. A gas has a pressure of 7.50 kPa at 420 K. What will the pressure be at 210 K if the volume does not change?

____

GUIDED PRACTICE PROBLEM 31 (page 434)

31. Determine the total pressure of a gas mixture that contains oxygen, nitrogen, and helium if the partial pressures of the gases are as follows:

P_{O_2} = 20.0 kPa, P_{N_2} = 46.7 kPa, and P_{He} = 26.7 kPa.

Analyze

a. What is the expression for Dalton's law of partial pressure?

____

b. What is the unknown in this problem? ______________

Calculate

c. Substitute the known quantities into the equation and solve.

Evaluate

d. Why is your answer reasonable?

____

____

Name ______________ Date ______________ Class ______________

15 WATER AND AQUEOUS SYSTEMS

SECTION 15.1 WATER AND ITS PROPERTIES (pages 445–449)

This section describes the properties of water in the liquid and solid states and explains how hydrogen bonding affects the surface tension and vapor pressure of water.

▶ Water in the Liquid State (pages 445–447)

1. What unique substance is essential to all life on Earth?

____

2. Approximately what fraction of Earth's surface is covered in water? ______________

3. Circle the letter next to each sentence that is true concerning water molecules.

a. Each O — H covalent bond in a water molecule is nonpolar.

b. In a water molecule, the less electronegative hydrogen atoms acquire a partial positive charge and the oxygen atom acquires a partial negative charge.

c. Because the water molecule has an H — O — H bond angle of 105°, the molecule as a whole is polar.

4. The diagram below depicts a water molecule. Complete the labels showing the locations of the hydrogen atoms, the oxygen atom, and the regions of positive and negative charge.

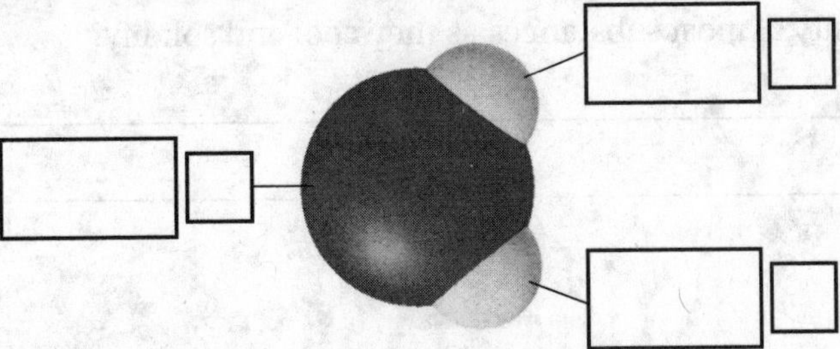

5. The diagram below depicts a collection of water molecules. Draw dotted lines showing where hydrogen bonding occurs.

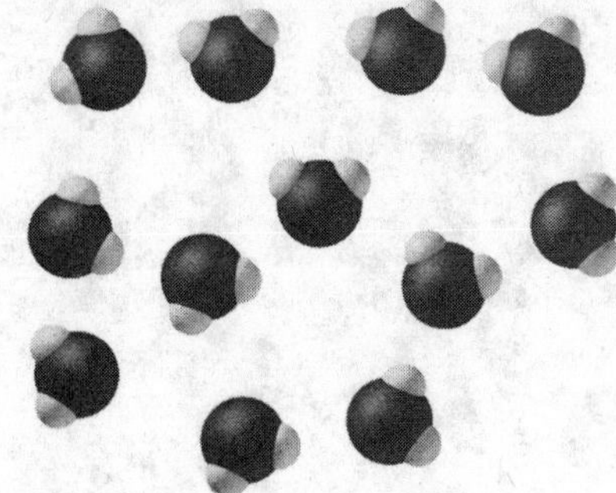

6. Circle the letter next to each sentence that describes a result of the surface tension of water.

   a. In a full glass of water, the water surface seems to bulge over the rim of the glass.

   b. Water beads up into small, nearly spherical drops on a paper towel.

   c. Water forms nearly spherical drops at the end of an eyedropper.

   d. An insect called a water strider is able to "walk" on water.

7. Using Figure 15.4 on page 447, explain why a water drop has surface tension.

   ____

   ____

   ____

8. Do liquids that have higher surface tension produce drops that are flatter or more nearly spherical than liquids with lower surface tension?

   ____

   ____

9. What is the name for an agent, such as a detergent, that has the ability to reduce surface tension? ______________

▶ Water in the Solid State (pages 448–449)

10. What happens to the density of most substances as they cool and solidify?

    ____

    ____

Name ______________________ Date __________ Class ______________

11. The diagrams below show hydrogen bonding between water molecules.

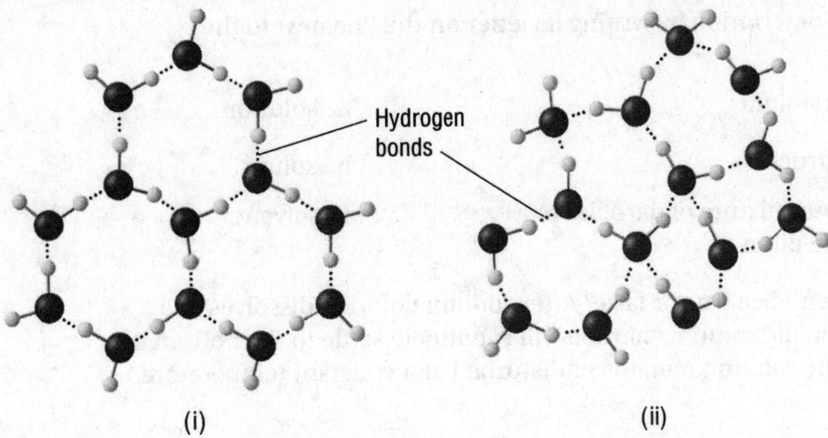

a. Which diagram depicts ice? ________

b. Which diagram depicts liquid water? ________

c. Why is ice less dense than liquid water? Refer to the diagrams to help you explain. ______________________________

____

____

12. Look at Table 15.1 on page 448. To four significant figures, list the density of

a. liquid water at 4°C ______________

b. liquid water at 0°C ______________

c. ice at 0°C ______________

13. What is unusual about the data in Question 12? Will ice float on liquid water?

____

____

____

SECTION 15.2 HOMOGENOUS AQUEOUS SYSTEMS (pages 450–457)

This section describes the process of solvation; distinguishes among strong electrolytes, weak electrolytes, and nonelectrolytes; and explains water of hydration.

▶ Solvents and Solutes (page 450)

1. Water samples containing dissolved substances are called

______________________________.

Name ______________________ Date ______________ Class ______________

Match each term to its description by writing its letter on the line next to the description.

______	**2.** dissolving medium	**a.** solution
______	**3.** dissolved particles	**b.** solute
______	**4.** homogeneous mixture of particles in a dissolving medium	**c.** solvent

5. Is the following sentence true or false? After sodium chloride dissolves in a container of water, the sodium chloride will eventually settle to the bottom of the container if the solution remains undisturbed at a constant temperature.

____

6. Circle the letter next to each sentence that is true about aqueous solutions.

a. Solute particles can be either ionic or molecular, and their average diameters are usually less than 1 nanometer.

b. When a solution is filtered, both solute and solvent will pass through the filter paper.

c. Ionic compounds and substances containing polar covalent molecules readily dissolve in water.

d. Nonpolar covalent molecules, such as those found in oil, grease, and gasoline, readily dissolve in water.

▶ The Solution Process (page 451)

7. What happens when a solid crystal of sodium chloride is placed in water?

____

8. What process occurs when solute ions become surrounded by solvent molecules? ______________________

9. Look at the model of solvation in Figure 15.7 on page 451. If enough solvent is present, what will eventually happen to the ionic solid depicted at the bottom of the diagram?

____

____

10. When a compound cannot be solvated to any significant extent, it is called

______________________.

Name _______________ Date _______________ Class _______________

11. Circle the letter next to the one sentence that best explains why the ionic compounds barium sulfate ($BaSO_4$) and calcium carbonate ($CaCO_3$) are nearly insoluble in water.

   a. The attractions between the ions in the crystals of these ionic compounds are weaker than the attractions between the ions and water molecules.

   b. The attractions between the ions in the crystals of these ionic compounds are stronger than the attractions between the ions and water molecules.

   c. There is no difference in the strength of the attractions between the ions in the crystals and the attractions between the ions and water molecules.

   d. These ionic compounds are easily dissolved in water.

12. What saying sums up the observation that, as a rule, polar solvents dissolve ionic compounds and polar molecules, but nonpolar solvents dissolve nonpolar compounds? _______________

▶ Electrolytes and Nonelectrolytes (pages 452–453)

13. What types of compounds can carry an electric current in the molten state or in aqueous solution? _______________

14. Is the following sentence true or false? All ionic compounds are electrolytes.

____

15. Compounds that do not conduct an electric current in either aqueous solution or the molten state are called _______________.

Look at the light bulbs in Figure 15.9 on page 453 to answer Questions 17, 18, and 19.

_______ 16. Which bulb, *a*, *b*, or *c*, indicates that the solution is nonconductive?

_______ 17. Which bulb, *a*, *b*, or *c*, indicates that the solution is weakly conductive?

_______ 18. Which bulb, *a*, *b*, or *c*, indicates that the solution is highly conductive?

▶ Hydrates (pages 454–457)

19. Water in a crystal that is an integral part of the crystal structure is called

_______________.

20. A compound that contains water as an integral part of its crystal structure is called _______________.

21. What does "$\bullet 5H_2O$" mean when included in a chemical formula?

____

Name ______________________ Date ______________ Class ______________

CHAPTER 15, Water and Aqueous Systems *(continued)*

22. Circle the letter next to each sentence that is true about hydrated compounds. Use Figures 15.10 on page 454 to help you.

a. Crystals of copper sulfate pentahydrate always contain five molecules of water for each copper and sulfate ion pair.

b. Heating blue crystals of copper sulfate pentahydrate above 100°C drives off the water of hydration, leaving a white anhydrous powder.

c. It is possible to regenerate copper sulfate pentahydrate by treating anhydrous copper sulfate with water.

d. Anhydrous cobalt(II) chloride is a good indicator for the presence of water because it changes from pink to blue when exposed to moisture.

23. If a hydrate has a vapor pressure greater than that of the water in the surrounding air, the hydrate will lose water to the air, or ______________________.

24. Hygroscopic substances that remove water from the air are used as drying agents called ______________________.

25. Look at Figure 15.13 on page 457. What happens to dry sodium hydroxide pellets that are exposed to normally moist air? What kind of compound exhibits this behavior?

____

____

____

Reading Skill Practice

By looking carefully at photographs and drawings in your textbook, you can better understand what you have read. Look carefully at Figure 15.8 on page 451. What important idea does this photograph communicate? Do your work on a separate sheet of paper.

Name ______________________ Date ______________ Class ______________

SECTION 15.3 HETEROGENEOUS AQUEOUS SOLUTIONS (pages 459–462)

This section describes how colloids and suspensions differ from solutions and from one another. It also explains the Tyndall effect.

▶ Suspensions (page 459)

1. Is the following sentence true or false? Heterogeneous mixtures are not true solutions. ______________

2. Heterogeneous mixtures in which particles settle out upon standing are called ______________.

3. Is the following sentence true or false? When a suspension of clay particles in water is filtered, both clay and water will pass through the filter paper.

____

▶ Colloids (pages 460–462)

4. Heterogeneous mixtures in which particles are of intermediate size between those of true solutions and suspensions are called ______________.

5. The scattering of light in all directions by colloidal particles is known as the ______________.

6. Identify each type of system shown in the figure below.

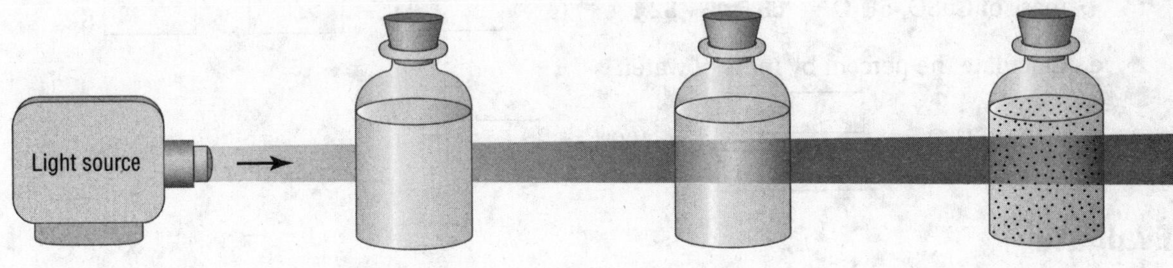

______________ ______________ ______________

Name ______________ Date ______________ Class ______________

GUIDED PRACTICE PROBLEM

GUIDED PRACTICE PROBLEM 6 (page 456)

6. What is the percent by mass of water in $CuSO_4 \cdot 5H_2O$?

Analyze

a. What formula do you use to find percent by mass of water in a hydrate?

$$\text{percent } H_2O = \frac{\boxed{}}{\boxed{}} \times \boxed{}$$

b. From the periodic table, what is the average atomic mass of each of the following elements?

Cu = ________ O = ________

S = ________ H = ________

Calculate

c. Determine the mass of water in the hydrate.

$$\text{mass of } 5H_2O = 5 \times [(2 \times \boxed{}) + \boxed{}] = 5 \times \boxed{} = \boxed{}\ \text{g}$$

d. Determine the mass of the hydrate.

$$\text{mass of } CuSO_4 \cdot 5H_2O = 63.5\ \text{g} + 32.1\ \text{g} + (4 \times \boxed{}) + \boxed{} = \boxed{}\ \text{g}$$

e. Calculate the percent by mass of water.

$$\text{percent } H_2O = \frac{\boxed{}}{\boxed{}} \times 100\% = \boxed{}\ \%$$

Evaluate

f. How do you know that your answer is correct?

____

____

EXTRA PRACTICE (similar to Practice Problem 6, page 456)

6. What is the percent by mass of water in $CaCl_2 \cdot 2H_2O$?

Name ______________________ Date ______________ Class ______________

16 SOLUTIONS

SECTION 16.1 PROPERTIES OF SOLUTIONS (pages 471–477)

This section identifies the factors that affect the solubility of a substance and determine the rate at which a solute dissolves.

▶ Solution Formation (pages 471–472)

Look at Figure 16.1 on page 471 to help you answer Questions 1 and 2.

1. Underline the condition that causes sugar to dissolve *faster* in water.

a. as a whole cube or in granulated form?

b. when allowed to stand or when stirred?

c. at a higher temperature or a lower temperature?

2. Name three factors that influence the rate at which a solute dissolves in a solvent.

a. ______________________

b. ______________________

c. ______________________

3. Is the following sentence true or false? Finely ground particles dissolve more rapidly than larger particles because finer particles expose a greater surface area to the colliding solvent molecules. ______________

▶ Solubility (pages 472–473)

4. Complete the following table showing the steps in a procedure to determine the total amount of sodium chloride that will dissolve in 100 g of water at 25°C.

Procedure	Amount Dissolved	Amount Not Dissolved
Add 36.0 g of sodium chloride to the water	36.0 g	0.0 g
Add an additional 1.0 g of sodium chloride		
Determine the total amount that dissolves		

5. The amount of a substance that dissolves in a given quantity of solvent at a constant temperature is called the substance's ______________ at that temperature.

6. If a solution contains the *maximum* amount of solute for a given quantity of solvent at a constant temperature, it is called a(n) ______________ solution.

Name ____________________ Date ______________ Class ______________

7. Look at Figure 16.2 on page 472. Circle the letter of each sentence that is true about a saturated solution.

   a. The total amount of dissolved solute remains constant.

   b. The total mass of undissolved crystals remains constant.

   c. When the rate of solvation equals the rate of crystallization, a state of dynamic equilibrium exists.

   d. If more solute were added to the container, the total amount of dissolved solute would increase.

8. If two liquids dissolve each other, they are said to be ____________________.

9. Look at Figure 16.3 on page 473. Why does the oil float on the vinegar?

   ____

   ____

▶ Factors Affecting Solubility (pages 474–477)

10. Is the following sentence true or false? The solubility of sodium chloride in water increases to 39.2 g per 100 g of water at 100°C from 36.2 g per 100 g of water at 25°C. ____________________

11. Circle the letter of the sentence that best answers the following question. How does the solubility of solid substances change as the temperature of the solvent increases?

    a. The solubility increases for all solids.

    b. The solubility increases for most solids.

    c. The solubility remains constant.

12. Look at Table 16.1 on page 474. Which solid substance listed in the table is nearly insoluble at any temperature? ____________________

13. How does the solubility of a gas change with an increase in temperature?

    ____

14. The directly proportional relationship between the solubility of a gas in a liquid and the pressure of the gas above the liquid is known as ____________________.

Name ______________________ Date ______________ Class ______________

15. Describe the two diagrams of a bottled carbonated beverage below as *greater pressure* or *lower pressure,* and then as *greater solubility* or *lower solubility.* How do these two examples illustrate the relationship between the solubility of a gas and its vapor pressure?

____

____

____

______________________________ ______________________________

16. How does a solution become supersaturated? ______________________________

____

____

____

SECTION 16.2 CONCENTRATIONS OF SOLUTIONS (pages 480–486)

This section explains how to solve problems involving molarity of a solution, how to prepare dilute solutions from more concentrated solutions, and what is meant by percent by volume and percent by mass.

▶ Molarity (pages 480–482)

1. A measure of the amount of solute dissolved in a given quantity of solvent is the ______________ of a solution.

2. The most important unit of concentration in chemistry is ______________.

3. Is the following sentence true or false? Molarity is the number of moles of dissolved solute per liter of solvent. ______________

CHAPTER 16, Solutions *(continued)*

4. Look at Figure 16.8 on page 481. Circle the letter of the best procedure for making a 0.50-molar (0.50*M*) solution in a 1.0-L volumetric flask.

a. Add distilled water exactly to the 1.0-L mark, add 0.50 mol of solute, and then agitate to dissolve the solute.

b. Place 0.50 mol of solute in the flask, add distilled water to the 1.0-L mark, and then agitate to dissolve the solute.

c. Combine 0.50 mol of water with 0.50 mol of solute in the flask, and then agitate to dissolve the solute.

d. Fill the flask with distilled water until it is about half full, add 0.50 mol of solute, agitate to dissolve the solute, and then carefully fill the flask with distilled water to the 1.0-L mark.

5. List the information needed to find the molarity of a 2.0-L solution containing 0.50 mol of sodium chloride.

Known	Unknown
____ of solution	Molarity = ?
____ of sodium chloride	

$$\text{molarity } (M) = \frac{\underline{\qquad\qquad}}{\text{liters of solution}}$$

▶ Making Dilutions (pages 483–484)

6. How do you make a solution less concentrated? ____________

7. On the diagram below, assume that each beaker contains an equal number of moles of solute. Label each solution as *concentrated* or *dilute*. Then indicate the approximate relative volumes of each solution by drawing in the surface level on each beaker.

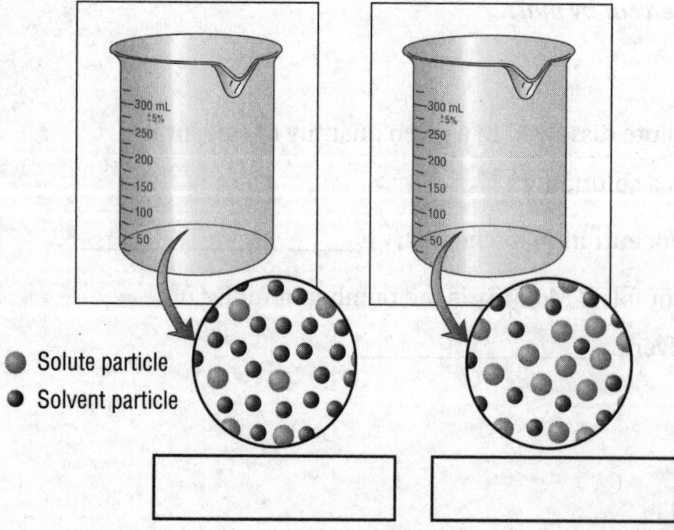

Name ______________________ Date ______________ Class ______________

Questions 8 and 9 refer to the following situation. Solvent is added to a solution until the total volume of the solution doubles.

8. What happens to the number of moles of solute present in the solution when the volume doubles?

____

9. Circle the letter of the correct description of the change in molarity of a solution when the volume doubles.

a. The molarity of the solution is cut in half.

b. The molarity of the solution doubles.

c. The molarity of the solution remains constant.

d. The molarity of the solution increases slightly.

10. List the information you need to find how many milliliters of a stock solution of 2.00*M* $MgSO_4$ you would need to prepare 100.0 mL of 1.00*M* $MgSO_4$.

Known	Unknown
M_1 = ______________	V_1 = ? mL of 2.00M $MgSO_4$
M_2 = ______________	
V_2 = ______________	
M_1 × ______ = ______ × ______	

▶ Percent Solutions (pages 485–486)

11. List the information needed to find the percent by volume of ethanol in a solution when 50 mL of pure ethanol is diluted with water to a volume of 250 mL.

Known	Unknown
Volume of ethanol = ______	% ethanol by volume = ? %
Volume of solution = ______	

% (v/v) = ______________________

Reading Skill Practice

Writing a summary can help you remember the information you have read. When you write a summary, include only the most important points. Write a summary of the information about percent solutions on pages 485–486. Your summary should be shorter than the text on which it is based. Do your work on a separate sheet of paper.

SECTION 16.3 COLLIGATIVE PROPERTIES OF SOLUTIONS (pages 487–490)

This section explains why a solution has a lower vapor pressure, an elevated boiling point, and a depressed freezing point compared with the pure solvent of that solution.

▶ Vapor Pressure Lowering (pages 487–488)

1. Properties of a solution that depend only on the number of particles dissolved, but not the identity of solute particles in the solution are called ______________.

2. Is the following sentence true or false? A nonvolatile substance is one that does not vaporize easily. ______________

3. Look at Figure 16.13 on page 487. What happens to the vapor pressure equilibrium when a nonvolatile solute is added to a pure solvent?

____

____

4. How is the decrease in vapor pressure of a solution with a nonvolatile solute related to the number of particles per formula unit of solute?

____

____

5. Assume 3 mol each of three different solutes have been added to three identical beakers of water as shown below. If the beakers are covered to form closed systems at constant temperature, rank the vapor pressures in each container from 1 (lowest) to 3 (highest).

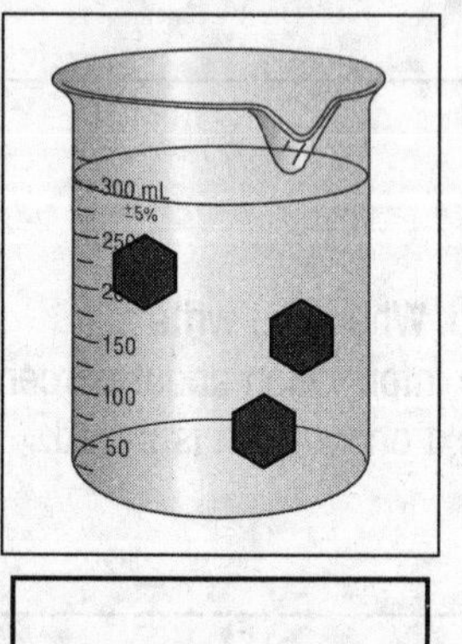

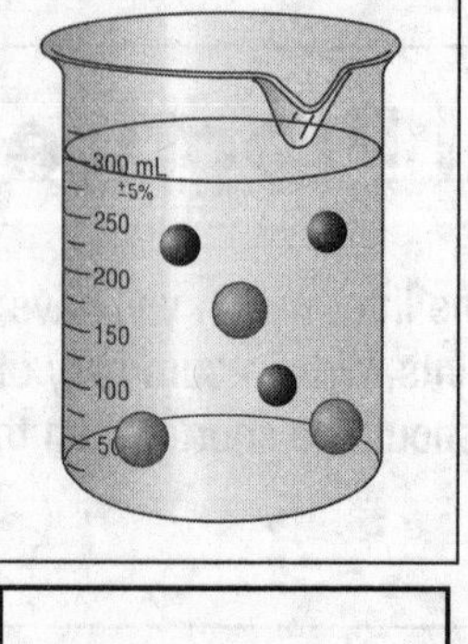

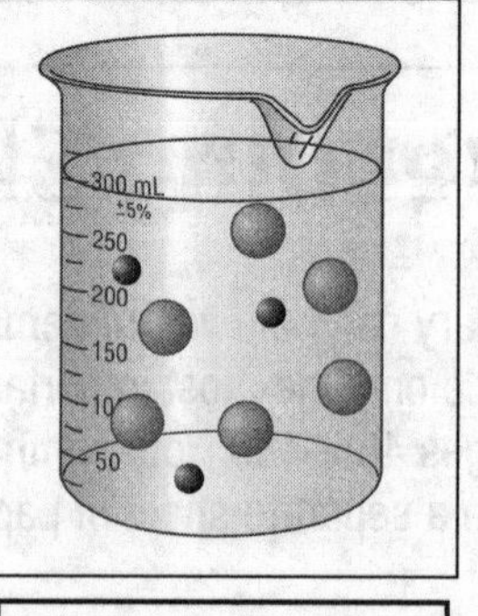

 Glucose  Na^+  Cl^- ● Ca^{2+}

Name ______________________ Date ______________ Class ______________

▶ Freezing-Point Depression (pages 488–489)

6. Circle the letter of each sentence that is true about the freezing point of a solution formed by a liquid solvent and nonvolatile solute.

a. When a substance freezes, the arrangement of its particles becomes less orderly.

b. The presence of a solute in water disrupts the formation of orderly patterns as the solution is cooled to the freezing point of pure water.

c. More kinetic energy must be withdrawn from a solution than from a pure solvent in order for the solution to solidify.

d. The freezing point of the solution is lower than the freezing point of the pure solvent.

7. One mole of which substance, glucose or sodium chloride, will produce more freezing-point depression when added to equal amounts of water? Why?

____

____

▶ Boiling-Point Elevation (page 490)

8. Circle the letter next to each sentence that is true concerning the boiling point of a solution formed by a liquid solvent and a nonvolatile solute.

a. The boiling point is the temperature at which the vapor pressure equals atmospheric pressure.

b. Adding a nonvolatile solute decreases the vapor pressure.

c. Because of the decrease in vapor pressure, additional kinetic energy must be added to raise the vapor pressure of the liquid phase to atmospheric pressure.

d. The boiling point of the solution is higher than the boiling point of the pure solvent.

9. The difference between the boiling point of a solution and that of the pure solvent is called the _______________________.

SECTION 16.4 CALCULATIONS INVOLVING COLLIGATIVE PROPERTIES (pages 491–496)

This section explains how to calculate the molality and mole fraction of a solution, and how to use molality to calculate the freezing-point depression or boiling-point elevation of a solution.

▶ Molality and Mole Fraction (pages 491–493)

1. For a solution, the ratio of moles of solute to mass of solvent in kilograms, represented by *m*, is the solution's _______________.

Name ______________ Date ______________ Class ______________

2. Is the following sentence true or false? Molarity and molality are always the same for a solution. ______________

3. What is the molality of a solution prepared by adding 1.0 mol of sodium chloride to 2.0 kg of water? ______________

4. The circle graph below shows the ratio of ethylene glycol (EG) to water in one antifreeze solution. Write the mole fractions for each substance.

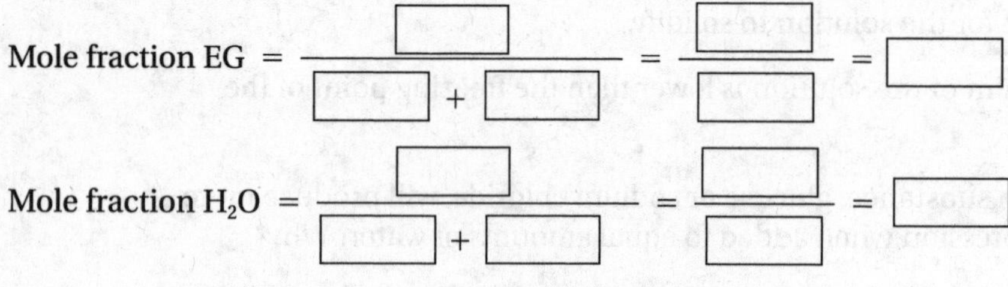

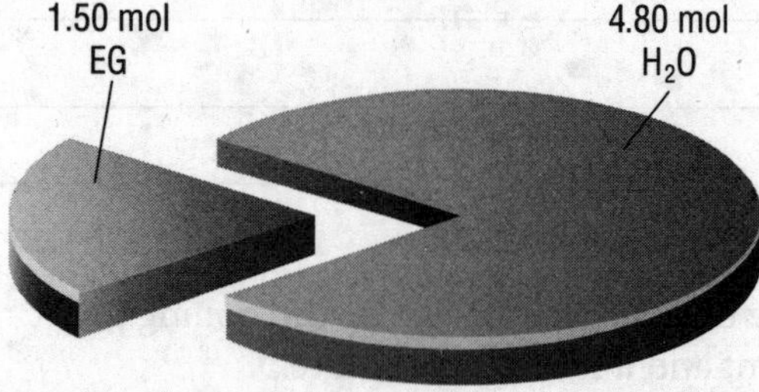

▶ Freezing-Point Depression and Boiling-Point Elevation (pages 494–496)

5. Assuming a solute is molecular and not ionic, the magnitude of the boiling-point elevation of the solution, ΔT_b, is directly proportional to

______________________________.

6. Look at Table 16.3 on page 495. What is the molal boiling-point elevation constant, K_b, for water? ______________

7. You need to find the freezing point of a 1.50*m* aqueous NaCl solution. You calculate ΔT_f to be 1.86°C/*m* × 3.00*m* or 5.86°C. What is the temperature at which the solution freezes? ______________

Name ______________________ Date ______________ Class ______________

GUIDED PRACTICE PROBLEMS

GUIDED PRACTICE PROBLEM 1 (page 477)

1. The solubility of a gas in water is 0.16 g/L at 104 kPa of pressure. What is the solubility when the pressure of the gas is increased to 288 kPa? Assume the temperature remains constant.

Analyze

Step 1. What is the equation for the relationship between solubility and

pressure? ______________

Step 2. What is this law called? ______________

Step 3. What are the known values in this problem?

P_1 = [ ]

S_1 = [ ]

[ ] = 288 kPa

Step 4. What is the unknown in this problem?

Calculate

Step 5. Rearrange the equation to solve for the unknown.

S_2 = [ ]

Step 6. Substitute the known values into the equation and solve.

$$S_2 = \frac{\boxed{}\ \text{g/L} \times \boxed{}\ \cancel{\text{kPa}}}{\boxed{}\ \cancel{\text{kPa}}} = \boxed{}$$

Evaluate

Step 7. How do you know that your answer is correct?

____

____

Step 8. Are the units correct? Explain.

____

____

GUIDED PRACTICE PROBLEM 8 (page 481)

8. A solution has a volume of 2.0 L and contains 36.0 g of glucose. If the molar mass of glucose is 180 g/mol, what is the molarity of the solution?

Step 1. What is the equation for molarity of a solution?

Molarity (M) = ______________

Step 2. How many moles of glucose are in the solution?

$\square$ g × $\frac{1 \text{ mol}}{\square \text{ g}}$ = $\square$ mol glucose

Step 3. Substitute the known values into the equation for molarity.

$M = \frac{\square}{2.0\ \square}$

Step 4. Solve.

M = ______________

GUIDED PRACTICE PROBLEM 9 (page 481)

9. A solution has a volume of 250 mL and contains 0.70 mol NaCl. What is its molarity?

Analyze

Step 1. List the knowns and the unknown.

Knowns

____

____

Unknown

____

The units of molarity, M, is mol solute/L solution.

Calculate

Step 2. Solve for the unknown.

As long as the units are correct, division gives the result.

$$\text{molarity} = \frac{\text{mol solute}}{\text{solution volume}} = \frac{0.70 \text{ mol NaCl}}{0.250 \text{ L}}$$

= ______________

Name ______________________ Date ______________ Class ______________

Evaluate

Step 3. Does the result make sense?

____

____

EXTRA PRACTICE (similar to Practice Problem 10, page 482)

10. How many moles of ammonium nitrate are in 375 mL of 0.40M NH_4NO_3?

GUIDED PRACTICE PROBLEM 12 (page 484)

12. How many milliliters of a solution of 4.00M KI is needed to prepare 250.0 mL of 0.760M KI?

Analyze

Step 1. List the knowns and the unknown.
Knowns

____

____

____

____

Unknown

____

Calculate

Step 2. Solve for the unknown.
Rearranging the equation above will give the result

$$V_1 = \frac{M_2 \times V_2}{M_1} = \frac{0.760M \text{ KI} \times 250.0 \text{ mL}}{4.00M \text{ KI}}$$

= __________________

Step 3. Evaluate Does the result make sense?

____

____

____

GUIDED PRACTICE PROBLEM 14 (page 485)

14. If 10 mL of pure propanone (or acetone) is diluted with water to a total solution volume of 200 mL, what is the percent by volume of acetone in the solution?

Step 1. What is the equation for calculating percent by volume? % (v/v) = ______________ × 100%

Step 2. What are the knowns in this problem?

____

____

Step 3. Substitute the known values into the equation and solve.

GUIDED PRACTICE PROBLEM 29 (page 492)

29. How many grams of sodium fluoride are needed to prepare a 0.400*m* NaF solution that contains 750 g of water?

Analyze

Step 1. List the knowns and the unknown.

Knowns

____

____

____

Unknown

____

The final solution must contain 0.400 mol of NaF per 1000 g of water. This information will provide a conversion factor. The process of conversion will be: grams of water → mol NaF → grams NaF

Calculate

Step 2. Solve for the unknown.
Multiply by the appropriate conversion factors:

$$750\ \cancel{g\ H_2O} \times \frac{0.400\ \cancel{mol\ NaF}}{100\cancel{g\ H_2O}} \times \frac{42.0\ g\ NaF}{\cancel{1\ mol\ NaF}}$$

= ______________________

Evaluate

Step 3. Does the result make sense?

____

____

____

EXTRA PRACTICE (similar to Practice Problem 31, page 493)

31. What is the mole fraction of each component in a solution made by mixing 230 g of ethanol (C_2H_5OH) and 450 g of water?

n_{ETH} = ______________________

n_{WAT} = ______________________

X_{ETH} = ______________________

X_{WAT} = ______________________

GUIDED PRACTICE PROBLEM 33 (page 495)

33. What is the freezing point depression of an aqueous solution of 10.0 g glucose ($C_6H_{12}O_6$) in 50.0 g H_2O?

Analyze

Step 1. List the knowns and the unknown.
Knowns

____

____

____

____

Unknown

____

To use the given equation, first convert the mass of solute to the number of moles, then calculate the molality, *m*.

Calculate

Step 2. Solve for the unknown.
Calculate the molar mass of $C_6H_{12}O_6$: 1mol $C_6H_{12}O_6$ = ______________

Calculate the number of moles of solute using this conversion:

$$\text{mol } C_6H_{12}O_6 = 10.0\ \cancel{\text{g } C_6H_{12}O_6} \times \frac{1\text{ mol } C_6H_{12}O_6}{180\ \cancel{\text{g } C_6H_{12}O_6}}$$

= ______________

Calculate the molality:

$$m = \frac{\text{mol solute}}{\text{kg solvent}} = \frac{0.0556\text{ mol } C_6H_{12}O_6}{0.0500\text{ kg } H_2O}$$

= ______________

Calculate the freezing point depression using the known formula:

____

Name ______________ Date ______________ Class ______________

Evaluate

Step 3. Does the result make sense?

____

____

____

GUIDED PRACTICE PROBLEM 35 (page 496)

35. What is the boiling point of a solution that contains 1.25 mol $CaCl_2$ in 1400 g of water?

Step 1. What is the concentration of the $CaCl_2$ solution?

$$\frac{1.25\ \text{mol}}{\square\ \text{g}} \times \frac{\square\ \text{g}}{1\ \text{kg}} = \square\ m$$

Step 2. How many particles are produced by the ionization of each formula unit of $CaCl_2$?

$CaCl_2(s) \longrightarrow Ca^{+} + \square\ Cl^{-}$,

therefore ______ particles are produced.

Step 3. What is the total molality of the solution?

______ $\times\ 0.89m = 2.7m$

Step 4. What is the molal boiling point elevation constant (K_b) for water?

K_b (water) = ______ °C/m

Step 5. Calculate the boiling point elevation.

ΔT_b = ______ °C/m × 2.7 ______

= 1.4 ______

Step 6. Add ΔT_b to 100°C to find the new boiling point.

______ °C + 100°C = ______ °C

GUIDED PRACTICE PROBLEM 36 (page 496)

33. What mass of NaCl would have to be dissolved in 1.000 kg of water to raise the boiling point by 2.00°C?

Analyze

Step 1. List the knowns and the unknown.

Knowns

____

____

____

____

Unknown

____

First calculate the molality, m, using the given equation. Then use a molar mass conversion to determine the mass of solute.

Calculate

Step 2. Solve for the unknown.
Calculate the molality by rearranging $\Delta T_b = K_b \times m$:

$$m = \Delta T_b / K_b = \frac{2.00°C}{1.86°C/m}$$

= ______________

Calculate the molar mass of NaCl: 1 mol NaCl = 58.5 g

= ______________ kg NaCl

Determine the number of moles of solute using the molality and the amount of solvent:

$$\text{moles NaCl} = \text{mass of solvent} \times \text{molality} = 1.000 \text{ kg } H_2O \times \frac{1.08 \text{ mol NaCl}}{1 \text{ kg } H_2O}$$

= ______________

Finally, convert the number of moles of NaCl to mass:

$$1.08 \text{ mol NaCl} \times \frac{5.85 \times 10^{-2} \text{ kg NaCl}}{1 \text{ mol NaCl}}$$

= ______________

Evaluate

Step 3. Does the result make sense?

____

____

Name ______________ Date ______________ Class ______________

17 THERMOCHEMISTRY

SECTION 17.1 THE FLOW OF ENERGY—HEAT AND WORK (pages 505–510)

This section explains the relationship between energy and heat, and distinguishes between heat capacity and specific heat.

▶ Energy Transformations (page 505)

1. What area of study in chemistry is concerned with the heat transfers that occur during chemical reactions? thermochemistry

2. Where the use of energy is concerned (in a scientific sense), when is work done?

work is done when energy is transferred.

3. Circle the letter next to each sentence that is true about energy.

a. Energy is the capacity for doing work or supplying heat.

b. Energy is detected only because of its effects.

c. Heat is energy that transfers from one object to another because they are at the same temperature.

d. Gasoline contains a significant amount of chemical potential energy.

4. Circle the letter next to each sentence that is true about heat.

a. One effect of adding heat to a substance is an increase in the temperature of that substance.

b. Heat always flows from a cooler object to a warmer object.

c. If two objects remain in contact, heat will flow from the warmer object to the cooler object until the temperature of both objects is the same.

▶ Exothermic and Endothermic Processes (pages 506–507)

5. What can be considered the "system" and what are the "surroundings" when studying a mixture of chemicals undergoing a reaction? Write your answers where indicated below.

System: Part being observed / the focus of the experiment.

Surroundings: the rest of the universe.

CHAPTER 17, Thermochemistry *(continued)*

6. In thermochemical calculations, is the direction of heat flow given from the point of view of the system, or of the surroundings?

It is in POV of the system.

7. What universal law states that energy can neither be created nor destroyed and can always be accounted for as work, stored potential energy, or heat?

The Law of Conservation of Energy

Questions 8 through 12 refer to the systems and surroundings illustrated in diagrams (a) and (b) below.

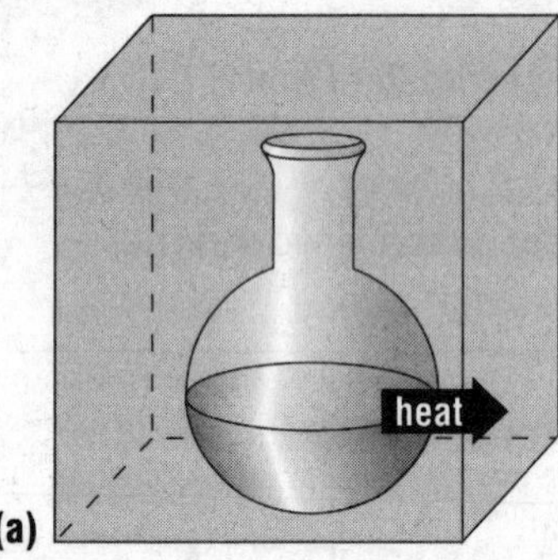

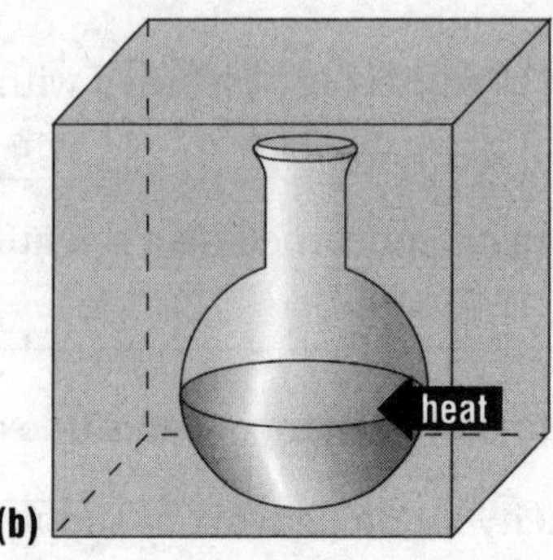

8. Which diagram illustrates an endothermic process? B

9. Is heat flow positive or negative in diagram (a)? Negative

10. Which diagram illustrates an exothermic process? A

11. Is heat flow positive or negative in diagram (b)? positive

12. What does a negative value for heat represent?

Heat is being lost, and is therefore −.

To answer Questions 13 and 14, look at Figure 17.2 on page 506.

13. A system is a person sitting next to a campfire. Is this system endothermic or exothermic? Explain why.

Endothermic b/c the person sitting is taking in heat so it is getting warmer.

14. A system is a person who is perspiring. Is this system endothermic or exothermic? Explain why.

Exothermic because the sweat released to cool the body down. This means heat is being released, hence it being exothermic.

Name ______________________ Date ______________ Class ______________

▶ Units for Measuring Heat Flow (page 507)

15. Heat generated by the human body is usually measured in units called

calories .

16. Describe the chemical reaction that generates heat in the human body.

Metabolism generates heat from the food we eat every day.

17. What is the definition of a calorie?

Amount of energy needed to heat 1g of H_2O by 1°C or 1K.

18. How is the calorie (written with a lower case c) related to the dietary Calorie (written with a capital C)?

The lowercase calorie is a smaller unit.

19. Circle the letter next to the SI unit of heat and energy.

a. calorie

b. Calorie

(c.) joule

d. Celsius degree

▶ Heat Capacity and Specific Heat (pages 508–510)

20. Is the next sentence true or false? Samples of two different substances having the same mass always have the same heat capacity. False

21. Compare the heat capacity of a 2-kg steel frying pan and a 2-g steel pin. If the heat capacities of these objects differ, explain why.

They are the same b/c they are both steel

22. Is the next sentence true or false? The specific heat of a substance varies with the mass of the sample. False

SECTION 17.2 MEASURING AND EXPRESSING ENTHALPY CHANGES (pages 511–517)

This section explains how to construct equations and perform calculations that show enthalpy changes for chemical and physical processes.

▶ Calorimetry (pages 511–513)

1. The property that is useful for keeping track of heat transfers in chemical and physical processes at constant pressure is called ______________.

Name ______________ Date ______________ Class ______________

CHAPTER 17, Thermochemistry *(continued)*

2. What is calorimetry? The precise measurement of heat flow.

3. Use Figure 17.5 on page 511. Circle the letter next to each sentence that is true about calorimeters.

(a.) The calorimeter container is insulated to minimize loss of heat to or absorption of heat from the surroundings.

(b.) Because foam cups are excellent heat insulators, they may be used as simple calorimeters.

c. A stirrer is used to keep temperatures uneven in a calorimeter.

d. In the calorimeter shown in Figure 17.5, the chemical substances dissolved in water constitute the system and the water is part of the surroundings.

4. Is the following sentence true or false? For systems at constant pressure, heat flow and enthalpy change are the same thing. true

5. Complete the table below to show the direction of heat flow and type of reaction for positive and negative change of enthalpy.

Sign of Enthalpy Change	Direction of Heat Flow	Is Reaction Endothermic or Exothermic?
ΔH is positive ($\Delta H > 0$)	in	endothermic
ΔH is negative ($\Delta H < 0$)	out	exothermic

6. Name each quantity that is represented in the equation for heat change in an aqueous solution.

$$q = \Delta H = m \times C \times \Delta T$$

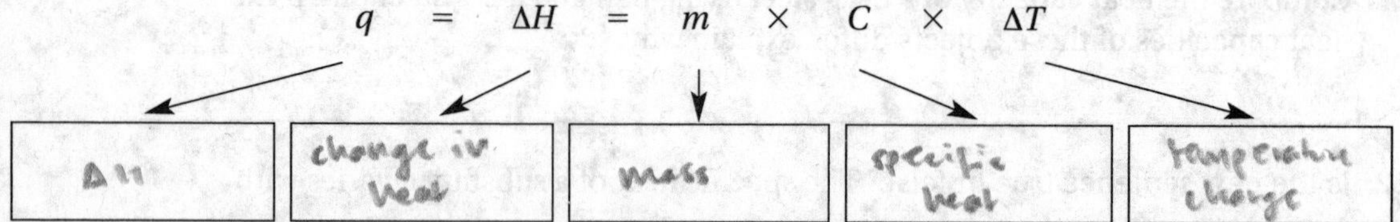

▶ Thermochemical Equations (pages 514–517)

7. What happens to the temperature of water after calcium oxide is added?

8. A chemical equation that includes the heat change is called a thermochemical equation.

9. Why is it important to give the physical state of the reactants and products in a thermochemical equation?

They may have different specific heats in different states of matter.

Name ______________________ Date ______________ Class ______________

10. Complete the enthalpy diagram for the combustion of natural gas. Use the thermochemical equation in the first paragraph on page 517 as a guide.

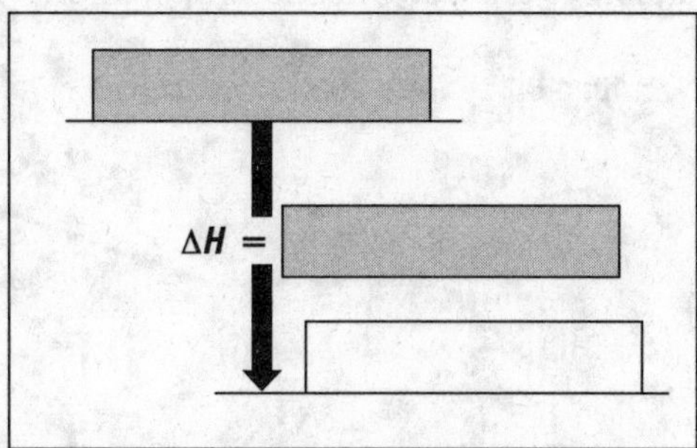

SECTION 17.3 HEAT IN CHANGES OF STATE (pages 520–526)

This section explains heat transfers that occur during melting, freezing, boiling, and condensing.

▶ Heats of Fusion and Solidification (pages 520–521)

1. Is the following sentence true or false? A piece of ice placed in a bowl in a warm room will remain at a temperature of 0°C until all of the ice has melted.

False

2. Circle the letter next to each sentence that is true about heat of fusion and heat of solidification of a given substance.

a. The molar heat of fusion is the negative of the molar heat of solidification.

b. Heat is released during melting and absorbed during freezing.

c. Heat is absorbed during melting and released during freezing.

d. The quantity of heat absorbed during melting is exactly the same as the quantity of heat released when the liquid solidifies.

3. Use Table 17.3 on page 522. Determine ΔH for each of these physical changes.

a. $H_2(s) \longrightarrow H_2(l)$ $\Delta H =$ ______________

b. $Ne(s) \longrightarrow Ne(l)$ $\Delta H =$ ______________

c. $O_2(s) \longrightarrow O_2(l)$ $\Delta H =$ ______________

▶ Heats of Vaporization and Condensation (pages 522–524)

4. Is the following sentence true or false? As liquids absorb heat at their boiling points, the temperature remains constant while they vaporize.

____

Name ______________________ Date ______________ Class ______________

Use the heating curve for water shown below to answer Questions 5, 6, and 7.

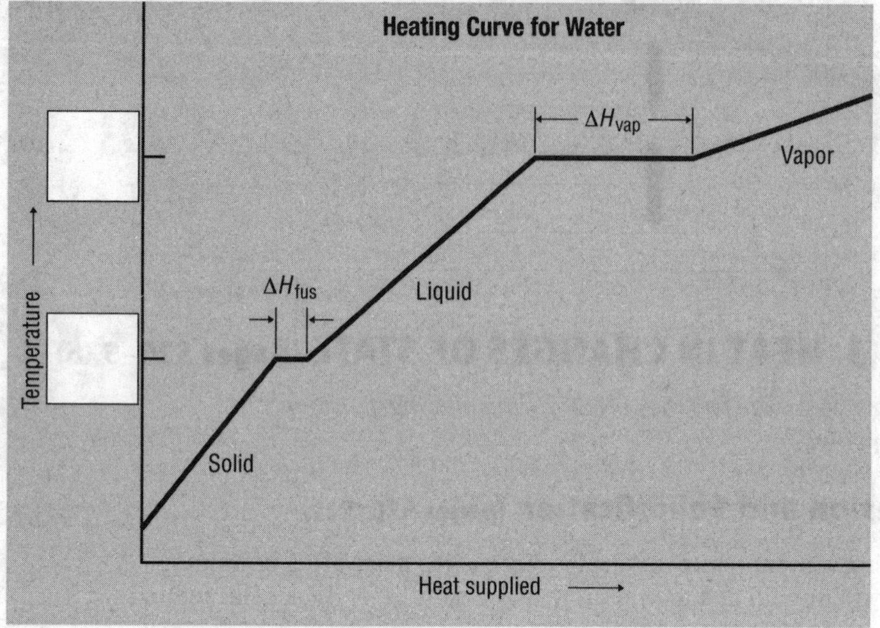

5. Label the melting point and boiling point temperatures on the graph.

6. What happens to the temperature during melting and vaporization?

____

____

7. Circle the letter next to the process that *releases* the most heat.

   a. Melting of 1 mol of water at 0°C

   b. Freezing of 1 mol of water at 0°C

   c. Vaporization of 1 mol of water at 100°C

   d. Condensation of 1 mol of water at 100°C

Look at Table 17.3 on page 522 to help you answer Questions 8 and 9.

8. How many of the 6 substances listed have a higher molar heat of vaporization than water? Which one(s)? ______________

9. It takes ______________ of energy to convert 1 mol of methanol molecules in the solid state to 1 mol of methanol molecules in the liquid state at the normal melting point.

Name ______________________ Date ______________ Class ______________

▶ Heat of Solution (pages 525–526)

10. The heat change caused by dissolution of one mole of a substance is the

______________________________.

11. How does a cold pack containing water and ammonium nitrate work?

____

____

____

Reading Skill Practice

Writing a summary can help you remember the information you have read. When you write a summary, write only the most important points. Write a summary for each of the five types of heat changes described on pages 520–526. Your summary should be much shorter than these six pages of text. Do your work on another sheet of paper.

SECTION 17.4 CALCULATING HEATS OF REACTION (pages 527–532)

This section explains how Hess's law of heat summation and standard heats of formation may be applied to find enthalpy changes for a series of chemical and physical processes.

▶ Hess's Law (pages 527–529)

1. For reactions that occur in a series of steps, Hess's law of heat summation says that if you add the thermochemical equations for each step to give a final equation for the reaction, you may also ______________________________

____.

2. Is the following sentence true or false? Graphite is a more stable form of elemental carbon than diamond at 25°C, so diamond will slowly change to graphite over an extremely long period of time. ______________

3. Look at Figures 17.13 and 17.14 on pages 528 and 529. According to Hess's law, the enthalpy change from diamond to carbon dioxide can be expressed as the sum of what three enthalpy changes?

a. ____

b. ____

c. ____

▶ Standard Heats of Formation (pages 530–532)

4. The change in enthalpy that accompanies the formation of one mole of a compound from its elements with all substances in their standard states at 25°C and 101.3 kPa is called the ______________________________.

5. Is the following sentence true or false? Chemists have set the standard heat of formation of free elements, including elements that occur in nature as diatomic molecules, at zero. ____________________

6. Complete the enthalpy diagram below by finding the heat of formation when hydrogen and oxygen gases combine to form hydrogen peroxide at 25°C. Use the data in Table 17.4 on page 530 and the equation $\Delta H^0 = \Delta H_f^0$ (products) – ΔH_f^0 (reactants) to find the answer.

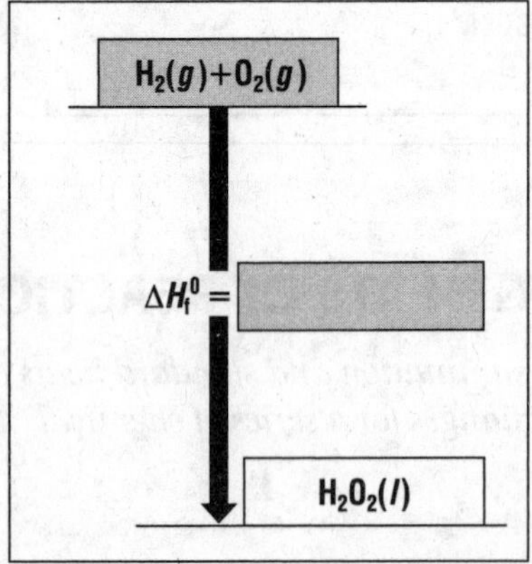

7. Look at Table 17.4. Methane burns to form carbon dioxide and water vapor.

$$CH_4(g) + 2O_2(g) \longrightarrow CO_2(g) + 2H_2O(g)$$

a. Will the heat of this reaction be positive or negative? How do you know?

____

____

____

b. How does your experience confirm that your answer to Question 7a is reasonable?

____

____

Name ______________ Date ______________ Class ______________

GUIDED PRACTICE PROBLEMS

GUIDED PRACTICE PROBLEM 3 (page 510)

3. When 435 J of heat is added to 3.4 g of olive oil at 21°C, the temperature increases to 85°C. What is the specific heat of the olive oil?

Analyze

a. What is the formula for calculating specific heat? ______________

b. What are the knowns and the unknown in this problem?

Knowns:

m = ______________

q = ______________

ΔT = ______________

Unknown:

____

Calculate

c. Substitute the known values into the equation for specific heat and solve.

$C_{\text{olive oil}}$ = [ ] = 2.0 [ ]

Evaluate

d. Explain why you think your answer is reasonable. Think about the time it takes to fry foods in olive oil versus the time it takes to cook foods in boiling water.

____

____

____

____

____

e. Are the units in your answer correct? How do you know?

____

____

GUIDED PRACTICE PROBLEM 12 (page 513)

12. When 50.0 mL of water containing 0.50 mol HCl at 22.5°C is mixed with 50.0 mL of water containing 0.50 mol NaOH at 22.5°C in a calorimeter, the temperature of the solution increased to 26.0°C. How much heat (in kJ) was released by this reaction?

a. Calculate the final volume of the water. $V_{final} = 50.0\text{ mL} + 50.0\text{ mL} =$ ______

b. Calculate the total mass of the water, using the density of water. $m =$ ______ $\text{mL} \times \frac{\square\text{ g}}{\text{mL}} =$ ______

c. Calculate ΔT. $\Delta T = 26.0\text{ °C} -$ ______ °C = ______ °C

d. Substitute the known quantities into the equation for changes in enthalpy (ΔH). $\Delta H =$ (______ g) × (4.18 ______) × ______ °C

e. Solve. ______ J

f. Convert joules to kilojoules (kJ) and round to three significant figures. ______ $\text{J} \times \frac{1\text{ kJ}}{1000\text{ J}} =$ ______ kJ

EXTRA PRACTICE (similar to Practice Problem 14, page 516)

14. When carbon disulfide is formed from its elements, heat is absorbed. Calculate the amount of heat (in kJ) absorbed when 8.53 g of carbon disulfide is formed.

$C(s) + 2S(s) \longrightarrow CS_2(l)$ $\quad \Delta H = 89.3\text{ kJ}$

GUIDED PRACTICE PROBLEM 22 (page 521)

22. How many grams of ice at 0°C could be melted by the addition of 0.400 kJ of heat?

a. Write the conversion factors from ΔH_{fus} and the molar mass of ice. $\frac{1\text{ mol ice}}{\square\text{ kJ}}$ and $\frac{\square\text{ g ice}}{1\text{ mol ice}}$

b. Multiply the known heat change by the conversion factors. $0.400\ \cancel{\text{kJ}} \times \frac{1\ \cancel{\text{mol ice}}}{\square\ \cancel{\text{kJ}}} \times \frac{\square\text{ g ice}}{1\ \cancel{\text{mol ice}}}$

$= \square$ g ice

EXTRA PRACTICE (similar to Practice Problem 23, page 524)

23. How much heat (in kJ) is absorbed when 88.45 g $H_2O(l)$ at 100°C and 101.3 kPa is converted to steam at 100°C? Express your answer in kJ.

Name ______________________ Date ______________ Class ______________

18 REACTION RATES AND EQUILIBRIUM

SECTION 18.1 RATES OF REACTION (pages 541–547)

This section explains what is meant by the rate of a chemical reaction. It also uses collision theory to show how the rate of a chemical reaction is influenced by the reaction conditions.

▶ Collision Theory (pages 541–544)

1. How are rates of chemical change expressed?

____

____

2. Look at Figure 18.3 on page 542. In a typical reaction, as time passes, the amount of ______________ decreases and the amount of ______________ increases.

3. What does collision theory say about the energies of atoms, ions, or molecules reacting to form products when they collide?

____

____

____

4. Look at the figures below. One shows a collision that results in the formation of product. Label it *effective collision.* Label the other collision *ineffective collision.*

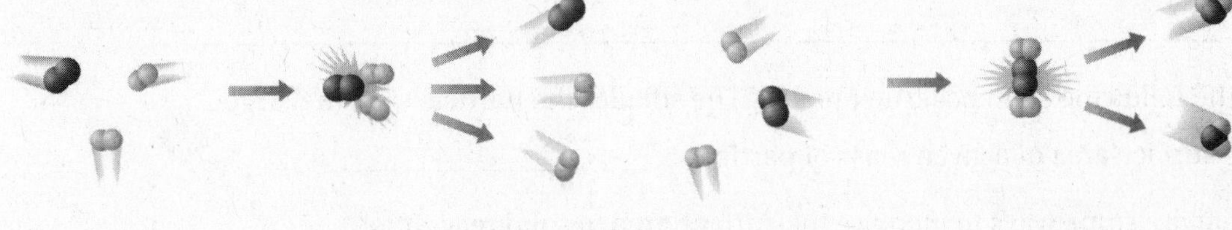

______________________ ______________________

5. Is the following sentence true or false? Particles lacking the necessary kinetic energy to react bounce apart unchanged when they collide. ______________

6. Look at Figure 18.5 on page 543. Which arrangement of atoms contains the least amount of energy?

a. reactants

b. activated complex

c. products

Name ______________________ Date ______________ Class ______________

7. Circle the letter of the term that completes the sentence correctly. The minimum amount of energy that particles must have in order to react is called the ______.

 a. kinetic energy c. potential energy

 b. activation energy d. collision energy

8. An activated complex is the arrangement of atoms at the ________________ of the activation-energy barrier.

9. Circle the letter of the term that best describes the lifetime of an activated complex.

 a. 10^{-15} s b. 10^{13} s c. 10^{-13} s d. 10^{-1} s

10. Why is an activated complex sometimes called the transition state?

____

____

▶ Factors Affecting Reaction Rates (pages 545–547)

11. Changes in the rate of chemical reactions depend on conditions such as

____.

12. The main effect of increasing the temperature of a chemical reaction is to

________________ the number of particles that have enough kinetic energy to react when they collide.

13. What happens when you put more reacting particles into a fixed volume?

____

____

14. Is the following sentence true or false? The smaller the particle size, the larger the surface area of a given mass of particles. ________________

15. What are some ways to increase the surface area of solid reactants?

____

16. A ________________ is a substance that increases the rate of a reaction without being used up itself during the reaction.

17. What does a catalyst do? ______________________________________

____

____

Name ______________________ Date ______________ Class ______________

The graph below shows the reaction rate of the same reaction with and without a catalyst. Use it to help you answer Questions 18 and 19.

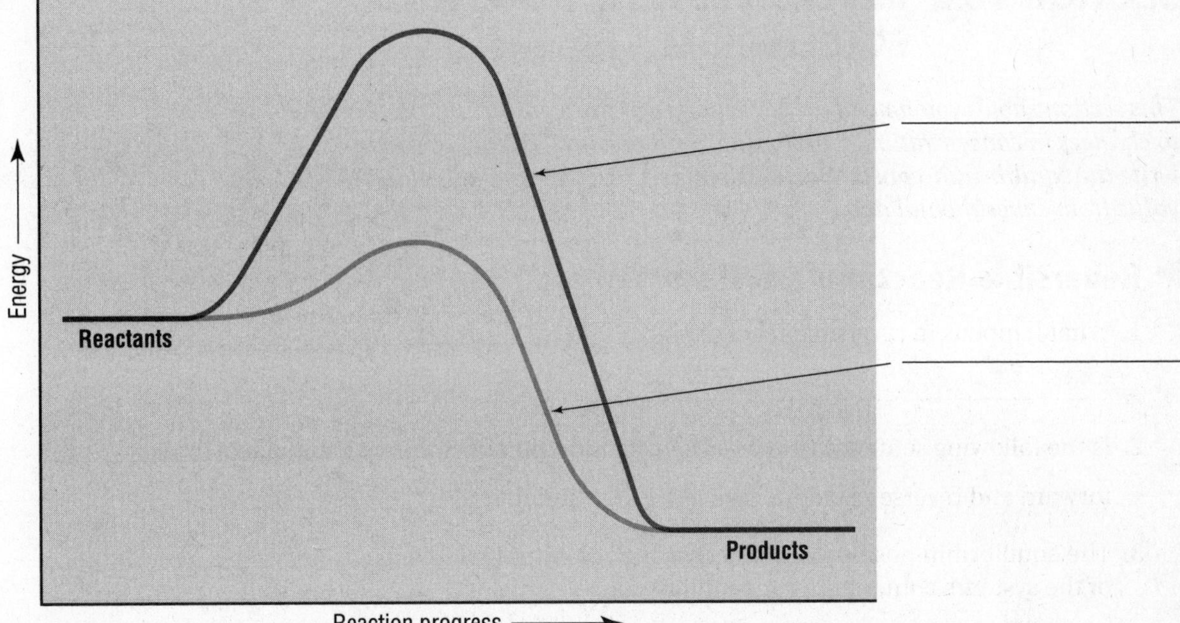

18. Label each curve as *with catalyst* or *without catalyst.*

19. What does the graph show about the effect of a catalyst on the rate of a reaction? ____

____

20. In a chemical equation, how do you show that catalysts are not consumed or chemically altered during a reaction? ______________________________

____

21. A(n) ______________________ is a substance that interferes with the action of a catalyst.

SECTION 18.2 REVERSIBLE REACTIONS AND EQUILIBRIUM (pages 549–559)

This section shows you how to predict changes in the equilibrium position due to changes in concentration, temperature, and pressure. It teaches you how to write the equilibrium-constant expression for a reaction and calculate its value from experimental data.

▶ Reversible Reactions (pages 549–551)

1. What happens in reversible reactions? ______________________________

____

2. Is the following sentence true or false? Chemical equilibrium is a state in which the forward and reverse reactions take place at different rates. ______________

3. The equilibrium position of a reaction is given by the relative ______________ of the system's components at equilibrium.

4. Fill in the missing labels on the diagram below with either the words *at equilibrium* or *not at equilibrium.* At equilibrium, how many types of molecules are present in the mixture? ______

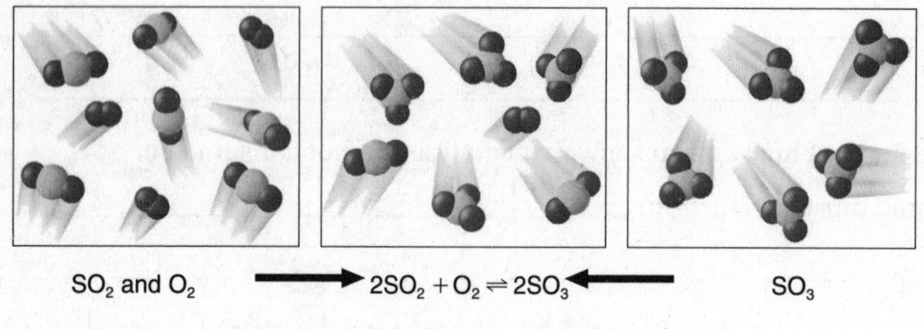

______________ ______________ ______________

5. Use Figure 18.10 on page 550 to answer these questions.

a. Which graph, left or right, shows an initial concentration of 100% SO_3 and no SO_2? ______________

b. Compare the initial concentrations of the substances shown in the other graph.

____

c. What is the favored substance at equilibrium? How can you tell?

____

▶ Factors Affecting Equilibrium: Le Châtelier's Principle (pages 552–555)

6. What is Le Châtelier's principle? ______________________________

____

Name ______________________ Date ______________ Class ______________

7. Circle the letters of the terms that complete the sentence correctly. Stresses that upset the equilibrium of a chemical system include changes in ______.

a. concentration
b. the amount of catalyst
c. pressure
d. temperature

8. When you add a product to a reversible chemical reaction, the reaction is always pushed in the direction of ______________. When you remove a product, the reaction is pulled in the direction of ______________.

9. Is the following sentence true or false? Increasing the temperature of a chemical reaction causes the equilibrium position of a reaction to shift in the direction that absorbs heat. ______________

10. How does increasing pressure affect a chemical system? ______________

____

____

11. Decreasing the pressure on the system shown in Figure 18.13 on page 554 results in a shift of equilibrium to favor ______________.

▶ Equilibrium Constants (pages 556–559)

12. The equilibrium constant (K_{eq}) is the ratio of ______________ concentrations to ______________ concentrations at equilibrium, with each concentration raised to a power equal to the number of ______________ of that substance in the balanced chemical equation.

13. What are the exponents in the equilibrium-constant expression?

____

14. What do the square brackets indicate in the equilibrium-constant expression?

____

____

15. Is the following sentence true or false? The value of K_{eq} for a reaction depends on the temperature. ______________

16. A value of K_{eq} greater than 1 means that ______________ are favored over ______________. A value of K_{eq} less than 1 means that ______________ are favored over ______________.

Name ______________________ Date ______________ Class ______________

SECTION 18.3 SOLUBILITY EQUILIBRIUM (pages 560–565)

This section explains how to calculate the solubility product constant of a slightly soluble salt.

▶ The Solubility Product Constant (pages 560–562)

1. What is the solubility product constant (K_{sp})?

____

____

2. Look at Table 18.1 on page 561. Which ionic compounds are exceptions to the general insolubility of carbonates, phosphates, and sulfites?

____

3. Look at Table 18.2 on page 562. Which salt is more soluble in water, silver bromide (AgBr) or silver chromate (Ag_2CrO_4)? ______________

▶ The Common Ion Effect (pages 563–565)

4. A common ion is an ion that is common to both ______________ in a solution.

5. Is the following sentence true or false? The raising of the solubility of a substance by the addition of a common ion is called the common ion effect. ______________

6. A solubility product can be used to predict whether a ______________ will form when solutions are mixed.

SECTION 18.4 ENTROPY AND FREE ENERGY (pages 566–573)

This section defines entropy and free energy, and characterizes reactions as spontaneous or nonspontaneous. It also describes how heat change and entropy change determine the spontaneity of a reaction.

▶ Free Energy and Spontaneous Reactions (pages 566–568)

1. Free energy is energy that is available to do ______________.

2. Is the following sentence true or false? All processes can be made 100% efficient. ______________

Name ______________ Date ______________ Class ______________

3. Make a concept map about balanced chemical reactions.

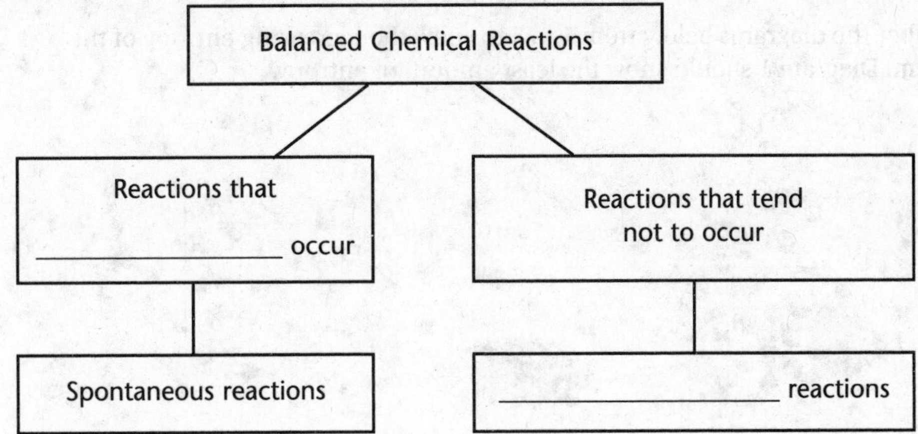

4. Spontaneous reactions are reactions that occur naturally and that favor the formation of ______________ at the specified conditions.

5. Describe four spontaneous reactions mentioned in this section.

a. ______________________________

b. ______________________________

c. ______________________________

d. ______________________________

6. What are nonspontaneous reactions?

____

____

7. Is the following sentence true or false? Some reactions that are non-spontaneous at one set of conditions may be spontaneous at other conditions. ______________

▶ Entropy (pages 568–570)

8. Some factor other than ______________ change must help determine whether a physical or chemical process is spontaneous.

9. What is entropy? ______________________________

10. The law of disorder states that processes move in the direction of ______________ disorder or randomness.

11. Is the following sentence true or false? Entropy decreases when a substance is divided into parts. ______________

Name ______________________ Date ________________ Class ________________

12. Number the diagrams below from 1 to 3 to show the increasing entropy of the system. Diagram 1 should show the least amount of entropy.

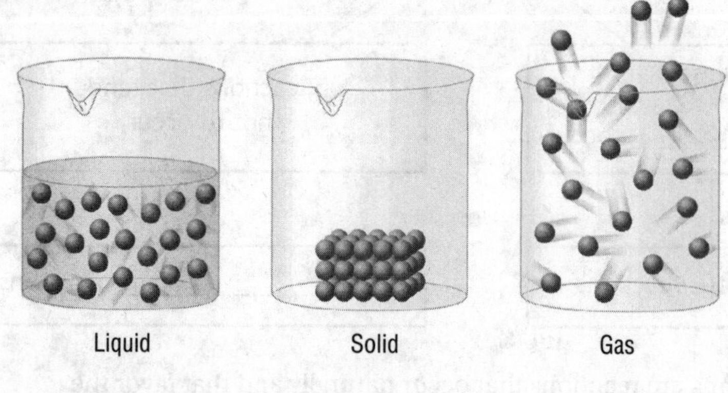

______ ______ ______

13. Does entropy tend to increase or decrease in chemical reactions in which the total number of product molecules is greater than the total number of reactant molecules? ________________

14. Entropy tends to ________________ when temperature increases.

▶ Heat, Entropy, and Free Energy (pages 571–572)

15. What determines whether a reaction is spontaneous?

____

____

16. Why is an exothermic reaction accompanied by an increase in entropy considered a spontaneous reaction? ________________________________

17. Is the following sentence true or false? A nonspontaneous reaction, one in which the products are not favored, has heat changes, entropy changes, or both working against it. ________________

18. What is the symbol for a change in entropy? ________________

▶ Gibbs Free-Energy (pages 572–573)

19. The Gibbs free-energy change (ΔG) is the maximum amount of energy that can be coupled to another process to do useful ________________.

20. What is the equation used to calculate the Gibbs free-energy change?

____

____

Name ______________________ Date ______________ Class ______________

21. The numerical value of ΔG is ________________ in spontaneous processes because the system loses free energy; the numerical value of ΔG is ________________ in nonspontaneous processes because the system requires that work be expended to make them go forward at the specified conditions.

Reading Skill Practice

Writing a summary can help you remember the information you have read. When you write a summary, include only the most important points. Write a summary of the information under the heading *Gibbs Free-Energy,* pages 572–573. Your summary should be shorter than the text on which it is based. Do your work on a separate sheet of paper.

SECTION 18.5 THE PROGRESS OF CHEMICAL REACTIONS (pages 575–579)

This section describes how to use experimental rate data to deduce the rate laws for simple chemical reactions. It also shows how to analyze the mechanism for a reaction from an energy diagram.

▶ Rate Laws (pages 575–577)

1. What is a one-step reaction? ____

____

2. Is the following sentence true or false? A rate law is an expression relating the rate of a reaction to the concentration of products. ________________

3. What is a specific rate constant (k) for a reaction? ________________________

____

4. The ________________ of a reaction is the power to which the concentration of a reactant must be raised to give the experimentally observed relationship between concentration and rate.

5. In a first-order reaction, the reaction rate is directly proportional to the concentration of _______ .

   a. two or more reactants

   b. both reactants and products

   c. only one reactant

Name ______________ Date ______________ Class ______________

6. How do you determine the actual kinetic order of a reaction?

____

▶ Reaction Mechanisms (page 578)

7. What is a reaction progress curve? ____

____

8. A(n) ______________ reaction is one in which reactants are converted to products in a single step.

9. Is the following sentence true or false? A reaction mechanism includes some of the elementary reactions of a complex reaction. ______________

10. What is an intermediate product of a reaction?

____

____

11. Look at Figure 18.28 on page 578. What is one difference between this graph and the chemical equation for this reaction?

____

____

____

____

Name ______________________ Date ______________ Class ______________

GUIDED PRACTICE PROBLEMS

GUIDED PRACTICE PROBLEM 6 (page 555)

6. How is the equilibrium position of this reaction affected by the following changes?

$C(s) + H_2O(g) + heat \rightleftharpoons CO(g) + H_2(g)$

a. lowering the temperature

b. increasing the pressure

c. removing hydrogen

d. adding water vapor

Analyze

Step 1. Plan a problem-solving strategy.
a-d Use Le Châtelier's principle to analyze the shift in the system effected by each stress.

Solve

Step 2. Apply the problem-solving strategy.

a. ____

____

b. ____

____

c. ____

____

d. ____

____

GUIDED PRACTICE PROBLEM 7 (page 557)

7. The reaction $N_2(g) + 3H_2(g) \rightleftharpoons 2NH_3(g)$ produces ammonia. At equilibrium, a 1-L flask contains 0.15 mol H_2, 0.25 mol N_2, and 0.10 mol NH_3. Calculate K_{eq} for the reaction.

Analyze

Step 1. List the knowns and the unknown.

Knowns

____

____

____

____

Unknown

____

Calculate

Step 2. Solve for the unknowns.

Use the concentrations given and the coefficients from the balanced equation to determine K_{eq}:

$$K_{eq} = \frac{[NH_3]^2}{[N_2] \times [H_2]^3}$$

$$= \frac{0.10^2}{0.25 \times 0.15^3} = 11.85$$

$= $ ______________

Name ____________________ Date ______________ Class ______________

GUIDED PRACTICE PROBLEM 9 (page 558)

9. Suppose the following system reaches equilibrium.

$N_2(g) + O_2(g) \rightleftharpoons 2NO(g)$

An analysis of the equilibrium mixture in a 1-L flask gives the following results: nitrogen, 0.50 mol; oxygen, 0.50 mol; nitrogen monoxide, 0.020 mol. Calculate K_{eq} for the reaction.

Step 1. List the known values and the unknowns.

Known	Unknown
$[N_2]$ = ______	$K_{eq} = ?$
$[O_2]$ = ______	
$[NO] = 0.020$ mol/L	

Step 2. Write the K_{eq} for the reaction. It should have three variables.

K_{eq} = ______

Step 3. Substitute the known values in the expression.

$$K_{eq} = \frac{(\square \text{ mol/L})^2}{\square \text{ mol/L} \times \square \text{ mol/L}}$$

Step 4. Solve. Write your answer in scientific notation.

$K_{eq} = 0.0016 = \square$

Name ______________________ Date ________________ Class ________________

GUIDED PRACTICE PROBLEM 18 (page 562)

18. What is the concentration of calcium ions in a saturated calcium carbonate solution at 25°C? ($K_{sp} = 4.5 \times 10^{-9}$)

Analyze

Step 1. List the knowns and the unknown.

Knowns

____

____

____

Unknown

____

At equilibrium $[Ca^{2+}] = [CO_3^{2-}]$. This fact will be used to solve for the unknown.

Calculate

Step 2. Solve for the unknown.

$K_{sp} = [Ca^{2+}] \times [CO_3^{2-}]$

Make a substitution based on the equilibrium condition stated above:

$K_{sp} = [Ca^{2+}] \times [Ca^{2+}] = [Ca^{2+}]^2 = 4.5 \times 10^{-9}$

Now solve for the unknown:

$[Ca^{2+}] =$ ______________________

Name ____________________ Date ______________ Class ______________

GUIDED PRACTICE PROBLEM 19 (page 564)

19. What is the concentration of sulfide ion in a 1.0-L solution of iron(II) sulfide to which 0.04 mol of iron(II) nitrate is added? The K_{sp} of FeS is 8×10^{-19}.

Analyze

Step 1. List the knowns and the unknown.
Knowns

____

____

____

____

____

Unknown

____

Let $x = [S^{2-}]$ so that $x + 0.04 = [Fe^{2+}]$

Calculate

Step 2. Solve for the unknown.
Because K_{sp} is very small, simplify by assuming $x << 0.04$, and becomes negligible. Thus $[Fe^{2+}]$ is approximately equal to 0.04 *M*.

Solve for x in the equation: $K_{sp} = [Fe^{2+}] \times [S^{2-}] = [Fe^{2+}] \times x = 8 \times 10^{-19}$

Rearranging for x gives the result:

$$x = \frac{8 \times 10^{-19}}{[Fe^{2+}]} = \frac{8 \times 10^{-19}}{0.04 \text{ mol}} = 2 \times 10^{-17} M$$

So $[S^{2-}] =$ ______________

GUIDED PRACTICE PROBLEM 36 (page 577)

36. Show that the unit of *k* for a first-order reaction is a reciprocal unit of time, such as a reciprocal second (s^{-1}).

Analyze

Step 1. Plan a problem-solving strategy
The definition of the reaction rate is the change in concentration of a substance per change in time. So using a unit, "concentration" for the numerator and "time" for the denominator, the reaction rate has units [concentration/time].

Use this knowledge algebraically to show the unit for *k*.

Solve

Step 2. Apply the problem solving strategy.
Because the change in concentration per unit time is proportional to the initial concentration, setting up an equation with units will show this proportionality.

$$\frac{A}{t} = k \times [A]$$

$$\frac{[\text{concentration}]}{[\text{time}]} = k \times [\text{concentration}]$$

Canceling the unit "concentration" from both sides of the equation gives the result:

$$\frac{1}{[\text{time}]} = k$$

The unit of *k* is $[\text{time}]^{-1}$

Name ______________________ Date ______________ Class ______________

19 ACIDS, BASES, AND SALTS

SECTION 19.1 ACID–BASE THEORIES (pages 587–593)

This section compares and contrasts acids and bases as defined by the theories of Arrhenius, Brønsted-Lowry, and Lewis. It also identifies conjugate acid–base pairs in acid–base reactions.

▶ Properties of Acids and Bases (pages 587–588)

1. Circle the letters of all the terms that complete the sentence correctly. The properties of acids include ______.

   a. reacting with metals to produce oxygen

   b. giving foods a sour taste

   c. forming solutions that conduct electricity

   d. causing indicators to change color

2. Bases are compounds that react with acids to form ______________ and a(n) ______________.

3. Circle the letters of all the terms that complete the sentence correctly. The properties of bases include ______.

   a. tasting bitter

   b. feeling slippery

   c. changing the color of an indicator

   d. always acting as a strong electrolyte

▶ Arrhenius Acids and Bases (pages 588–590)

4. Match the number of ionizable hydrogens with the type of acid.

C one	a. diprotic
A two	b. triprotic
B three	c. monoprotic

5. Is the following sentence true or false? Only the hydrogens in weak polar bonds are ionizable. False

6. Hydrogen is joined to a very electronegative element in a very polar bond.

7. Alkali metals react with water to produce basic solutions.

Name ______________ Date ______________ Class ______________

8. How do concentrated basic solutions differ from other basic solutions?

Concentrated basic solutions is easily prepared.

▶ Brønsted-Lowry Acids and Bases (pages 590–592)

9. How does the Brønsted-Lowry theory define acids and bases?

Acids are hydrogen ion donors and bases are hydrogen ion acceptors

10. Is the following sentence true or false? Some of the acids and bases included in the Arrhenius theory are not acids and bases according to the Brønsted-Lowry theory. true

11. Is the following sentence true or false? A conjugate acid is the particle formed when a base gains a hydrogen ion. false

12. A conjugate base is the particle that remains when an acid has donated a hydrogen ion.

13. What is a conjugate acid–base pair? Two substances related by the loss or gain of a hydrogen ion.

14. A substance that can act as both an acid and a base is said to be amphoteric.

15. In a reaction with HCl, is water an acid or a base?

Water is base

▶ Lewis Acids and Bases (pages 592–593)

16. What is a Lewis acid? A Lewis Acid is a substance that can accept a pair of electrons

17. A Lewis base is a substance that can donate a pair of electrons to form a covalent bond.

Name ______________________ Date ______________ Class ______________

18. Is the following sentence true or false? All the acids and bases included in the Brønsted-Lowry theory are also acids and bases according to the Lewis theory.

false

19. Complete this table of acid-base definitions.

Acid–Base Definitions		
Type	**Acid**	**Base**
Brønsted-Lowry	H^+ donor	H^+ acceptor
Lewis	electron-pair acceptor	electron-pair donor
Arrhenius	H^+ producer	H^+ user

SECTION 19.2 HYDROGEN IONS AND ACIDITY (pages 594–604)

This section classifies solutions as neutral, acidic, or basic, given the hydrogen-ion or hydroxide-ion concentration. It explains how to convert hydrogen-ion concentrations into pH values and hydroxide-ion concentrations into pOH values.

▶ Hydrogen Ions from Water (pages 594-595)

1. What does a water molecule that loses a hydrogen ion become?

It becomes OH^-

2. What does a water molecule that gains a hydrogen ion become?

It becomes H_3O

3. The reaction in which water molecules produce ions is called the self-ionization of water.

4. In water or aqueous solution, hydrogen ion are always joined to water molecules as hydronium ions (H_3O^+).

5. Is the following sentence true or false? Any aqueous solution in which $[H^+]$ and $[OH^-]$ are equal is described as a neutral solution. true

▶ Ion Product Constant for Water (pages 595–596)

6. What is the ion-product constant for water (K_w)? Give the definition, the expression, and the value. ______________________

____

____

Name ______________________ Date ______________ Class ______________

7. A(n) ____acidic____ solution is one in which $[H^+]$ is greater than $[OH^-]$.

A(n) ____basic____ solution is one in which $[H^+]$ is less than $[OH^-]$.

8. Match the type of solution with its hydrogen-ion concentration.

__B__ acidic		**a.** less than $1.0 \times 10^{-7} M$
__C__ neutral		**b.** greater than $1.0 \times 10^{-7} M$
__A__ basic		**c.** $1.0 \times 10^{-7} M$

▶ The pH Concept (pages 596–600)

9. The __pH__ of a solution is the negative logarithm of the hydrogen-ion concentration.

10. Match the type of solution with its pH.

__C__ acidic		**a.** pH > 7.0
__B__ neutral		**b.** pH = 7.0
__A__ basic		**c.** pH < 7.0

11. Look at Table 19.5 on page 598. What is the approximate $[H^+]$, the $[OH^-]$, and the pH of washing soda? ______________________

12. The pOH of a solution is the negative logarithm of the ______________________ concentration.

13. What is the pOH of a neutral solution? __7__

14. For pH calculations, in what form should you express the hydrogen-ion concentration? __express in an exponent__

15. Look at the pH scale below. Label where you would find acids, bases, and neutral solutions.

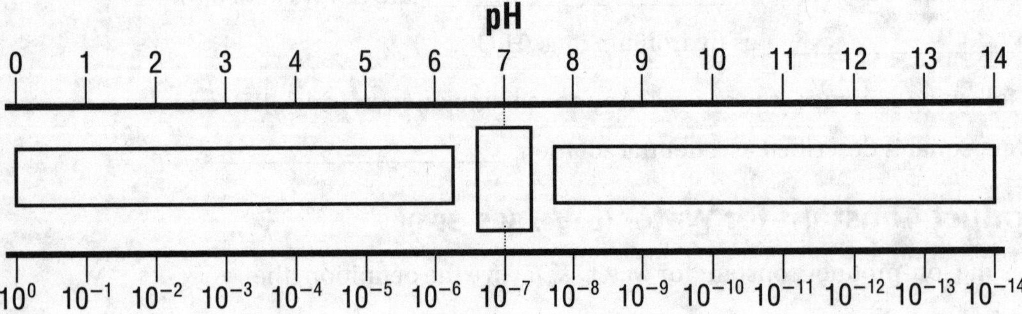

Name ______________________ Date ______________ Class ______________

16. Is the following sentence true or false? Most pH values are whole numbers.

false

17. If $[H^+]$ is written in scientific notation but its coefficient is not 1, what do you need to calculate pH? ______________________

18. Is the following sentence true or false? You can calculate the hydrogen-ion concentration of a solution if you know the pH. ______________

▶ Measuring pH (pages 600–603)

19. When do you use indicators and when do you use a pH meter to measure pH?

20. Why is an indicator a valuable tool for measuring pH?

21. Why do you need many different indicators to span the entire pH spectrum?

22. Look at the figure below. Fill in the missing pH color change ranges for the indicators.

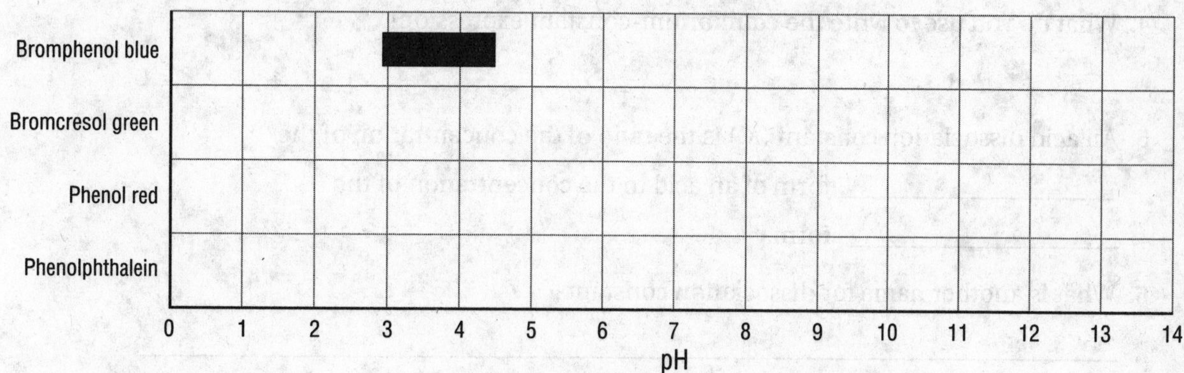

23. List three characteristics that limit the usefulness of indicators.

a. ______________________

b. ______________________

c. ______________________

24. What is the pH of each of the following liquids?

a. water ______

b. vinegar ______

c. milk of magnesia ______

25. Is the following sentence true or false? Measurements of pH obtained with a pH meter are typically accurate to within 0.001 pH unit of the true pH.

____

SECTION 19.3 STRENGTHS OF ACIDS AND BASES (pages 605–611)

This section defines strong and weak acids and bases. It explains how to calculate acid and base dissociation constants (K_a) and (K_b).

▶ Strong and Weak Acids and Bases (pages 605–609)

1. What factor is used to classify acids as strong or weak?

____

2. Strong acids are ______________ ionized in aqueous solution; weak acids ionize ______________ in aqueous solution.

3. Look at Table 19.6 on page 605. Which acid is the weakest acid in the table? Which base is the weakest base?

____

4. What do you use to write the equilibrium-constant expression?

____

5. An acid dissociation constant (K_a) is the ratio of the concentration of the

______________ form of an acid to the concentration of the

______________ form.

6. What is another name for dissociation constants?

____

7. Is the following sentence true or false? The stronger an acid is, the smaller its K_a value. ______________

8. A diprotic acid has ______________ dissociation constants.

Name ______________ Date ______________ Class ______________

9. Look at Table 19.7 on page 607. What is the second dissociation constant for the triprotic phosphoric acid? ______________

10. Weak bases react with water to form the hydroxide ion and the ______________ of the base.

11. A base dissociation constant (K_b) is the ratio of the concentration of the ______________ times the concentration of the hydroxide ion to the concentration of the ______________.

12. What does the magnitude of the base dissociation constant (K_b) indicate?

____

____

13. The words *concentrated* and *dilute* indicate how much acid or base is ______________ in solution.

14. Is the following sentence true or false? The words strong or weak refer to the extent of ionization or dissociation of an acid or base. ______________

▶ Calculating Dissociation Constants (pages 609–610)

15. Is the following sentence true or false? You can calculate the acid dissociation constant (K_a) of a weak acid from experimental data. ______________

16. To measure the equilibrium concentrations of all substances present at equilibrium for a weak acid, what two conditions must you know?

____

____

Reading Skill Practice

By looking carefully at photographs and drawings in textbooks, you can better understand what you have read. Look carefully at Figure 19.16 on page 606. What important idea does this drawing communicate? Do your work on a separate sheet of paper.

Name Bobby Date ______ Class ______

CHAPTER 19, Acids, Bases, and Salts *(continued)*

SECTION 19.4 NEUTRALIZATION REACTIONS (pages 612–616)

This section explains how acid–base titration is used to calculate the concentration of an acid or a base. It also explains the concept of equivalence in neutralization reactions.

▶ Acid–Base Reactions (pages 612–613)

1. Is the following sentence true or false? Acids react with compounds containing hydroxide ions to form water and a salt. true

2. What does the reaction of an acid with a base produce?

It produces water and salt

3. In general, reactions in which an acid and a base react in an aqueous solution to produce a salt and water are called neutralization reactions.

4. Look at Table 19.9 on page 613. Circle the letter of the salt that is used for photographic emulsions.

a. calcium chloride

b. potassium chloride

c. silver bromide

d. sodium chloride

5. Salts are compounds consisting of a(n) anion from an acid and a(n) cation from a base.

▶ Titration (pages 613–616)

6. How can you determine the concentration of an acid or base in a solution?

By doing a neutralization reaction

7. Complete the flow chart below showing the steps of a neutralization reaction.

A measured volume of an acid solution of ______ concentration is added to a flask.

↓

Several drops of the ______ are added to the solution while the flask is gently swirled.

↓

Measured volumes of a base of ______ concentration are mixed into the acid until the indicator changes ______.

Name ______________ Date ______________ Class ______________

8. The process of adding a known amount of solution of known concentration to determine the concentration of another solution is called titration.

9. What is the solution of known concentration called?

It is called a standard solution

SECTION 19.5 SALTS IN SOLUTION (pages 618–622)

This section demonstrates with equations how buffers resist changes in pH. It also explains how to calculate the solubility product constant of a slightly soluble salt.

▶ Salt Hydrolysis (pages 618–620)

1. What is salt hydrolysis? ______________

2. Complete this table of the rules for hydrolysis of a salt.

Reactants	Products
______ acid + ______ base	Neutral solution
Strong acid + Weak base	______ solution
______ acid + ______ base	Basic solution

▶ Buffers (pages 620–622)

3. What are buffers? ______________

4. A buffer is a solution of a ______________ acid and one of its salts, or a solution of a ______________ base and one of its salts.

5. Is the following sentence true or false? The buffer capacity is the amount of acid or base that can be added to a buffer solution before a significant change in pH occurs. ______________

GUIDED PRACTICE PROBLEMS

EXTRA PRACTICE PROBLEM (similar to Practice Problem 13, page 600)

13. Find the value of $[OH^-]$ for a solution with a pH of 8.00.

GUIDED PRACTICE PROBLEM 16b (page 601)

16b. Calculate the pH of this solution: $[H^+] = 8.3 \times 10^{-10} M$.

	Known	**Unknown**
Step 1. Identify the known and unknown values.	$[H^+] = \square \times 10^{-10} M$	pH = ?

Step 2. Substitute values into the pH equation.

$$pH = -\log [H^+]$$
$$= -\log (8.3 \times \square)$$

Step 3. The logarithm of a product equals the sum of the logs of its factors.

$$= -(\log \square + \log \square)$$

Step 4. Evaluate log 8.3 by using a calculator. Evaluate $\log 10^{-10}$ by using the definition of logarithm.

$$= -(0.919 + \square)$$

Step 5. Add and simplify. Write your answer with two significant figures to the right of the decimal point.

$$= -(-9.081) = \square$$

Name ______________________ Date ______________ Class ______________

GUIDED PRACTICE PROBLEM 22 (page 610)

22. For a solution of methanoic acid exactly 0.1 M, $[H^+] = 4.2 \times 10^{-3} M$. Calculate the K_a of methanoic acid.

Analyze

Step 1. What is known about the acid?

____

____

Step 2. What is the unknown? ____

Step 3. What is the expression for the K_a of methanoic acid? $K_a =$

Calculate

Step 4. What expression can you write to find the equilibrium concentration of HCOOH? ______________________

Step 5. Substitute values into the formula for K_a and solve.

____

Evaluate

Step 6. Look at Table 19.7 on page 607. Explain why your answer is reasonable.

____

Name ______________________ Date ______________ Class ______________

20 OXIDATION–REDUCTION REACTIONS

SECTION 20.1 THE MEANING OF OXIDATION AND REDUCTION (pages 631–638)

This section explains oxidation and reduction in terms of the loss or gain of electrons, and describes the characteristics of a redox reaction. It also explains how to identify oxidizing and reducing agents.

▶ What are Oxidation and Reduction? (pages 631–635)

1. What was the original meaning of the term *oxidation*? ______________________

____

2. Circle the letter of each sentence that is true about oxidation.

a. Gasoline, wood, coal, and natural gas (methane) can all burn in air, producing oxides of carbon.

b. All oxidation processes involve burning.

c. Bleaching is an example of oxidation.

d. Rusting is an example of oxidation.

3. Look at Figure 20.2 and Figure 20.3 on page 632. Describe what is happening in each chemical reaction.

a. $C(s) + O_2(g) \longrightarrow CO_2(g)$ ______________________

____

b. $4Fe(s) + 3O_2(g) \longrightarrow 2Fe_2O_3(s)$ ______________________

____

4. What is the name of the process that is the opposite of oxidation?

____

5. Circle the letter of each sentence that is true about oxidation and reduction.

a. Oxidation never occurs without reduction and reduction never occurs without oxidation.

b. You need to add heat in order to reduce iron ore to produce metallic iron.

c. When iron oxide is reduced to metallic iron, it gains oxygen.

d. Oxidation–reduction reactions are also known as redox reactions.

Name ______________________ Date ________________ Class ________________

6. What substance is heated along with iron ore in order to reduce the metal oxide to metallic iron? ________________

7. Look at the chemical equation for the reduction of iron ore on page 632. When iron ore is reduced to metallic iron, what oxidation reaction occurs at the same time? ____

8. Is the following sentence true or false? The concepts of oxidation and reduction have been extended to include many reactions that do not even involve oxygen. ________________

9. What is understood about electrons in redox reactions?

____

10. In the table below, fill in either "Gain" or "Loss" to correctly describe what happens to electrons or oxygen during oxidation or reduction.

	Oxidation	Reduction
Electrons		
Oxygen		

11. Look at Figure 20.4 on page 633. Circle the letter of each sentence that is true about the reaction of magnesium and sulfur.

a. When magnesium and sulfur are heated together, they undergo a redox reaction to form magnesium sulfide.

b. Electrons are transferred from the metal atoms to the nonmetal atoms in this reaction.

c. When magnesium atoms lose electrons and sulfur atoms gain electrons, the atoms become less stable.

d. Magnesium is the oxidizing agent and sulfur is the reducing agent in this reaction.

12. Is the following sentence true or false? In any redox reaction, complete electron transfer must occur. ________________

13. Is the following sentence true or false? A redox reaction may produce covalent compounds. ________________

Name ______________________ Date ______________ Class ______________

14. Draw arrows showing the shift of bonding electrons during formation of a water molecule. Then complete the table listing the characteristics of this reaction.

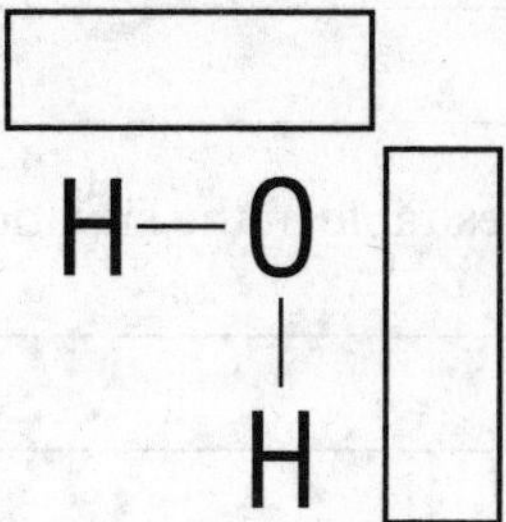

Formation of Water by Reaction of Hydrogen and Oxygen	
Chemical equation	
Shift of bonding electrons	
Reduced element	
Oxidized element	
Reducing agent	
Oxidizing agent	
Is heat released or absorbed?	

15. For each process described below, label it *O* if it is an oxidation or *R* if it is a reduction.

_______ **a.** Addition of oxygen to carbon or carbon compounds

_______ **b.** Removal of a metal from its ore

_______ **c.** Complete gain of electrons in an ionic reaction

_______ **d.** Shift of electrons away from an atom in a covalent bond

_______ **e.** Gain of hydrogen by a covalent compound

▶ Corrosion (pages 636–638)

16. Circle the letter of each sentence that is true about corrosion.

a. Preventing and repairing damage from corrosion of metals requires billions of dollars every year.

b. Iron corrodes by being oxidized to ions of iron by oxygen.

c. Water in the environment slows down the rate of corrosion.

d. The presence of salts and acids increases the rate of corrosion by producing conducting solutions that make the transfer of electrons easier.

Name ______________________ Date ______________ Class ______________

17. Why are gold and platinum called noble metals? ______________________

____

18. Look at Figure 20.6 on page 636. Why is corrosion desirable in the situation shown? ______________________

____

19. Look at Figure 20.7 on page 636. Complete the sketch below to show how oxides form on the surface of each metal. Explain how differences between the oxides affect further corrosion of the metals.

____

____

____

Iron

Aluminum

SECTION 20.2 OXIDATION NUMBERS (pages 639–643)

This section explains how to determine the oxidation number of an atom of any element in a pure substance and defines oxidation and reduction in terms of a change in oxidation number.

▶ Assigning Oxidation Numbers (pages 639–641)

1. Is the following sentence true or false? As a general rule, a bonded atom's oxidation number is the charge that it would have if the electrons in the bond were assigned to the more electronegative element. ______________

2. For each binary ionic compound listed in the table, write the symbols for both ions, their ionic charges, and their oxidation numbers.

Compound	Ions	Ionic Charges	Oxidation Numbers
NaCl			
CaF_2			

Name ______________________ Date ______________ Class ______________

3. Is the following sentence true or false? Even though water is a molecular compound, you can still obtain oxidation numbers for the bonded elements by imagining that the electrons contributed by the hydrogen atoms are completely transferred to oxygen. ______________

4. Write the oxidation number, or the sum of the oxidation numbers, for the given atoms, ions, or compounds.

   ______ **a.** Cu(II) ion

   ______ **b.** Hydrogen in water

   ______ **c.** Hydrogen in sodium hydride (NaH)

   ______ **d.** Potassium sulfate (K_2SO_4)

▶ Oxidation-Number Changes in Chemical Reactions (page 642)

5. Label each change *O* if it describes oxidation or *R* if it describes reduction.

   ______ **a.** Decrease in the oxidation number of an element

   ______ **b.** Increase in the oxidation number of an element

SECTION 20.3 BALANCING REDOX EQUATIONS (pages 645–654)

This section explains how to use the oxidation-number-change and half-reaction methods to balance redox equations.

▶ Identifying Redox Reactions (pages 645–647)

1. Name two kinds of reactions that are not redox reactions.

   ____

2. Look at Figure 20.15b on page 645. Write the oxidation numbers of all the elements in the reactants and products. Then answer the questions about the reaction.

	Reactants			Products		
	Zinc		Hydrochloric acid		Zinc chloride		Hydrogen
Oxidation numbers	________		________		________		________
Chemical equation	Zn(*s*)	+	HCl(*aq*)	⟶	$ZnCl_2$(*aq*)	+	H_2(*g*)

   a. Is this a redox reaction? ______________

   b. Which element is oxidized? How do you know?

   ____

   c. Which element is reduced? How do you know?

   ____

3. When a solution changes color during a reaction, what can you conclude about the reaction that has taken place?

____

▶ Two Ways to Balance Redox Equations (pages 647–652)

4. Answer these questions to help you balance the following equation using the oxidation-number-change method.

$H_2(g) + O_2(g) \longrightarrow H_2O(l)$ (unbalanced)

a. What are the oxidation numbers for each atom in the equation?

b. Which element is oxidized in this reaction? Which is reduced?

____

c. Use your answers to question *a* above to balance the equation. Write the coefficients needed to make the total change in oxidation number equal to 0.

$$\overset{0}{H_2}(g) + \overset{0}{O_2}(g) \longrightarrow \overset{+1\,-2}{H_2O}(l)$$

☐ × +1

☐ × −2

d. What is the final balanced equation? ______________

5. The equations for which reactions are balanced separately when using the half-reaction method? ______________

____

6. For what kind of reaction is the half-reaction method particularly useful?

____

Name ______________________ Date ______________ Class ______________

▶ Choosing a Balancing Method (page 653)

7. When would you choose to use oxidation-number changes to balance an equation?

____

____

8. What method would you choose to balance an equation for a reaction that takes place in an acidic or alkaline solution?

____

Reading Skill Practice

A flowchart can help you to remember the order in which events occur. On a separate sheet of paper, create a flowchart that describes the steps for the oxidation-number-change method. This process is explained on page 648 of your textbook.

Name ________________ Date ________________ Class ________________

GUIDED PRACTICE PROBLEM

GUIDED PRACTICE PROBLEM 9 (page 641)

9. Determine the oxidation number of each element in these substances.

a. S_2O_3

Step 1. What is the oxidation number for oxygen? Use rule 3. ________

Step 2. What is the oxidation number for all of the oxygen atoms?

____

Step 3. What is the oxidation number for all of the sulfur atoms? ________

Step 4. What is the oxidation number for each sulfur atom? ________

Step 5. How do you know your answers are correct?

____

b. Na_2O_2

Step 1. What is the oxidation number of oxygen? Use rule 3.

(Hint: This compound is a peroxide.) ________

Step 2. What is the oxidation number of sodium? ________

Step 3. How do you know your answer is correct?

The oxidation number for both oxygen atoms is ________. The sum of the oxidation numbers for all the atoms must be ________. Therefore, the oxidation number for both sodium atoms must equal ________.

c. P_2O_5

Step 1. What is the oxidation number for oxygen? Use rule 3. ________

Step 2. What is the oxidation number for all of the oxygen atoms?

$-2 \times 5 =$ ________

Step 3. What is the oxidation number for all of the phosphorous atoms? ________

Step 4. What is the oxidation number for each phosphorous atom?

$+10 \div 2 =$ ________

Step 5. How do you know your answers are correct?

____

Name ______________________ Date ______________ Class ______________

d. NH_4^+

Step 1. What is the oxidation number for hydrogen? Use rule 2. __________

Step 2. What is the oxidation number for all of the oxygen atoms?

$+1 \times 4 =$ __________

Step 3. What is the oxidation number for the nitrogen atom? __________

Step 4. How do you know your answers are correct?

____

____

e. $Ca(OH)_2$

Step 1. What is the oxidation number for oxygen? Use rule 3. __________

Step 2. What is the oxidation number for all of the oxygen atoms?

$-2 \times 2 =$ __________

Step 3. What is the oxidation number for hydrogen? Use rule 2. __________

What is the oxidation number for the hydroxide (OH)?

$-2 + +1 =$ __________

Step 5. What is the oxidation number for all of the hydroxide?

$-1 \times 2 =$ __________

Step 6. What is the oxidation number for the calcium atom? __________

Step 7. How do you know your answers are correct?

____

f. $Al_2(SO_4)_3$

Step 1. What is the charge of the polyatomic sulfate ion? __________

Step 2. What is the oxidation number of oxygen? Use rule 3. __________

Step 3. What is the oxidation number of all of the oxygen atoms? __________

Step 4. What is the oxidation number of the sulfur atom? __________

Step 5. What is the oxidation number of the aluminum ion? __________

Name ____________________ Date ____________ Class ____________

EXTRA PRACTICE (similar to Practice Problem 19, page 649)

19. Balance this redox equation using the oxidation-number-change method.

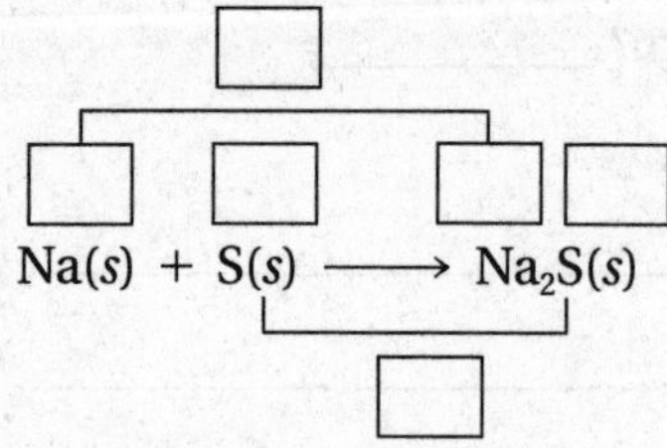

To make the oxidation numbers balance, you must multiply the oxidation number of sodium by __________. Add a coefficient of ________ in front of elemental sodium, but not in front of sodium sulfate because the sodium in sodium sulfate has a subscript of ______. The balanced equation is

______________________________.

Name ______________________ Date ______________________ Class ______________________

ELECTROCHEMISTRY

SECTION 21.1 ELECTROCHEMICAL CELLS (pages 663–670)

This section describes how redox reactions interconvert electrical energy and chemical energy. It also explains the structure of a dry cell and identifies the substances that are oxidized and reduced.

▶ Electrochemical Processes (pages 663–665)

1. What do the silver plating of tableware and the manufacture of aluminum have in common?

____

Look at Figure 21.1 on page 663 and the related text to help you answer Questions 2–6.

2. In what form are the reactants when the reaction starts?

____

3. What kind of reaction occurs? Is it spontaneous?

____

4. Which substance is oxidized in the reaction? ______________________

5. Which substance is reduced? ______________________

6. Which atoms lose electrons and which ions gain electrons during the reaction?

____

7. Look at Table 21.1 on page 664. What information in this table explains why the reaction in Figure 21.1 occurs spontaneously?

____

____

____

____

8. What happens when a copper strip is placed in a solution of zinc sulfate? Explain.

____

____

9. The flow of ______________________ from zinc to copper is an electric ______________________.

Name ______________________ Date ______________ Class ______________

10. Circle the letter of each sentence that is true about electrochemical cells.

a. An electrochemical cell either produces an electric current or uses an electric current to produce a chemical change.

b. Redox reactions occur in electrochemical cells.

c. For an electrochemical cell to be a source of useful electrical energy, the electrons must pass through an external circuit.

d. An electrochemical cell can convert chemical energy to electrical energy, but not electrical energy into chemical energy.

▶ Voltaic Cells (pages 665–667)

For Questions 11–15, match each description with the correct term by writing its letter in the blank.

_______ **11.** Any electrochemical cell used to convert chemical energy into electrical energy

_______ **12.** One part of a voltaic cell in which either reduction or oxidation occurs

_______ **13.** The electrode at which oxidation occurs

_______ **14.** A tube containing a strong electrolyte, which allows transport of ions between the half-cells

_______ **15.** The electrode at which reduction occurs

a. cathode

b. salt bridge

c. voltaic cell

d. half-cell

e. anode

▶ Using Voltaic Cells as Energy Sources (pages 667–670)

16. Look at Figure 21.4 on page 667. How is a common dry cell constructed?

____

____

____

17. Why are alkaline cells better and longer lasting than common cells?

____

____

18. Which element is oxidized in a dry cell? Which element is reduced?

____

Name ________________ Date ________________ Class ________________

19. What is a battery? ________________

20. How many voltaic cells are connected inside a lead storage battery typically found in a car? About how many volts are produced by each cell and what is the total voltage of such a battery?

____

____

21. Look at Figure 21.5 on page 668. In the diagram below label the following parts of a lead storage battery: electrolyte, anode, and cathode. Also indicate where oxidation and reduction occur while the battery is discharging.

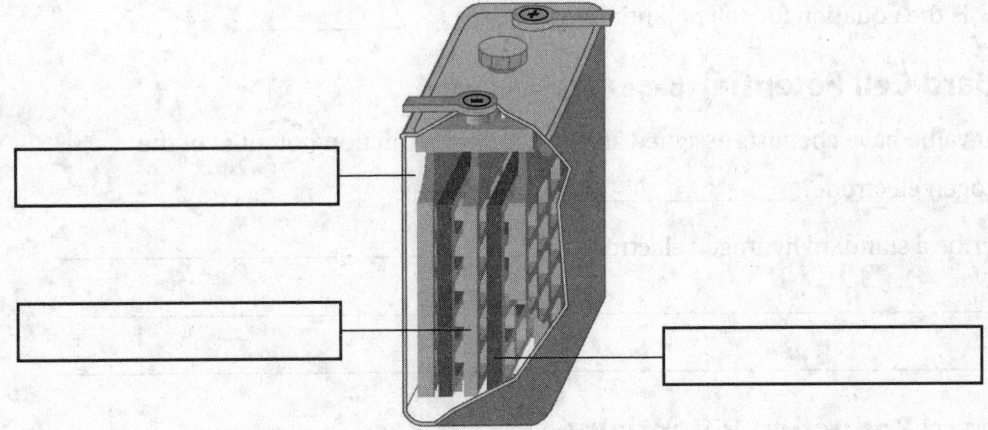

22. Are the following sentences true or false? As a lead storage battery discharges, lead sulfate builds up on the electrodes. Recharging the battery reverses this process. ________________

23. Name two advantages of fuel cells. ________________

____

Reading Skill Practice

Outlining is a way to help you understand and remember what you have read. Write an outline for Section 21.1 *Electrochemical Cells*. Begin your outline by copying the headings in the textbook. Under each heading, write the main idea. Then list details that support, or back up, the main idea. Do your work on a separate sheet of paper.

SECTION 21.2 HALF-CELLS AND CELL POTENTIALS (pages 671–677)

This section defines standard cell potential and standard reduction potential. It also explains how to use standard reduction potential to calculate standard cell potential.

▶ Electrical Potential (page 671)

1. What unit is usually used to measure electrical potential?

____

2. What is the equation for cell potential? ______________

▶ Standard Cell Potential (page 672)

3. What value have chemists assigned as the standard reduction potential of the hydrogen electrode? ______________

4. Describe a standard hydrogen electrode. ______________

____

____

▶ Standard Reduction Potentials (pages 672–675)

5. Use of a standard hydrogen electrode allows scientists to determine the ______________ for many half-cells.

6. Look at Figure 21.10 on page 673. Which substance, zinc metal or hydrogen gas, has a greater potential to be oxidized? How can you tell?

____

____

7. In the diagram below use the value given for E^0_{cell} above the voltmeter and Table 21.2 to identify the chemical substances in the left half-cell. Use symbols to label the metal electrode and the ions in the half-cell. Also label the cathode and the anode.

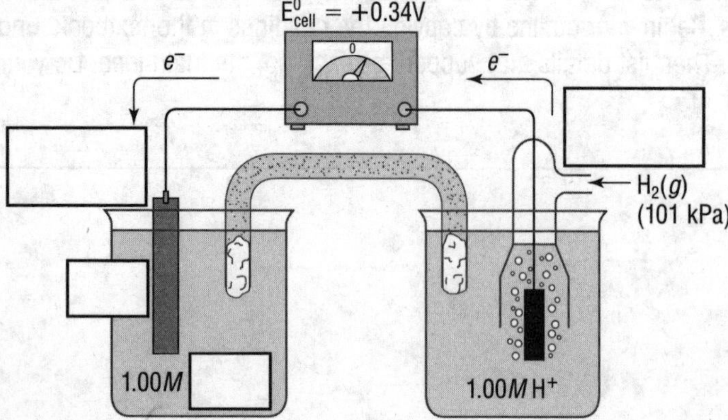

Name ______________________ Date ______________ Class ______________

▶ Calculating Standard Cell Potentials (pages 675–677)

8. If the cell potential for a given redox reaction is ______________, then the reaction is ______________. If the cell potential is ______________, then the reaction is ______________.

SECTION 21.3 ELECTROLYTIC CELLS (pages 678–683)

This section differentiates electrolytic cells from voltaic cells, and lists uses of electrolytic cells. It also identifies the products of the electrolysis of brine, molten sodium chloride, and water.

▶ Electrolytic vs. Voltaic Cells (pages 678–679)

1. An electrochemical cell used to cause a chemical change through the application of electrical energy is called ______________.

2. For each sentence below, fill in *V* if it is true about voltaic cells, *E* if it is true about electrolytic cells, and *B* if it is true about both voltaic and electrolytic cells.

_______ **a.** Electrons are pushed by an outside power source.

_______ **b.** Reduction occurs at the cathode and oxidation occurs at the anode.

_______ **c.** The flow of electrons is the result of a spontaneous redox reaction.

_______ **d.** Electrons flow from the anode to the cathode.

▶ Electrolysis of Water (page 680)

3. Write the net reaction for the electrolysis of water.

____

▶ Electrolysis of Brine (page 681)

4. Which three important industrial chemicals are produced through the electrolysis of brine?

____

5. Why are the sodium ions not reduced to sodium metal during the electrolysis of brine?

____

▶ Other Applications of Electrolytic Cells (page 682)

6. Deposition of a thin layer of metal on an object in an electrolytic cell is called ______________.

7. The object to be plated is made the ______________ in the cell.

GUIDED PRACTICE PROBLEM

GUIDED PRACTICE PROBLEM 8 (page 676)

8. A voltaic cell is constructed using the following half-reactions.

$Cu^{2+}(aq) + 2e^- \longrightarrow Cu(s)$ $\quad E^0_{Cu^{2+}} = +0.34\ V$

$Al^{3+}(aq) + 3e^- \longrightarrow Al(s)$ $\quad E^0_{Al^{3+}} = -1.66\ V$

Determine the cell reaction and calculate the standard cell potential.

Analyze

Step 1. What are the known values?

____

Step 2. Which half-reaction is a reduction? An oxidation?

Reduction: _______________________________

Oxidation: _______________________________

Step 3. Write both half-reactions in the direction they actually occur.

____

Step 4. What is the expression for the standard cell potential?

E^0_{cell} = _______________

Calculate

Step 5. Write the cell reaction by adding the half-reactions, making certain that the number of electrons lost equals the number of electrons gained. The electrons gained and lost will cancel out.

☐ $[Cu^{2+}(aq) + 2e^- \longrightarrow Cu(s)]$

☐ $[Al(s) \longrightarrow Al^{3+}(aq) + 3e^-]$

____

☐

Step 6. Calculate the standard cell potential.

E^0_{cell} = _______________

Evaluate

Step 7. How do you know that the cell reaction is correct?

____

Step 8. When a reaction is spontaneous, will the standard cell potential be positive or negative?

____

Name ______________________ Date ______________ Class ______________

22 HYDROCARBON COMPOUNDS

SECTION 22.1 HYDROCARBONS (pages 693–701)

This section describes the bonding in hydrocarbons and distinguishes straight-chain from branched-chain alkanes. It also provides rules for naming branch-chained alkanes.

▶ Organic Chemistry and Hydrocarbons (pages 693–694)

1. What is organic chemistry? ______________________

2. Organic compounds that contain only carbon and hydrogen are called ______________________.

3. Is the following sentence true or false? Hydrogen atoms are the only atoms that can bond to the carbon atoms in a hydrocarbon. ______________

4. Circle the letter of each statement that is true about carbon's ability to form bonds.

a. Carbon atoms have four valence electrons.

b. Carbon atoms always form three covalent bonds.

c. Carbon atoms can form stable bonds with other carbon atoms.

▶ Alkanes (pages 694–699)

5. Is the following sentence true or false? Alkanes contain only single covalent bonds. ______________

6. What is the simplest alkane? ______________

7. What are straight-chain alkanes? ______________________

____

8. The names of all alkanes end with the suffix ______________.

Match the name of the straight-chain alkane with the number of carbon atoms it contains.

______	**9.** nonane	**a.** 3
______	**10.** propane	**b.** 4
______	**11.** heptane	**c.** 7
______	**12.** butane	**d.** 9

13. The straight-chain alkanes form a(n) ______________________ because there is an incremental change of a CH_2 group from one compound in the series to the next.

CHAPTER 22, Hydrocarbon Compounds *(continued)*

14. Circle the letter of each condensed structural formula for pentane.

a. C_5H_{12}

b. $CH_3CH_2CH_2CH_2CH_3$

c. $CH_3(CH_2)_3CH_3$

d. C—C—C—C—C

15. The IUPAC system uses ______________ to show the number of carbon atoms in a straight-chain alkane.

16. A(n) ______________ is an atom or group of atoms that replaces a hydrogen in a hydrocarbon molecule.

17. Alkyl groups are named by removing the *-ane* ending of the parent hydrocarbon and adding ______________.

18. What is a branched-chain alkane? ______________

19. Circle the letter of the correct IUPAC name for the molecule below.

```
      CH3      CH3
      |        |
CH3—  C — CH2— CH — CH3
      |
      CH3
```

a. 2,2,4-triethylpentane

b. 3-methylpentane

c. 2,2,4-trimethylpentane

20. Draw a condensed structural formula for 2-methylhexane.

▶ Properties of Alkanes (page 700)

21. Why are hydrocarbon molecules such as alkanes nonpolar? ______________

____

____

22. Hydrocarbons and other nonpolar molecules are not attracted to ______________.

Name ______________________ Date ______________ Class ______________

Reading Skill Practice

A flowchart can help you to remember the order in which events occur. On a separate sheet of paper, create a flowchart that describes the steps for naming branched-chain alkanes using the IUPAC system. This process is explained on page 698.

SECTION 22.2 UNSATURATED HYDROCARBONS (pages 702–703)

This section explains the difference between unsaturated and saturated hydrocarbons. It also describes the difference between alkenes and alkynes.

▶ Alkenes (page 702)

1. What is an alkene?

____

2. Organic compounds that contain the maximum number of hydrogen atoms per carbon atoms are called ______________ compounds.

3. Which family of hydrocarbons are always saturated compounds?

____

4. Circle the letter of the correct name for the alkene shown below.

$$\begin{array}{ccc} CH_3 & & CH_3 \\ & C{=}C & \\ CH_3 & & CH_2CH_3 \end{array}$$

a. 2,3-dimethyl-3-pentene

b. 2-methyl-3-methyl-2-pentene

c. 2,3-dimethyl-2-pentene

d. 3-ethyl-2-methyl-2-butene

5. Is the following sentence true or false? Rotation can occur around a carbon–carbon double bond. ______________

▶ Alkynes (page 703)

6. Hydrocarbons that contain one or more ______________ covalent bonds between carbons are called alkynes.

7. ______________ is the simplest alkyne, and is also known by the common name ______________.

Name ______________ Date ______________ Class ______________

8. Circle the letter of each compound that is an aliphatic compound.

a. 1-butene

b. acetylene

c. 2-methylpropane

9. What are the major attractive forces between alkane, alkene, or alkyne molecules?

____

10. Complete the table below with the names of the indicated alkanes, alkenes, and alkynes. For the alkenes and alkynes, assume that the multiple bond occurs between the first two carbons.

Number of Carbons	Alkane	Alkene	Alkyne
C_6			
C_7			
C_8			

11. Is the following sentence true or false? The angle between the carbon atoms in a carbon–carbon triple bond is 120°. ______________

SECTION 22.3 ISOMERS (pages 704–707)

This section explains how to distinguish among structural, geometric, and stereoisomers. It also describes how to identify the asymmetric carbon or carbons in stereoisomers.

▶ Structural Isomers (page 704)

1. What are structural isomers?

____

____

2. Is the following sentence true or false? Structural isomers have the same physical properties. ______________

3. How many structural isomers are there for C_4H_{10}? ______________

4. Name the structural isomers of C_4H_{10}. ______________

5. In general, what determines which of two structural isomers will have the lower boiling point? ______________

____

Name ______________________ Date ______________________ Class ______________________

▶ Stereoisomers (pages 705–706)

6. Stereoisomers differ only in the ______________________ in space.

7. What two things need to be present for geometric isomers to exist?

   a. ______________________

   b. ______________________

8. What are the names of the molecules represented by the ball-and-stick models below?

______________________ ______________________

9. Objects that are ______________________ will produce a reflection that is indistinguishable from the original object.

10. Mirror images of a right hand and a left hand cannot be ______________________.

11. What is an asymmetric carbon?

____

12. Is the following sentence true or false? The relationship of optical isomers is similar to that between right and left hands. ______________________

13. Look at Figure 22.9 on page 705. Why are these two molecules optical isomers?

____

____

14. Circle the two asymmetric carbons in the structure shown below.

```
CH3—CH2—CH2—CH—CH—CH—CH3
             |   |   |
            CH2 CH3 CH3
             |
            CH3
```

Name ______________ Date ______________ Class ______________

SECTION 22.4 HYDROCARBON RINGS (pages 709–711)

This section describes how to identify and classify cyclic hydrocarbons. It also explains the bonding in benzene.

▶ Cyclic Hydrocarbons (page 709)

1. What is a cyclic hydrocarbon?

____

2. The most abundant cyclic hydrocarbons contain ______________ or ______________ carbons.

3. What are the names of the cyclic hydrocarbons represented below?

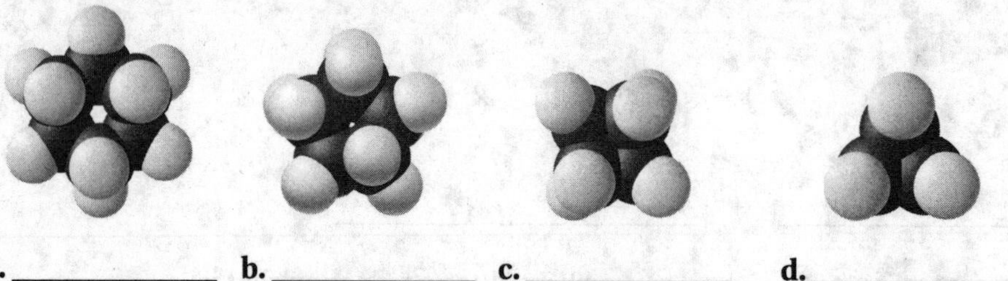

a. ______________ b. ______________ c. ______________ d. ______________

4. Is the following sentence true or false? Cyclic hydrocarbons that contain only single carbon–carbon bonds are called cycloalkanes. ______________

▶ Aromatic Hydrocarbons (pages 710–711)

5. What is the origin of the name *aromatic compounds?*

____

6. Benzene has the chemical formula ______________.

7. Is the following sentence true or false? Any substance that has carbon–carbon bonding like that of benzene is called an aromatic compound. ______________

8. Another name for an aromatic compound is a(an) ______________.

9. What does it mean to say that benzene exhibits resonance?

____

10. Molecules that exhibit resonance are more ______________ than similar molecules that do not exhibit resonance.

11. The actual bonds in a benzene ring are identical ______________ of single and double bonds.

12. When ______________ is a substituent on an alkane, it is called a phenyl group.

Name ____________________ Date ______________ Class ____________

13. Circle the letter of the name of the compound shown below.

CH_2CH_3 (benzene ring)

a. ethylhexene

b. dimethylbenzene

c. ethylbenzene

14. Derivatives of benzene that have ____________________ substituents are called disubstituted benzenes.

15. Why do disubstituted benzenes always have three structural isomers?

____

Match the terms for naming a disubstituted benzene with the substituent positions they represent.

_______ 16. *meta* a. 1,2

_______ 17. *ortho* b. 1,3

_______ 18. *para* c. 1,4

19. What is another name for the dimethylbenzenes? ____________________

SECTION 22.5 HYDROCARBONS FROM EARTH'S CRUST (pages 712–715)

This section describes the origin, composition, and uses of natural gas, petroleum, and coal.

▶ Natural Gas (page 712)

1. What are fossil fuels?

____

2. List three factors needed to produce fossil fuels from organic residue.

a. ____________________

b. ____________________

c. ____________________

3. Petroleum and natural gas contain mostly ____________________ hydrocarbons.

4. What are the four main components of natural gas?

____

5. Which noble gas is found in natural gas? ____________________

CHAPTER 22, Hydrocarbon Compounds *(continued)*

6. Fill in the missing reactants and products in the equation for the combustion of methane.

   $CH_4(g)$ + 2 ________ $(g) \longrightarrow$ ________ (g) + 2 ________ (g) + heat

7. Propane and butane are sold in ____________________ form to be used as ____________________ fuels.

8. ____________________ combustion of a hydrocarbon produces a blue flame; ____________________ combustion produces a yellow flame.

9. What toxic gas is formed during incomplete combustion of a hydrocarbon?

   ____

▶ Petroleum (page 713)

10. The first oil well was drilled in ____________________ in the late 1850s.

11. Is the following sentence true or false? Petroleum is commercially useful without refining. ____________________

12. How is petroleum refined?

    ____

    ____

13. Circle the letter of the distillation fraction that represents the highest percent of crude oil.

    a. natural gas

    b. gasoline

    c. kerosene

    d. lubricating oil

14. Using a catalyst and heat to break hydrocarbons down into smaller molecules is called ____________________ .

Name ______________________ Date ______________ Class ______________

15. Complete the table below about four fractions obtained from crude oil. Indicate where each fraction will be collected from the fractionating column shown at the right.

Fraction	Composition of Carbon Chains	Where in Column?
Fuel oil		
Gasoline		
Lubricating oil		

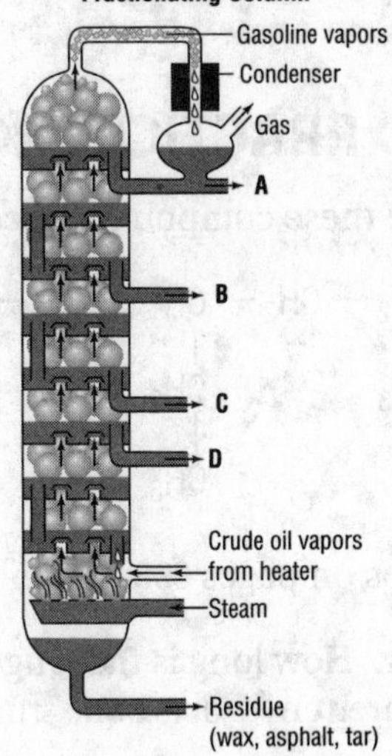

▶ Coal (pages 714–715)

16. ______________________ is the intermediate material that is the first stage in coal formation.

17. Name the three types of coal and the carbon content of each.

a. ______________________

b. ______________________

c. ______________________

18. Is the following sentence true or false? Coal mines in North America are usually at least a kilometer below Earth's surface. ______________

19. Coal consists primarily of ______________________ compounds of extremely high molar mass.

20. Aromatic compounds produce more ______________________ when burned than do ______________________ fuels.

21. What major air pollutants are produced by burning coal that contains sulfur?

____

22. List four products that can be obtained by distilling coal.

a. ______________________ c. ______________________

b. ______________________ d. ______________________

23. Which of these products can be distilled further?

____

GUIDED PRACTICE PROBLEM

GUIDED PRACTICE PROBLEM 3 (page 699)

3. Name these compounds according to the IUPAC system.

a. $CH_2—CH_2—CH—CH_2—CH_3$, with CH_3 attached to the first CH_2 and $CH_2—CH_3$ attached to CH

b. $CH_3—CH_2—CH—CH_3$, with CH_3 attached to CH

Use the steps on pages 698–699 to name each compound.

Step 1. How long is the longest string of carbon atoms? What is the name of the parent hydrocarbon structure?

a. ______________ **b.** ______________

Step 2. From which side will you number the carbon chain? Why?

a. ______________________________

b. ______________________________

Step 3. What are the names and positions of the substituents?

a. ______________ **b.** ______________

Step 4. Explain why neither name will contain a prefix.

a. ______________________________

Step 5. Does the name contain any commas or hyphens?

a. ______________________________

b. ______________________________

Step 6. What is the complete name of each compound?

a. ______________ **b.** ______________

EXTRA PRACTICE PROBLEM (similar to Practice Problem 18, page 706)

18. Circle the symmetric carbon, if there is one, in each of these structures.

a. $CH_3—CH—CH—CH_3$, with CH_3 attached to each CH

b. $CH_3—CH—CH_2—CH_2$, with $CH_2—CH_3$ attached to CH and CH_3 attached to the last CH_2

Name ______________ Date ______________ Class ______________

23 FUNCTIONAL GROUPS

SECTION 23.1 INTRODUCTION TO FUNCTIONAL GROUPS (pages 725–729)

This section defines a functional group and gives several examples. It also describes halocarbons and the substitution reactions they undergo.

▶ Functional Groups (pages 725–726)

1. Is the following sentence true or false? The saturated hydrocarbon skeletons of organic molecules are chemically reactive. ______________

2. What is a functional group? ______________

____

Use Table 23.1 on page 726 to answer Questions 3 and 4.

3. Name the functional group for each compound structure.

a. R—O—R ______________ **b.** R—OH ______________ **c.** $R-NH_2$ ______________

4. Name two compound types that have a carbonyl group as a functional group.

a. ______________ **b.** ______________

▶ Halogen Substituents (pages 726–728)

5. What are halocarbons? ______________

____

6. Give the IUPAC and common names for the following halocarbons.

a. $CH_3-CH_2-CH_2-Br$ ______________

b. $H_2C=CHI$ (H, H on one carbon; I, H on the other) ______________

7. A halogen attached to a carbon of an aliphatic chain produces a halocarbon called a(n) ______________.

Match the prefix used in naming alkyl groups with its description.

a. *iso-* **b.** *sec-* **c.** *tert-*

______ **8.** The carbon joining this alkyl group to another group is bonded to three other carbons.

______ **9.** The carbon joining this alkyl group to another group is bonded to two other carbons.

______ **10.** The carbon joining this alkyl group to another group is bonded to one other carbon.

Name ______________________ Date ______________ Class ______________

11. What is an aryl halide? ____

____

▶ Substitution Reactions (pages 728–729)

12. Why do reactions involving organic compounds often proceed more slowly than those involving inorganic molecules and ions?

____

13. Is the following sentence true or false? The products of organic reactions are often a complex mixture of compounds. ______________

14. Organic reactions that involve the replacement of one atom or group of atoms with another atom or group of atoms are called ______________ reactions.

15. Label the compounds in this generalized equation. (*X* stands for a halogen.)

$$R—H \quad + \quad X_2 \longrightarrow R—X \quad + \quad HX$$

______________ ______________ ______________ ______________

16. Hydroxide ions can displace most halogens on carbon chains to produce a(n) ______________.

SECTION 23.2 ALCOHOLS AND ETHERS (pages 730–736)

This section describes the structures and naming of alcohols and ethers, as well as comparing their properties. It also defines and gives examples of addition reactions.

▶ Alcohols (pages 730–731)

1. What are alcohols?

____

2. The functional group in an alcohol is called a(n) ______________ group.

Match each structural category of aliphatic alcohols with its description.

______	3. primary alcohol	a. three R groups attached to C — OH
______	4. secondary alcohol	b. one R group attached to C — OH
______	5. tertiary alcohol	c. two R groups attached to C — OH

6. Circle the letter of the IUPAC ending used for an alcohol with two — OH substitutions.

a. *-ol* **b.** *-tetrol* **c.** *-triol* **d.** *-diol*

Name ____________________ Date ______________ Class ______________

7. ______________ is the common name for alcohols with more than one —OH substituent.

8. Write the IUPAC name and the common name for each alcohol shown.

a. $CH_3—CH_2—OH$ ______________________________

b. $CH_3—CH(OH)—CH_3$ ______________________________

c. $CH_2(OH)—CH(OH)—CH_2(OH)$ ______________________________

▶ Properties of Alcohols (pages 732–733)

9. Is the following sentence true or false? Alcohols cannot form intermolecular hydrogen bonds. ______________

10. What are the two parts of an alcohol molecule?

____

11. Why are alcohols with four or more carbons not soluble in water?

____

____

12. Name two uses for isopropyl alcohol.

a. ____

b. ____

13. Which alcohol is used in many antifreezes? ______________

14. The action of yeast or bacteria on sugars to produce ethanol is called ______________.

15. How is ethanol denatured?

____

▶ Addition Reactions (pages 733–735)

16. Adding new functional groups at the double or triple bond of an alkene or alkyne is called a(n) ______________ reaction.

17. Is the following sentence true or false? Adding a hydrogen halide to an alkene results in a disubstituted halocarbon. ______________

Name ______________ Date ______________ Class ______________

18. Look at the reaction between ethene and water:

$$\mathrm{H_2C{=}CH_2} + \mathrm{H{-}OH} \xrightarrow[100^\circ C]{H^+}$$

a. Draw the structure of the product.

____

b. What type of compound is the product? ______________

c. What is this type of addition reaction called? ______________

d. What is the role of the hydrogen ions? ______________

19. What type of reaction is used to manufacture margarine from unsaturated vegetable oils? ______________

20. Which hydrocarbon resists addition reactions? ______________

▶ Ethers (pages 735–736)

21. An ether is a compound in which ______________ is bonded to two carbon groups.

22. How are ethers named? ______________

____

23. Circle the letter of each symmetrical ether.

a. ethylmethyl ether

b. diethyl ether

c. diphenyl ether

d. methylphenyl ether

24. Is the following sentence true or false? Ethers have higher boiling points than alcohols of comparable molar mass. ______________

Reading Skill Practice

By looking carefully at photographs and diagrams in your textbook, you can better understand what you have read. Look carefully at Figure 23.8 on page 734. What important idea do these photographs communicate? Do your work on a separate sheet of paper.

Name ______________________ Date ______________ Class ______________

SECTION 23.3 CARBONYL COMPOUNDS (pages 737–746)

This section explains how to distinguish among the carbonyl groups of aldehydes, ketones, carboxylic acids, and esters. It also describes the reactions of compounds that contain the carbonyl group.

▶ Aldehydes and Ketones (pages 737–740)

1. A ____________________ consists of a carbon joined by a double bond to an oxygen atom.

2. What is the difference between an aldehyde and a ketone? ____________________

____

____

3. What ending is used in the IUPAC system to indicate an aldehyde? a ketone?

____

4. Circle the letter of each statement that is true about aldehydes and ketones.

a. In an aldehyde or ketone sample, the molecules cannot form intermolecular hydrogen bonds.

b. The molecules in an aldehyde or ketone sample do not attract each other through polar–polar interactions.

c. Most aldehydes and ketones are gases at room temperature.

d. Aldehydes and ketones can form weak hydrogen bonds with water.

Match the aldehyde or ketone with its use.

______	**5.** methanal	**a.** almond flavoring
______	**6.** propanone	**b.** preservative
______	**7.** benzaldehyde	**c.** oil of cinnamon
______	**8.** 3-phenyl-2-propenal	**d.** solvent

9. Aromatic aldehydes are often used as ____________________ agents.

▶ Carboxylic Acids (pages 740–741)

10. What is a carboxyl group?

____

11. Is the following sentence true or false? Carboxylic acids are weak acids. __________

12. What ending is used under the IUPAC system to designate a carboxylic acid?

____

13. Carboxylic acids with three or more carbons in a straight chain are also known as ____________________ acids.

CHAPTER 23, Functional Groups *(continued)*

14. Complete the table about saturated aliphatic carboxylic acids.

IUPAC Name	Common Name	Carbon Atoms	Formula
		4	$CH_3(CH_2)_2COOH$
Octanoic acid			$CH_3(CH_2)_6COOH$
	Acetic acid	2	
Octadecanoic acid	Stearic acid		

15. What form do all aromatic carboxylic acids have at room temperature?

____

▶ Esters (pages 742–743)

16. An ester is a derivative of a ______________ that has an —OR substituted for the —OH.

17. Write the general formula for an ester. ______________

18. What two products are formed when an ester is hydrolyzed in the presence of a strong acid or base?

____

▶ Oxidation–Reduction Reactions (pages 743–745)

19. Are triple carbon–carbon bonds more or less oxidized than double and single carbon–carbon bonds? ______________

20. What is a dehydrogenation reaction? ______________

____

21. Circle the letter of the compound that is the final product of methane oxidation.

a. methanol

b. formic acid

c. methanal

d. carbon dioxide

22. Primary alcohols are oxidized to form ______________, but secondary alcohols form ______________ when oxidized.

23. Why are tertiary alcohols resistant to oxidation? ______________

____

Name ______________________ Date ______________ Class ______________

24. Is the following sentence true or false? The oxidation of organic compounds is exothermic. ______________

25. What property of aldehydes do Fehling's test and Benedict's test take advantage of? What color is the precipitate that forms?

____

SECTION 23.4 POLYMERIZATION (pages 747–752)

This section defines polymers and monomers. It also names and describes the uses of some important addition and condensation polymers.

▶ Addition Polymers (pages 747–749)

1. What are polymers? ______________________________

____

2. Is the following sentence true or false? Polymers can only contain one type of monomer. ______________

3. Most polymerization reactions require a ______________.

4. Complete the table by naming each polymer.

Polymer	Structure
	$H\text{-}(CH_2-CH_2)_x\text{-}H$
	$\text{-}(CH_2-CH(CH_3))_x\text{-}$
	$\text{-}(CH_2-CH(Cl))_x\text{-}$
	$\text{-}(CF_2-CF_2)_x\text{-}$

Match the polymer with its use.

_____ 5. polyethylene

_____ 6. polystyrene

_____ 7. polytetrafluoroethene

_____ 8. polyisoprene

_____ 9. polyvinyl chloride

a. foam coffee cups

b. rubber tubing

c. nonstick cookware

d. plastic wrap

e. plumbing pipes

Name ______________________ Date ______________ Class ______________

▶ Condensation Polymers (pages 750–752)

10. How is a polyester formed? ________________________________

____

11. For condensation polymerization to occur, each monomer molecule must have ______________ functional groups.

12. Name the two monomer molecules that are joined to form the polyester PET.

____

13. Garments made from PET fibers are ______________ resistant.

14. Is the following sentence true or false? The polymer produced by the condensation of a carboxylic acid and an amine is called an amide. ______________

15. What common group of synthetic materials is made up by polyamides?

____

16. ______________ are an important group of naturally occurring polyamides made from monomers called ______________.

Match each common polymer to its structural representation.

_____ **17.** $\left(\overset{O}{\overset{\|}{C}} - C_6H_4 - \overset{O}{\overset{\|}{C}} - O - CH_2CH_2 - O \right)_x$

_____ **18.** $\left(CH_2 \left(CH_2 \right)_4 \overset{O}{\overset{\|}{C}} - \overset{H}{\overset{|}{N}} \right)_x$

_____ **19.** $\left(\overset{O}{\overset{\|}{C}} - C_6H_4 - \overset{O}{\overset{\|}{C}} - \underset{H}{\underset{|}{N}} - C_6H_4 - \underset{H}{\underset{|}{N}} \right)_x$

_____ **20.** $\left(\overset{O}{\overset{\|}{C}} - C_6H_4 - \overset{O}{\overset{\|}{C}} - \overset{H}{\overset{|}{N}} - C_6H_4 - \overset{H}{\overset{|}{N}} \right)_x$

a. Kevlar™
b. Nomex™
c. nylon
d. PET

Name ______________________ Date ______________ Class ______________

24 THE CHEMISTRY OF LIFE

SECTION 24.1 A STRATEGY FOR LIFE (pages 763–765)

This section describes the structure of a typical eukaryotic cell. It also explains the relationship between photosynthesis and all life on Earth.

▶ The Structure of Cells (pages 763–764)

1. What are the two major types of cell design?

a. ______________________ **b.** ______________________

2. Which of the two cell types are found in humans?

____

3. Fill in the missing labels for structures in the drawing of a eukaryotic cell.

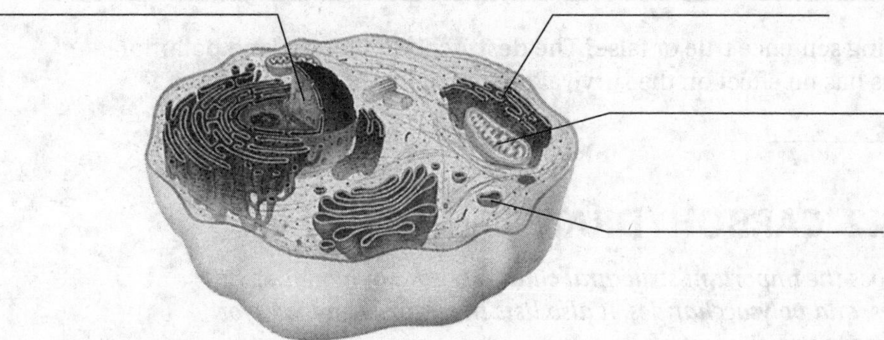

4. Is the following sentence true or false? Both cell types are surrounded by a cell membrane that acts as a selective barrier to the passage of chemicals into or out of the cell. ______________

5. Only eukaryotic cells contain membrane-enclosed ______________ in which specialized functions of the cell occur.

Match the organelle to its function.

_______	**6.** mitochondrion	**a.** manufacture of proteins
_______	**7.** nucleus	**b.** cell reproduction
_______	**8.** lysosome	**c.** energy production
_______	**9.** endoplasmic reticulum	**d.** digestion

Name ______________________ Date ______________ Class ______________

▶ Energy and Carbon Cycle (pages 764–765)

10. What is the source of all energy for life on Earth? ______________

11. Circle the letter of the process by which organisms capture solar energy and use it to make food.

a. oxidation **b.** photosynthesis **c.** digestion **d.** respiration

12. How do plants use the energy they obtain from sunlight?

____

13. Explain how animals obtain the energy they need.

____

____

14. What are the products of the oxidation of glucose?

____

15. Is the following sentence true or false? The destruction of forests and pollution of the oceans has no effect on the survival of animal life.

____

SECTION 24.2 CARBOHYDRATES (pages 766-768)

This section describes the important structural characteristics of monosaccharides, disaccharides, and polysaccharides. It also lists the sources and uses for a number of important carbohydrates.

▶ Monosaccharides (pages 766–767)

1. Carbohydrates are made from aldehydes and ketones that contain many

______________ groups.

2. Name the three elements present in carbohydrates.

a. ______________ **b.** ______________ **c.** ______________

3. What is the general formula for a carbohydrate? ______________

4. What is another name for simple sugars? ______________

5. Circle the letter of each simple sugar.

a. glucose **b.** sucrose **c.** fructose **d.** starch

▶ Disaccharides and Polysaccharides (pages 767–768)

6. Sugars formed by linking two monosaccharides are called ______________.

7. What compound is lost in the reaction that links two monosaccharides?

____

8. Is the following sentence true or false? Sucrose, or table sugar, is formed by the polymerization of two glucose molecules. ________________

9. What are polysaccharides? ____

____

10. Complete the following table about polysaccharides.

Polysaccharide	Source	Function
starch		
		energy storage
	plants	

SECTION 24.3 AMINO ACIDS AND THEIR POLYMERS (pages 769–773)

This section explains how to write a general formula for an amino acid and describes the bonding between amino acids. It also describes the effect of enzymes on biochemical reactions.

▶ Amino Acids (pages 769–770)

1. What is an amino acid? How many amino acids are found in living organisms?

____

____

____

2. What determines the physical and chemical properties of an amino acid?

____

Match the amino acid to its abbreviation.

_____ 3. Glutamine — a. Ile

_____ 4. Isoleucine — b. Trp

_____ 5. Methionine — c. Pro

_____ 6. Proline — d. Gln

_____ 7. Tryptophan — e. Met

CHAPTER 24, The Chemistry of Life *(continued)*

▶ Peptides (page 770)

8. What is a peptide?

____

____

9. The bond between amino acids is called a(n) ________________ bond.

10. Is the following sentence true or false? The bond between amino acids always involves the side chains. ________________

11. The formula for peptides is written so that the free ________________ group is on the left end and the free ________________ group is on the right end.

12. Is the following sentence true or false? The order of the amino acids in a peptide can be reversed and still represent the same peptide. ________________

▶ Proteins (pages 770–771)

13. A(n) ________________ contains more than ten amino acids, but a(n) ________________ has more than 100 amino acids.

14. The chemical and physiological properties of a protein are determined by its ________________ sequence.

15. Name each type of structure that can be formed by folding long peptide chains.

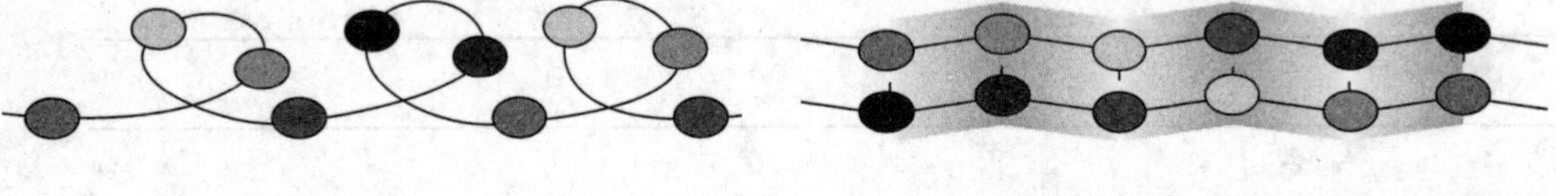

________________ ________________

16. What types of bonds maintain the three-dimensional shape of a folded protein? ____

____

17. Is the following sentence true or false? A single protein can be made from separate polypeptide chains, held together by bonds between side-chain groups. ________________

▶ Enzymes (pages 772–773)

18. What are enzymes?

____

19. What three properties of a catalyst do enzymes have?

   a. ______________________________

   b. ______________________________

   c. ______________________________

20. Is the following sentence true or false? Because an active site fits a specific substrate, each enzyme catalyzes only one chemical reaction.

   ____

21. What is the enzyme molecule joined to its substrate molecule called?

   ____

Match the enzyme to its substrate.

______	22. urease	a. carbonic acid
______	23. carbonic anhydrase	b. hydrogen peroxide
______	24. catalase	c. urea

25. What is a coenzyme? Give two examples. ______________________________

   ____

SECTION 24.4 LIPIDS (pages 775–777)

This section characterizes the molecular structure of triglycerides, phospholipids, and waxes. It also describes the functions of phospholipids and proteins in cell membranes.

▶ Triglycerides (pages 775–776)

1. Fats provide an efficient means of ______________ for your body.

2. What are lipids? ______________________________

3. Triglycerides are triesters of one ______________ molecule and three ______________ molecules.

4. Complete the following table about two types of triglycerides.

Triglyceride Type	State at Room Temperature	Primary Source
fats		
		plants

5. Circle the letter of the process used to make soap.

   a. hydrogenation

   b. saponification

   c. denaturation

   d. polymerization

Name ______________________ Date ________________ Class ________________

▶ Phospholipids (pages 776–777)

6. What is the molecular structure of a phospholipid?

____

7. How does the chemical nature of a phospholipid affect its solubility?

____

____

8. When phospholipids are added to water, they spontaneously form a lipid

________________, with the hydrophobic tails located in the

________________.

9. How does a cell membrane accomplish selective absorption?

____

____

____

▶ Waxes (page 777)

10. What is the molecular structure of waxes?

____

11. Is the following sentence true or false? Waxes are liquid at room temperature.

____

12. Name two functions of waxes in plants.

____

SECTION 24.5 NUCLEIC ACIDS (pages 778–785)

This section describes the structural components of nucleotides and nucleic acids, including DNA, and gives simple examples of genetic mutations. It also explains what is meant by recombinant DNA technology.

▶ DNA and RNA (pages 778–779)

1. What are the functions of the two types of nucleic acids?

____

____

2. The monomers that make up nucleic acids are called ________________.

3. Name the three parts of a nucleotide.

a. ______________ b. ______________ c. ______________

4. What nitrogen bases are found in DNA? in RNA?

____

____

5. DNA molecules consist of two chains of nucleotides that are bound together into a double ______________.

6. Name the complementary base pairs found in DNA.

a. ______________ b. ______________

▶ The Genetic Code (pages 780–781)

7. What is a gene?

____

8. How many nucleotides are needed to code for one amino acid? ______________

9. The ______________ is the arrangement of code words in DNA that provides the information to make specific proteins.

10. Is the following sentence true or false? Each amino acid has only one DNA code word. ______________

11. Use Table 24.2 on page 781. Which amino acids are coded in the nucleotide sequence TACAGCCTCGACAAG?

____

12. Circle the letter of each code word that represents a termination signal.

a. ATT b. AAC c. ATC d. AAT

▶ Gene Mutations (pages 782–783)

13. Circle the letter of each event that could cause a gene mutation.

a. substitution of one or more nucleotides

b. addition of one or more nucleotides

c. deletion of one or more nucleotides

14. What is the effect of mutations on the production of proteins?

____

____

____

Name ______________________ Date ______________ Class ______________

15. Is the following sentence true or false? Diseases resulting from gene mutations are called inborn errors. ______________

16. Name two diseases that are caused by mutations in the hemoglobin gene.

____

▶ DNA Fingerprinting (pages 783–784)

17. DNA base sequences differ for everyone except ______________.

18. Complete the flowchart about DNA fingerprinting.

Obtain a small sample of DNA from ______________ .
↓
______________ the amount of DNA by millions of times.
↓
Use ______________ to cut the DNA into fragments.
↓
Separate and ______________ the fragments.
↓
Compare the DNA fingerprint, or ______________, with a DNA sample from a known individual.

19. What are the disadvantages of DNA fingerprinting in criminal cases?

____

____

▶ Recombinant DNA Technology (pages 784–785)

20. Describe the three steps in the production of recombinant DNA.

a. ____

b. ____

c. ____

21. Name three medicines that are produced by recombinant DNA technology.

a. ______________ **b.** ______________ **c.** ______________

22. What is a clone? ____

Name ______________________ Date ______________ Class ______________

SECTION 24.6 METABOLISM (pages 786–790)

This section describes the role of ATP in energy production and energy use in the cell. It also defines metabolism and explains the relationship between catabolism and anabolism.

▶ ATP (pages 786–787)

1. What is ATP and what is its function?

____

2. Energy is captured when a ____________________ group is added to adenosine diphosphate (ADP).

3. a. How much energy is stored when one mole of ATP is produced? ______________

b. How much energy is released when one mole of ATP is hydrolyzed back to ADP? ______________

4. ATP is important because it occupies an ____________________ position between higher-energy ____________________ reactions and other cellular processes.

▶ Catabolism (pages 787–788)

5. The entire set of all chemical reactions that are carried out in a living organism is called ____________________.

6. What is catabolism? ______________________________________

____

7. Circle the letter of each product of catabolism.

a. heat

b. ATP

c. complex biological molecules

d. building blocks for new compounds

8. One of the most important catabolic processes is the complete oxidation of ____________________ to form ____________________ and water.

9. How much energy is released by the complete combustion of one mole of glucose? ____________________

10. How many moles of ATP are produced by the complete oxidation of one mole of glucose? ______________________________

11. Is the following sentence true or false? All the reactions involved in the complete oxidation of glucose are shown in Figure 24.25.

____

Name ______________________ Date ______________ Class ______________

12. Use Figure 24.25 to fill in the names of the carbon-containing molecules and ions represented.

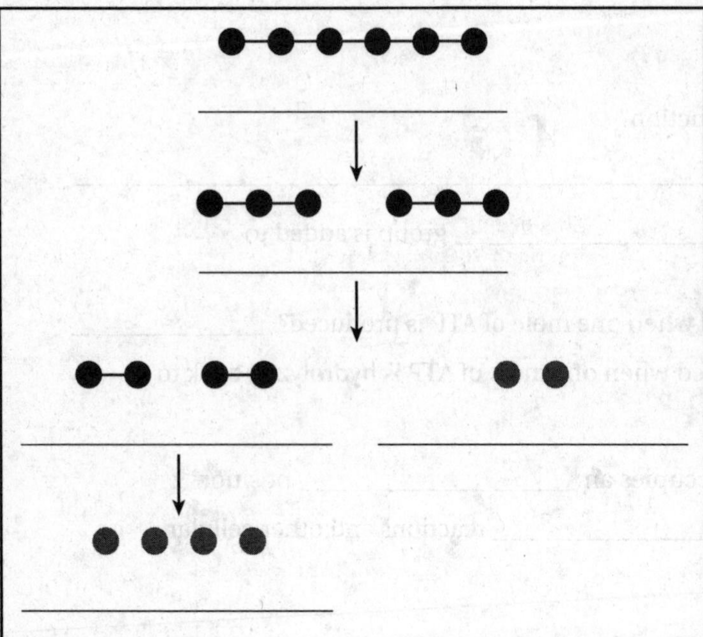

▶ Anabolism (page 788)

13. Anabolic reactions are ____________________ reactions that produce more-complex biological molecules.

14. Catabolic reactions ____________________ energy, whereas anabolic reactions ____________________ energy.

15. Look at Figure 24.26. Explain why all the terms that appear in the yellow ovals also appear in the blue ovals.

____

____

____

▶ The Nitrogen Cycle (pages 789–790)

16. Is the following sentence true or false. Animals can use atmospheric nitrogen to produce nitrogen-containing compounds. ____________________

17. Certain bacteria reduce atmospheric nitrogen to ammonia in a process called ____________________.

Name ______________ Date ______________ Class ______________

18. How do nitrogen fertilizers enter the biosphere?

____

____

Reading Skill Practice

By looking carefully at photographs and drawings in your textbook, you can better understand what you have read. Look carefully at Figure 24.27 on page 789. What important ideas does this drawing communicate? Do your work on a separate sheet of paper.

Name _______________ Date _______________ Class _______________

25 NUCLEAR CHEMISTRY

SECTION 25.1 NUCLEAR RADIATION (pages 799–802)

This section describes the nature of radioactivity and the process of radioactive decay. It characterizes alpha, beta, and gamma radiation in terms of composition and penetrating power.

▶ Radioactivity (pages 799–800)

1. Which French chemist noticed that uranium salts could fog photographic plates, even without being exposed to sunlight?

   ____

2. What name did Marie Curie give to the process by which materials give off rays capable of fogging photographic plates? _______________

3. An isotope that has an unstable nucleus is called a(n) _______________.

4. Complete the table below to show basic differences between chemical and nuclear reactions.

Type of Reaction	Is Nucleus of Atom Changed?	Is Reaction Affected by Temperature, Pressure, or Catalysts?
Chemical		
Nuclear		

5. Complete the flowchart below, which describes the radioactive decay process.

The presence of too many or too few _______________ relative to protons leads to an unstable nucleus.

↓

At some point in time, an unstable nucleus will undergo a reaction and lose energy by emitting _______________.

↓

During the process of radioactive decay, an _______________ radioisotope of one element is transformed eventually into a _______________ isotope of a different element.

Name ______________________ Date ______________ Class ______________

▶ Types of Radiation (pages 800–802)

6. Complete the following table showing some characteristics of the main types of radiation commonly emitted during radioactive decay.

Type			
Consists of	2 protons and 2 neutrons	electron (or positron)	high-energy electromagnetic radiation
Mass (amu)			
Penetrating power (low, moderate, or high)			
Minimum shielding			

7. Look at Figure 25.2a on page 801. It shows the alpha decay of uranium-238 to thorium-234.

a. What is the change in atomic number after the alpha decay?

____

b. What is the change in mass number after the alpha decay?

____

8. When are radioisotopes that emit alpha particles dangerous to soft tissues?

____

9. Look at Figure 25.2b on page 801. This diagram shows the beta decay of carbon-14 to nitrogen-14.

a. What is the change in atomic number after the beta decay?

____

b. Which quantity changes in beta decay, the mass number or the charge of the nucleus? ______________

10. Explain how gamma radiation is similar to visible light, and how it is different.

Similar: ____

Different: ____

11. When are gamma rays emitted? ______________________________

____

12. Is the following sentence true or false? Gamma rays have no mass and no electrical charge. ________________

13. Look at the diagram below. Below each material indicate with a checkmark which type of radiation—alpha, beta, or gamma—can be stopped by each material.

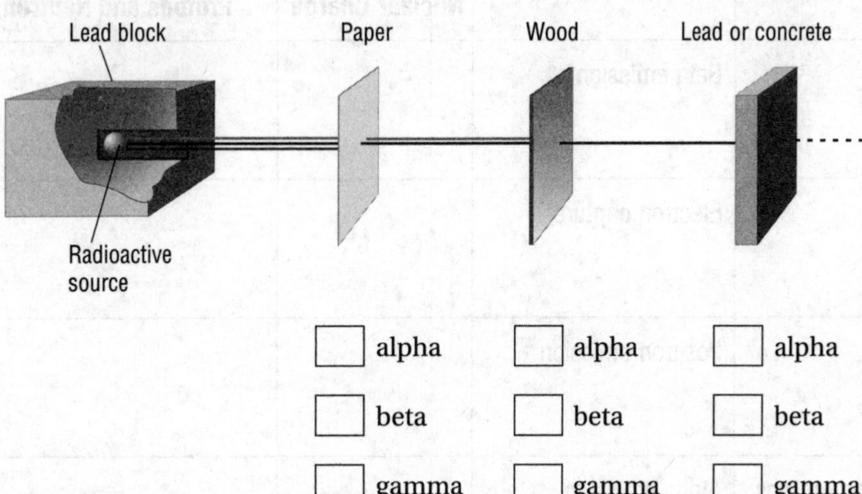

Paper	Wood	Lead or concrete
☐ alpha	☐ alpha	☐ alpha
☐ beta	☐ beta	☐ beta
☐ gamma	☐ gamma	☐ gamma

SECTION 25.2 NUCLEAR TRANSFORMATIONS (pages 803–808)

This section relates nuclear stability and decay to the ratio of neutrons to protons in a nucleus. It explains the use of half-life to describe the decay rate of unstable nuclei and gives examples of transmutations.

▶ Nuclear Stability and Decay (pages 803–804)

1. Of the more than 1500 different nuclei that are known to exist, about what portion are stable?

a. 1 of 10 **b.** 1 of 6 **c.** 1 of 3 **d.** 1 of 2

2. For elements with low atomic numbers, stable nuclei have roughly ________________ numbers of neutrons and protons.

3. Look at Figure 25.4 on page 803. How does the ratio of neutrons to protons for stable nuclei change as atomic number increases from 1 to 82?

____

4. A positron has the mass of a(n) ________________ but its charge is ________________.

CHAPTER 25, Nuclear Chemistry *(continued)*

5. Complete the table below showing changes in charge and number of neutrons and protons for different types of nuclear decay.

Reason Nucleus Is Unstable	Type of Decay	Change in Nuclear Charge	Change in Number of Protons and Neutrons
Too many neutrons	Beta emission		
Too many protons	Electron capture		
Too many protons	Positron emission		
Too many protons and neutrons	Alpha emission		

▶ Half-Life (pages 804–806)

6. What is half-life? ______________________________

____

7. Look at Table 25.3 on page 805 to help you answer the following questions.

a. What is the half-life in years of carbon-14? ______________

b. How many years old is an artifact that contains 50% of its original carbon-14? An artifact that contains 25% of its original carbon-14?

____

c. What radiation is emitted when potassium-40 decays?

____

d. What is the half-life of potassium-40? ______________

e. Which isotopes listed in Table 25.3 have a half-life similar to that of potassium-40? ______________________________

Name ____________________ Date ______________ Class ______________

8. The decay reaction below shows how a radioactive form of potassium found in many minerals decays into argon (gas). Fill in the missing mass number and atomic number for the argon isotope that results from the decay of potassium-40.

$$^{40}_{19}\text{K} + ^{0}_{-1}\text{e} \longrightarrow ^{\square}_{\square}\text{Ar}$$

▶ Transmutation Reactions (pages 807–808)

9. The conversion of an atom of one element to an atom of another element is called ____________________ .

10. What are two ways transmutation can occur? ____________________

____

11. Uranium-238 undergoes 14 transmutations before it reaches the stable isotope ____________________ .

12. Is the following sentence true or false? All transuranium elements were synthesized in nuclear reactors and accelerators. ____________________

Reading Skill Practice

By looking carefully at photographs and graphs in your textbook, you help yourself understand what you have read. Look carefully at Figure 25.5 on page 804. What important idea does this graph communicate? If you were to extend the curve indefinitely, would the percent of radioisotope remaining ever cross 0%? Why or why not? Do your work on a separate sheet of paper.

Name ______________________ Date ______________ Class ______________

SECTION 25.3 FISSION AND FUSION OF ATOMIC NUCLEI (pages 810–813)

This section describes nuclear fission and nuclear fusion. It discusses their potential as sources of energy, methods used to control them, and issues involved in containment of nuclear waste.

▶ Nuclear Fission (pages 810–811)

1. When certain heavy isotopes are bombarded with ______________________, they split into smaller fragments.

2. Use the following labels to complete the diagram below: *fission, fission fragments,* and *neutrons/chain reaction.*

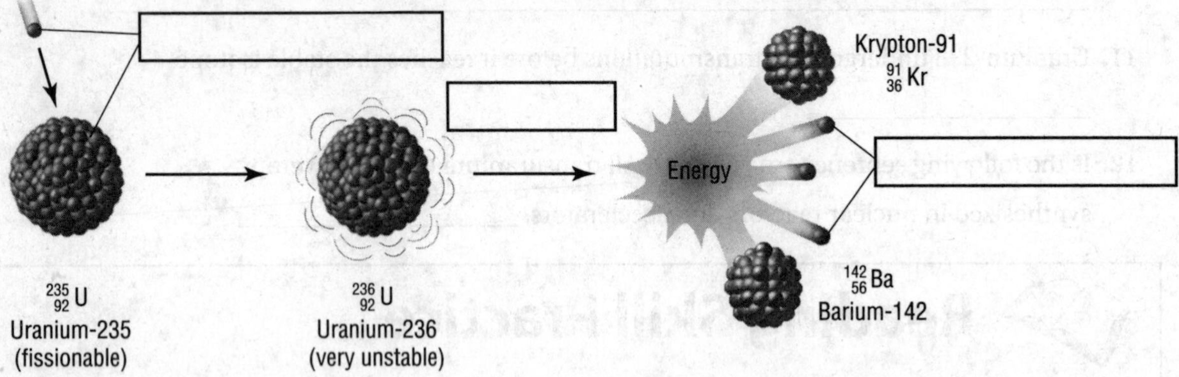

3. The uncontrolled fission of 1 kg of uranium-235 can release energy equal to ______________________ tons of dynamite.

4. Look at Figure 25.11 on page 811. This figure shows the basic components of a nuclear power reactor.

   a. What part of the reactor contains the nuclear fuel?

   ____

   b. What are the two parts of the reactor that control the fission reaction, one by reducing the speed of neutrons, the other by absorbing neutrons?

   ____

   c. What is the role of the coolant? ______________________

   ____

Name ____________ Date ____________ Class ____________

▶ Nuclear Waste (page 812)

5. Which parts of a nuclear reactor must be removed and replaced periodically?

____

6. Look at Figure 25.12 on page 812. Where are spent fuel rods stored in a typical nuclear power plant?

____

▶ Nuclear Fusion (page 813)

7. Look at Figure 25.13 on page 813. What happens to each pair of hydrogen nuclei during nuclear fusion?

____

____

8. What problem has prevented the practical use of nuclear fusion?

____

____

SECTION 25.4 RADIATION IN YOUR LIFE (pages 816–819)

This section explains three methods of detecting radiation and describes applications of radioisotopes in medicine and research.

▶ Detecting Radiation (page 816–817)

1. Why are beta particles called ionizing radiation? _______________

____

2. A device that detects flashes of light after ionizing radiation strikes a specially coated phosphor surface is called a _______________ .

▶ Using Radiation (pages 818–819)

3. How is neutron activation analysis used?

____

4. Look at Figure 25.15 on page 819. How is radioactive iodine-131 being used as a diagnostic tool? _______________

____

Name ______________________ Date ________________ Class ______________

GUIDED PRACTICE PROBLEMS

GUIDED PRACTICE PROBLEM 7 (page 806)

7. Manganese-56 is a beta emitter with a half-life of 2.6 h. What is the mass of manganese-56 in a 1.0-mg sample of the isotope at the end of 10.4 h?

Analyze

Step 1. What are the known values?

____

Step 2. How many half-lives have passed during the elapsed time?

$$\text{Number of half-lives} = \frac{\text{elapsed time}}{t_{1/2}} = \frac{\square}{2.6\ \text{h/half-life}} = \square\ \text{half-lives}$$

Calculate

Step 3. Multiply the initial mass by $\frac{1}{2}$ for each half-life.

1.0 mg × ____________________ = ________________ mg Mn-56

Evaluate

Step 4. How do you know your answer is correct? ____________________________

____

EXTRA PRACTICE (similar to Practice Problem 7, page 806)

7. Iodine-126 is a beta emitter with a half-life of 13 days. What is the mass of iodine-126 in a 8.0-mg sample of the isotope at the end of 39 days?

GUIDED PRACTICE PROBLEM 8 (page 806)

8. A sample of thorium-234 has a half-life of 24.1 days. Will all the thorium undergo radioactive decay in 48.2 days? Explain.

Step 1. How many half-lives have passed in 50 days?

$$\frac{48.2\ \text{days}}{\square} = \square\ \text{half-lives}$$

____

Step 2. What fraction of the thorium will remain after 50 days?

____

Step 3. Will all the thorium decay in 50 days? Explain.

____